D1555588

STUDIES ON GREEK AMERICANS

BY
GEORGE A. KOURVETARIS

E
184
.G7
K83
1997
West

EAST EUROPEAN MONOGRAPHS, BOULDER
DISTRIBUTED BY COLUMBIA UNIVERSITY PRESS, NEW YORK

1997

EAST EUROPEAN MONOGRAPHS, NO. CDLXXX

Copyright © 1997 by George A. Kourvetaris
ISBN 0-88033-377-4
Library of Congress Catalog Card Number 97-60363

Printed in the United States of America

Dedication

To all the *protoporoi* (pioneers, first generation Greek immigrants) who through the hard work, thriftiness, and perseverance paved the way for a prosperous and respected Greek-American community.

PREFACE

This volume represents the distillation of the author's work on Greek Americans for the last quarter of a century. It covers a wide spectrum of topics of Greek American experience. The following essays and studies reflect a continuous interest in Greek American ethnicity. The reader consists of 12 chapters dealing with various aspects of the Greek American experience(s) and three chapters on the Greeks in other countries. Chapter one briefly gives a socio-historical and sociological profile of early and late Greek immigrants through such issues as education, work experiences, lifestyles, problems of adjustment, community life, ethnic organizations, and the Orthodox church. It has been noted that while both early and late Greek immigrants followed similar patterns of employment and problems of adjustment, by far the early Greek immigrants faced greater difficulties of social adjustment and acceptance in the United States.

Chapter two examines the social class and mobility patterns of first and second generation Greeks in Chicago. A number of socioeconomic indices and mobility changes such as economic, political, educational, residential, and other dimensions were compared between first and second generational units. While first generation struggled for economic success, the second generation was more concerned with status and acceptability by their American peers, and embraced the Anglo-conformity model.

Chapter three deals with the Greek Orthodox and Greek American ethnic identity by looking at the religious and secular dimensions of Greek American identity. While most respondents prefer both ethnic and Orthodox Greek identities, if they had to choose between the two, the religious Orthodox identity would be more important to them than the secular Greek American identity.

Chapter four explores patterns of intermarriage and subculture among three generations of Greeks in the United States. Each generation is analyzed in terms of its subculture and interethnic, interfaith, and interclass marriages. It is pointed out that as one moves from first to second to third generation, there is a steady increase of intermarriage across ethnic and faith lines. American born Greek women are more likely to marry within the Greek Orthodox faith; if they marry outside, they are more likely to bring the non-Greek spouse into the Greek Orthodox church.

Chapter five covers the Greek American family of three generations of Greeks and Greek Americans. A number of dimensions of marriage and family organization is examined, including gender roles (both ideal and real aspects) of

Greek American subculture, work experiences, authority relations, kinship relations, and problems of adjustment and discord. As one moves from the first generation to the second to the third generation and subsequent generations, the Greek American family is moving away from intraethnic cultural patterns of the old world to more and more of middle class American ones. By third generation, the Greek American family adopts the more general values of middle class America.

Chapter six deals with the historical and more contemporary aspects of Greek American professionals and entrepreneurs. Greeks are known more often as entrepreneurs rather than as professionals. Since World War II, Greek Americans have made tremendous inroads in various professions. While Greek Americans have achieved social mobility and professional status, they still have not reached top and elite levels within the American professional structure. While we find hundreds of professional practitioners among the Greek-Americans, we notice very few outstanding professionals, scholars, and scientists.

In chapter seven an effort was made to test empirically Gordon's ethclass hypothesis. The findings support the ethclass hypothesis. Italian Catholic, Swedish Lutheran, and Greek Orthodox couples in a medium-sized community in the Midwest tend to confine their primary group relations to persons of their own ethnicity and class.

In chapter eight, the Greeks of Asia Minor and Egypt as middleman economic minorities during the late 19th and 20th centuries are explored. The once thriving Greek communities in Asia Minor and Egypt no longer exist. Similarly, in other regions and countries, especially in the United States, Greek ethnicity will be defined as an Anglo-Saxonic phenomenon.

In chapter nine a number of issues which cause conflicts and identity crises among Greek Americans and Greeks of the diaspora are discussed. Among the most salient issues examined are the Greek language, Greek Orthodox faith, Greek Orthodox community, old and new wealth among the Greeks, and the like.

Chapter ten examines the Greek brain drain thesis within the context of international migration of scientists. It is argued that Greece, along with a number of other countries, has lost many of its most gifted professionals and students who have remained in the United States due to the lack of employment and underemployment in their own mother country.

Chapter eleven looks at the Bahamian Greek community in the Caribbean. This was a joint project with my three children during our Christmas stay at Nassau, Bahamas in 1994. The Greek Bahamians evolved from an original

vi

Greek sponge colony to a full fledged Greek Bahamian community branching out in various other small scale enterprises and occupations.

Finally, in chapter twelve the futuristics of Greek America into the twenty-first century are discussed. Five major issues are explored: demographics, institutional/organizational issues, stratification-mobility patterns, attitudinal surveys, and factors of continuity and discontinuity of Greek American ethnicity. The last part of this chapter includes a commentary on "Greece, American Greeks and Philhellenism."

The author wishes to express his appreciation to Dan Georgakas and Stavros Constantinou who read the entire volume and made useful suggestions for improvement of the manuscript. Also, I would like to express my thanks and appreciation to Karen Blaser, Susan Harshman, Elizabeth Mehren, and Kim Isaacs who worked at different phases of this project. They all work at Manuscript Services in the College of Liberal Arts & Sciences. In addition, I wish to express my deepest appreciation and love to our son Andrew who aspires to be a sociologist and who read the entire manuscript and made useful suggestions. Andrew is very much part of the story of Greek American experience. He is working for his Ph.D. at Columbia University. It must be stressed, however, that any omissions or shortcomings are mine alone. Also, I would like to acknowledge the editors of the journals that some of the articles in this volume were originally published. These include: *International Review of Sociology, Sociology and Social Research, Greek National Research, Ethnic Groups, Greek American Review, Journal of Hellenism, International Sociology of the Family, The Journal of Hellenic Diaspora, The Journal of Contemporary Sociology*, and Elseview Publishers.

TABLE OF CONTENTS

INTRODUCTION
GREEK AMERICAN ETHNICITY[*]

The study of ethnic groups as a substantive area of inquiry in the United States has been the mainstream of much research and theory by social scientists. Since the 1960s, "ethnicity" in the United States has become fashionable. Long ago, the American writer Walt Whitman accurately described the United States as a nation of immigrants. Every successive generation of immigrants to the United States has followed somewhat similar patterns upon its entrance into the American society and culture. Both early and late immigrants to the United States followed similar patterns of acculturation and assimilation into the predominantly Anglo-Saxonic culture. The concepts of "ethnic groups", "ethnicity" and new "multiculturism" have been described interchangeably with such terms as "aliens," "immigrants," "minorities," "races," "refugees," "ethnics," and the like.

In this paper "ethnic groups" will be defined as social aggregates characterized by distinct national, socio-historical, socio-cultural, and religious orientations or combinations of these patterns and socio-cultural traits. Greek Americans and Greeks in other countries represent an ethno-religious cultural group with its own historical national identification and cultural and religious physiognomy. In short, Greek Americans can be studied as an ethnic group with its own historical and socio-cultural dynamics, characterized by a sense of peoplehood and ethnic consciousness.

Two major principles seem to contribute to the formation of an ethnic group. First, there is a selective receptivity on the part of the Anglo-Saxonic majority, and secondly, there is a partial closure by the ethnic minority. Thus, it has been suggested (Warner, 1945) that "ethnic minorities typically become partially or wholly assimilated into the larger American society as a result of the opportunities for class mobility open to these members. As members of ethnic groups seek and achieve class mobility, they tend to detach themselves from their ethnic identification and therefore lessen their cohesiveness and distinctive identity."

The Greek American experience must be understood within the broader socio-historical and political economic context of European immigration. Both

---

[*]Portions of this chapter, especially those dealing with "The Dionysian and Apollonian Dimensions of Ethnicity: A Convergence Model," were presented at the Illinois Sociological Association meeting, Peoria, IL, October 19-21, 1994. The paper was published in the *Journal of International Sociology*.

Psomiades (1987) and Moskos (1990) believe that this experience is better understood not primarily as part of a Hellenic diaspora, but in the broad context of ethnic experience in the United States. However, the Greek American experience cannot be understood if severed from its roots in modern Greek culture. The Greek pioneer immigrants along with other Southern, Eastern, and Central Europeans represent the "new" immigrants vis-à-vis the "old" immigrants from Northwestern Europe. Every new generation of immigrants experienced social and economic hardships and discrimination at the hands of the groups that preceded it. Thus the Greeks and other Southern and Eastern European immigrants faced social discrimination from earlier generations of European immigrants.

Before we discuss the Greek American experience in subsequent chapters, we must look at the conceptual frameworks which guide the United States ethnic and racial intergroup policies. One such perspective stresses an assimilation path while the second views the ethnics engaged in perpetual conflict with themselves to maintain their ethnic identity and ethnic subcultures. Assimilation theories stress the systemic integrative functions of ethnic groups. This means that ethnic groups are viewed as social subsystems. Through the process of class mobility these ethnic groups lose their distinct ethnic identities and merge into the more universalistic American culture by adopting and internalizing the values and norms of the Anglo-Saxonic dominant core culture.

Pressured from the earlier Anglo-Saxon Protestant groups, the majority of European immigrants surrendered most of their ethnic subcultures and ethnic particularities in a period of three generations and adopted the Anglo-Saxonic core culture. By Anglo-Saxonic core culture is meant the basic American values that cut across any particular ethnic or cultural group. Certainly, the early ethnic groups who came to the United States primarily, from countries of North Western Europe such as Britain, Scotland, Ireland, Germany, Netherlands, Scandinavia, had established the basic institutions of government and the character of the present capitalist system and its social structures. This is what African Americans refer to as Eurocentric culture. Subsequent European and other ethnic groups alike maintained some of their in-group ethnic ties and identities, particularly those pertaining to family and kinship relationships, religion, and the "Dionysian" aspects of their ethnic subcultures (those pertaining to food, dance, and other external material aspects of their subcultures). They gave up most of their esoteric or Apollonian ethnic traditions, such as language, literature, and music beyond the third and subsequent generations in exchange for social mobility and accommodations in the larger Anglo-American dominant culture.

The majority of late European immigrants and their progenies strove for equality with the early dominant groups by adopting their values. This is known as an "assimilation" process along a continuum of *cultural, civic, structural, attitudinal, and behavioral dimensions* of assimilation.[1] The assimilationist or "straight line" model posits a decline in ethnic diversity for successive generations of immigrants. The assimilationist policy is a fusionist or "McDonaldization" model which works against the maintenance of distinct ethnic identities in the United States. The assimilationist perspective and its variants, "Americanization," "Anglo-conformity," and, to a lesser extent, "melting pot" were, and to some extent still are, the explicit and implicit policies of the United States' social institutions.

The assimilationist model is in congruence with the dominant Anglo-Saxonic model. Using the Noel hypothesis (1968:163), "If two or more groups come together in a contact situation which is characterized by ethnocentrism, competition, and a differential in power, then some form of racial or ethnic stratification will result." The Northwestern Europeans and their descendants established a system of dominant-minority group relations through the processes of ethnocentric-Eurocentric institutions, economic domination, and political power.

The "assimilationist" model has elicited considerable criticism in recent years. Some of the criticisms include the following: a) It is a one way street; b) It has a built-in bias in favor of the Anglo-Saxonic dominant culture; c) It applies mostly to European immigrants; d) It is a conservative perspective; e) It does not allow for diversity and change; and f) It does not explain the persistence of ethnicity. The critics of the assimilationist model argue that the ethnic and racial composition of the United States is changing. It becomes more and more ethnically, racially, and culturally diverse. The United States' Census recognizes four broad racial and ethnic groupings: Caucasian/White, African Americans, Hispanics, and Asians.

In response to the assimilationist perspective an alternative approach has been suggested by a number of social scientists, including the view of "cultural pluralism," according to which ethnic groups maintain certain ethnic and cultural characteristics. For example, Glazer and Moynihan (1967:16-17) argued that European immigrant groups remained culturally distinct in terms of name, values, religion, and other cultural traits. However, the loss of the language, customs, and traditions by the third generation does not always mean the decline of ethnicity. Ethnicity becomes transformed into something else. The authors found that ethnic groups become like "interest groups." However, even in cultural pluralism, assimilation takes place in various degrees among different ethnic groups beyond the second generation.

A third perspective is known as the power-conflict perspective that sees each succeeding ethnic group in an embattled position, fighting for its survival as a culturally distinct group. In this struggle, an ethnic group is subject to a perpetual conflict between its own ethnic subculture and its resistance to absorption into the dominant culture. Greek Americans, like other Southern European and non-European ethnic groups, are caught between these two perspectives. They find themselves between the Scylla and Charybdis. They want to be part of the dominant culture and the political economy of the United States, but at the same time they would like to maintain their ethnic and religious identity. Greek Americans along with other non-Anglo-Saxonic ethnic groups are caught in this dilemma.

On a different level of analysis, Patterson (1979:103-105) argues that while "today's Greek, Polish, or Italian Americans want to be exactly that. . . . we should be wary of accepting these loosely related groups as examples of 'ethnicity.'" The author believes that "many of them lack sufficient knowledge of the cultures as they exist in the 'old countries' to recognize how they have evolved in the 'new world' and therefore purport to study and demonstrate ethnic individuality where, indeed none exists." Greek Americans, like other Euro-Americans, share similar American cultural traits and experiences, just as their forbearers did when they came to the United States of America. At the same time, Greek Americans share a broader view of Greek cultural ethnic identity. Concepts like ethnic identification, ethnic heritage, and ethnic culture are part of what Greeley (1971) refers to as "ethnogenesis." The ethnogenesis perspective is mostly defined by "nationality" and "religion." It is an extension of cultural pluralism without assimilation. Ethnicity in this sense follows a natural development. It posits an adaptation process of the ethnic group which implies more than one way, straight line, or assimilationist experience. Greek Americans perceive themselves as an ethnic group but at the same time feel very much American. They have a dual hyphenated identity. More and more, Greek ethnic identity is defined within an Eastern Orthodox ethno-religious pluralistic and denominational model.

In contrast to western Christianity, the Eastern Orthodox Christian ethno-religious denominational model derives its historical and cultural traditions from Byzantium. Byzantine civilization followed a Christian Orthodox faith in which Greek culture and language were the most dominant. In western Christianity, (both Roman Catholic and Protestant), Latin was the common language. The Byzantine empire lasted longer (400 A.D. to 1453 A.D.) than the western Roman empire.

Following the sack of Constantinople, the capital of the Byzantine Empire, in 1453 by the Ottomans, Byzantine civilization and Greek culture were dominated by the Ottomans and Islamic religion. The Ottoman empire was one of the largest political structures that the western world had known since the Roman Empire disintegrated (Hourani, 1991:215). It ruled many ethnic groups—Greeks, Serbs, Bulgarians, Rumanians, Armenians, Arabs, and various religious communities including Muslims, Christians and Jews (Hourani, 1991:216).

The head of the Orthodox Christian communities in Ottoman territory was the patriarch of Constantinople. In the East nationality was usually thought to be synonymous with religion (Runciman, 1991:2). The Ottoman Sultans organized their state into a number of horizontal religious communities known as Millets. The "Rum Millet" was the Orthodox Christian community. The patriarch, as head of the Orthodox Christian communities, was given the title of the ethnarch or the ruler of the Orthodox nation (Rum Milleti) (quoted in Runciman, 1991: 167-68).

Under the Ottoman imperial structure, the Orthodox Millet subsystem was subordinate to the authority of the Ottoman Sultan. The Sultans ruled their vast empire through these millet subsystems. In addition to the ecclesiastical and religious duties of the Orthodox prelates (patriarchs, archbishops, and bishops), they also exercised authority over civil matters including marriage and divorce, the guardianship of minors, testaments and successions all according to Byzantine canon law. The ethnarch was responsible for its flock and to collect the taxes, which were heavy for non-Muslims. This system lasted for over 400 years until Greece became a nation state in the middle of the 19th century.

The patriarch of the Greek Orthodox Millet is still in existence in Modern Turkey without a flock (only a couple of thousand Greek Orthodox Christians still remain in modern Turkey). At present the patriarch is more of a symbol and tradition, rather than an ecclesiastical authority equivalent to that of the Pope in the Vatican. More and more the archbishops of the Greek Orthodox faith have become independent of the Patriarch's jurisdiction. Due to the fact that there is no more Greek emigration, the Greek Americans, Greek Canadians, and Greek Australians have become more and more homegrown and less and less Greeks of the Diaspora. The Greek American Orthodox Church with a few exceptions has ceased to be an immigrant Orthodox church.

It is for this reason that Orthodox laity and panorthodox unity movements have appeared in the last few years in the United States. In short, as Greek Americans, we move away from the "Diaspora model" to the "Orthodox Millet model." The difference, however, is that while our ancestors lived under the oppressive Ottoman imperial system, which lasted for 400 years the Greek Americans and their progenies live and work in an American, Anglo-Saxonic system in which western Christianity (both Protestantism and Roman

Catholicism) is the predominant form of Christianity while Eastern Orthodoxy is a minority ethno-denominational subsystem of Christianity.

Although the United States is predominantly an Anglo-Saxon Eurocentric culture, one can argue it has some features of the Ottoman Millet system. Like the Ottoman Empire, the United States continental empire is a multi-ethnic, multi-religious, and multi-racial nation. The authority of the United States government and its armed forces are in the hands of the Anglo-Saxon White Protestant elite or commonly known as the WASP establishment. In a similar vein the Ottoman empire (Circa 1400s-1900s) was a multi-ethnic, multi-religious, and multi-racial imperial system ruled by Sultans (a sort of emperors). The Turkish islamic elite was the Anglo-Saxonic elite of the Ottoman empire. The difference between the two systems is this: while the United States is a nation of immigrants, the Ottoman empire was an Islamic Turkish State made up of conquered minorities and ethnic groups (Greeks, Jews, Armenians, Slavs, etc.). Assimilation in the form of intermarriage (inter-ethnic and interfaith) is not prohibited in the United States with the exception of interracial marriages in the past. In the Ottoman empire, and indeed in most Islamic states today, unless one converts to the Islamic religion, intermarriage was not condoned.

Gans (1979) employs the term "symbolic ethnicity" to describe the ethnicity of third generation American ethnics. In Gans' view "symbolic ethnicity" takes an expressive rather than instrumental function in people's lives. Expressive behavior often involves the use of symbols or cultural practices taken from the older ethnic culture. According to Gans, "symbolic ethnicity" is characterized by "a nostalgic allegiance to the culture of the immigrant generation, or that of the old country; a love for and a pride in a tradition that can be felt without having to be incorporated into everyday behavior" (1979: 204). Gans argues that this symbolic "expressive ethnicity" takes different forms for different ethnic cultural groups such as rites de passage, religious and national holidays, politics, consumer goods, ethnic pride, and even ethnic nationalism. For example, the Holocaust has become a symbol of ethnic identity of all Jews throughout the world. Similarly, for Greeks, Greek Independence Day (March 25) has become an ethnic symbol of freedom of the Greek nation from the Turkish oppression. Gans predicts that eventually even "symbolic ethnicity" will disappear. Ethnic groups "may retain American forms of religions that their ancestors brought to America, but their secular cultures will be only a dim memory" (1979: 218). In other words, Gans believes that eventually all ethnic groups will follow an assimilationist straight line model. Gans' "symbolic ethnicity" model is more applicable to the European ethnic groups and as such can be thought of as a variant of the assimilationist model.

Arriving in America, the Greek male immigrant brought with him a way of life that was folk-oriented, ethnocentric, and traditional. With the oncoming of the second generation, this ethnic outlook was challenged. Culture conflict between parents and children was inevitable. Out of this generational conflict two major types of Greeks emerged, namely the "traditionalists" and the "environmentalists" (Saloutos, 1964:312).

The traditionalists attempted to rear their Greek American born offsprings as those reared in Greece. The parental group proved unyielding. These traditionalists usually were found in cities with large Greek communities. They insisted upon preserving their ethnic institutions, particularly those pertaining to religion, language, endogamous marriage, and family. They tried to socialize their children in the traditional Greek folkways. Thus, they attempted to convince their children of the "mystique" of their illustrious Hellenic ancestry, warned them against the dangers of intermarriage, and made an effort to instill in them a sense of Greek "ethnic consciousness" and "peoplehood."

On the other hand, the environmentalists (known also as the "assimilationists") believed that their children should be raised as Americans, but wanted them to retain membership in the Greek Orthodox Church, keep their Greek names, and be able to communicate in the Greek language. These Greeks felt that the assimilation process, a fusion of cultures and nationalities into an Anglo-American core culture, could not be curtailed but only temporarily delayed. The environmentalists were more realistic and experienced less conflict with their offspring. They were more cognizant of the fact that powerful social and cultural forces operate in American society which exert an unprecedented influence upon their offspring and compel them toward Anglo-Saxonic conformity.

Following Saloutos' (1964) analysis of second generation Greek American environmentalist/assimilationist perspective, Moskos (1987, 1990) argues that "embourgeoisement" has been the dominant characteristic of the Greek American experience which is closer to the assimilationist model, due to the class mobility of Greek Americans. The embourgeoisement thesis proposed first by Saloutos and advanced by Moskos is one of the major reasons why the majority of Greek Americans vis-à-vis other ethnic groups tend to be more conservative. Against the Moskos embourgeoisement thesis, Georgakas (1987) has proposed a left wing working class thesis among Greek Americans. Trying to resolve the Moskos-Georgakas debate, Kitroeff (1987) concluded that "there is still too little qualitative evidence to resolve the question of the relative importance of working class and left wing political activity of the Greek American experience."

It seems to me that both of these characterize the Greek American experience. As we move from the immigrant first generation to the second and subsequent generations, a process of embourgeoisement or middle class is taking place. It is precisely this embourgeoisement and class mobility among subsequent generations of Greek Americans that function as a depressant of Greek American ethnicity. In general, first generation Greeks both early and late immigrants, particularly the traditionalists, were faced with major difficulties in carrying out their intent to socialize their children (second generation) in the Greek ways of life. These difficulties, along with their fear of losing control over their children, were intensified when the children came into contact with the larger American society, particularly when they were of school age, began working, and became of marital age. In other words, the issue of Greek American ethnicity is not so much a phenomenon of first generation, but rather it begins with the second and subsequent generations.

THE APOLLONIAN AND DIONYSIAN DIMENSIONS OF GREEK ETHNICITY

In a more general way, when we think of new immigrants and new ethnic groups, we think in terms of their ethnic food culture. Food is an important material component of most ethnic cultures. Food has a social and cultural function of cementing ethnic relationships and promoting ethnic group solidarity. Eating together is a group ritual which has a festive and a religious character, a sort of celebration of life and social existence. The transition from the more festive, or what I refer to as the "Dionysian" way of life, to the more symbolic or "Apollonian" world view, has been gradual. Dionysian aspects of an ethnic subculture include the more external or material and experiential manifestations of that culture such as food, cultural artifacts, and rituals. The Apollonian components represent the more symbolic, esoteric, and abstract aspects of an ethnic culture such as literature, philosophy, values, history, language and the like. Americans know very little about the Apollonian and only a fraction of the Dionysian aspects of various ethnic and racial groups.

Originally, the terms Dionysian and Apollonian came from the two cults and mythological deities of the ancient Greeks, Apollo and Dionysus. Both deities had a special place in Greek pantheon mythology. They were not simply two of the many Greek deities but they were special gods usually of an adversarial nature and relationship. Apollo, was considered the god of music and medicine and averter of evil. Guthrie (1950:73) argues that "Apollo is the very embodiment of the Hellenic spirit. Everything that marks of the Greek outlook from that of other peoples . . . beauty of every sort, whether of art, music, poetry or youth, sanity and moderation--all are summed up in Apollo." In a way, Apollo symbolizes the "golden age of Greece," the miracle of the Hellenic culture. The "Golden Age" represents the multiple contributions of ancient Greeks to Western civilization in the arts, philosophy, poetry, sculpture, music, religion, as well as qualities such as sobriety, rationality, moderation, wisdom, virtue, symmetry, harmony, and beauty.

In contrast, the depiction of Dionysus' attributes and qualities in Greek art and mythology are less illustrious and complimentary. The cult of Dionysus represents two natures or two aspects of the god's personality. One, the wild and orgiastic as depicted in the Dionysiac worship of the *Bacchae*; and second, the god of annual festivals, held in Winter and Spring of each year, characterized by exuberance and phallic obscenity with very little trace of orgiastic ritual (Dodds, 1951). In more modern times both terms were originally coined and used by the German philosopher Nietzsche (1844-1900) and later applied to patterns of culture by the American anthropologist Ruth Benedict (1887-1948).

Nietzsche (1872) used both of the Greek deities as artistic modalities and two opposing perspectives of culture. He linked the "rational" with the Apollonian and the "irrational" with the Dionysian. He considered the Apollonian and, its opposite, the Dionysian as artistic energies. Following Aristotle's definition of art, Nietzsche thought of every artist as an "imitator" of either an Apollonian type found in "dreams" or of a Dionysian artistic expression found in "ecstasies." Through the mediation of the artist and through both the Apollonian dream and the Dionysian ecstasies, Nietzsche thought the artist gave birth to a higher form of art, namely, that of the "Greek tragedy."

The Apollonian motif was adopted by western culture and represents qualities such as sobriety, harmony, moderation, and rationality. Apollo embodies the shining dream of the inner world of ideas, higher truth, perfection, and excellence. The Greeks believed that this deep consciousness of nature, which finds its soothing expression in the arts, has its dark side: "human irrationality" and emotional states of human consciousness represented by the Dionysian deity. The latter personifies the human instincts, the primordial impulses in man which manifest themselves through ecstasy induced by intoxication and festive celebrations.

In Nietzsche's view, the Apollonian and Dionysian represent two different forms of Greek religion. One is the Olympian, which is represented by Apollo and other deities of the Olympian pantheon, the other form is the *chthonic* or underworld deities such as Pluto (Hades), Demeter, including Dionysus. While Apollo was perceived as the god suited for warriors, as in Homer's *Odyssey* and *Iliad* epic poems, Dionysus represents the humble or folk religion associated with people close to plants and animals or rural life in general. However, Nietzsche's gods exist beyond socio-political stratification. The Dionysiac worship is essentially communal (mass of worshippers) which is represented in *Greek tragedy* by the chorus as against the aristocratic heroes of the drama itself, which reflects the Apollonian.

On this point of the "Olympian" vs. the "chthonian" analogies of Apollo and Dionysus, respectively, Dodds (1960) says: "Dionysus was in the archaic age as much of a social necessity as Apollo; each ministered in his own way to the anxieties characteristic of a guilt-culture. Apollo promised security: "Understand your station as may; do as the father tells you; and you will be safe tomorrow." Dionysus offered freedom: "Forget the difference, and you will find the identity; join the *thiasos* (festival), and you will be happy today. . . ." And his joys were accessible to all, including slaves. While Apollo moved only in the best society, Dionysus was at all periods *demotikos* or the god of the people. Dionysus was the liberator, the god who enables you to stop being yourself.

Indeed, Nietzsche's distinction between the Apollonian and the Dionysian as ideal types were similar to other ideal types proposed later by a number of sociologists and social thinkers during the early 20th century such as Töennies' gemeinschaft vs gesellschaft, Durkheim's mechanical vs. organic solidarity, Sorokin's ideational, sensate, idealistic, and mixed systems of culture or what he called the "internal" and "external" social and cultural dynamics of culture (Sorokin, 1962). Furthermore, Benedict (1934: 72, 162, 168), the American anthropologist, used Nietzsche's conceptualization of Dionysian and Apollonian as patterns of culture. She applied them to the cultures of native American Indians of North America and Mexico. According to her, most American Indians and those of Mexico were Dionysian with the exception of the Southwest Pueblos who she termed Apollonian. All the tribes of the Northwest Coast, according to Benedict, were Dionysian. In general, most Indian tribes strove for ecstasy through their religious ceremonies. According to Benedict, (1934: 162) Indian dance songs celebrated their frenzy and madness as a supernatural spirit that destroys man's reason.

CONTEMPORARY APPLICATIONS OF THE APOLLONIAN-DIONYSIAN DICHOTOMY

Since the 1960s there has been a greater anti-rationalist, anti-intellectual, and anti-Apollonian way of life. Ferner (1987) argues that Fromm's psychoanalytic analysis of the Apollonian and Dionysian traditions set certain classical standards of intellectual posture. Failure to adhere to these standards of excellence stems from the romantic orientation in which the primary emphasis is compassion at the expense of quality, originality, scholarship, and enlightenment. Munoz (1978) uses the Apollonian and Dionysian dichotomy as polar principles expressed in human activities such as nationalism, order, preestablished power versus expressiveness, spontaneity, freedom, and suspension of predetermined rules. According to the Munoz these principles are inherent in a number of socio-cultural systems, e.g. religion, philosophy, law, the arts, politics, daily life, and science. The controversy between hard and soft methodology in social sciences, the Munoz contends, reflects the Apollonian vs. Dionysian ideal types respectively. The "Apollonian modality" represents hard methodology which is based on the logical positivism while the revival of soft methodology, e.g. phenomenology and ethnomethodology, are close to the Dionysian or more unstructured participant observation type methodology. Casadio's (1990) study of Greek thought and drama provide a discussion of Apollonian and Dionysian tendencies in historical religious thought. Casadio argues that the Dionysian is believed to reflect the "feminist" perspective while the Apollonian is linked to "masculine" solidarity and prophecy. He notes the failure of both models to underscore their common morphological basis.

Viewed from a different vantage point, the Apollonian and Dionysian polarity is interpreted as the east-west dimensions of preferred cognitive styles and value orientations (Krus and Kennedy, 1980; Krus and Krus, 1978). Indeed, the eastern cultures reflect a more *chthonian* and festive way of life which is closer to the Dionysian ideal type while the western European cultures emphasize a more rational, bureaucratic, military-industrial ethic which is closer to the Apollonian-Olympian model. In the Middle East, for example, the rise of Islamic fundamentalism can be seen as a resistance of the western Apollonian model.

In a more recent study, Maffesoli (1990) develops several themes regarding Dionysian aesthetics and the sociology of senses. In his book, two major themes predominate: a) the depth of appearances and b) the birth of a new postmodern culture. The author argues that contemporary social life is characterized by an irresponsible and powerful (often marginalized) hedonism which has become the pivotal point of modern life. This transformation, Maffesoli contends, has tremendous intellectual, affective, rational, emotional, and sensual implications in general. The ecstatic cult of *anastenarides* in Macedonia, northern Greece is close to the cult of the Dionysian deity in ancient Greece, which also can be traced to the *Enthusiasti* during the Byzantine and post-Byzantine eras (Villa, 1988). The ethnic food festivals and picnics like Octoberfest (mostly by Germans in Chicago) or Greek *panygyria* (Greek food festivals during the summer months), organized by various Greek Orthodox parishes, are mostly Dionysian in nature. Similar festivals are found among many other ethnic groups both in the United States and other countries.

THE DIONYSIAN-APOLLONIAN ETHNICITY: A CONVERGENCE MODEL

Both the Dionysian and Apollonian duality can be understood and explained as an ideal type of value orientations, cultural, and ideological modalities. As we pointed out the Dionysian-Apollonian dichotomy is somewhat similar to other typologies advanced by early social theorists in their effort to describe the changes and dynamics of western societies. The Dionysian and Apollonian motifs are two ways of conceptualizing of western and eastern world views and ethnic cultures. Classical Greece, which influenced western thought and social institutions, represents both the Dionysian and Apollonian world views blended into one. Athens and most other city states of Greece contained both the Dionysian and Apollonian world views. Both the rational and irrational were present, which culminated in what Nietzsche referred to as the *Birth of Greek Tragedy*, or the combination of both the Dionysian and Apollonian which emerged during the Persian wars. This duality is found not only in classical Greece but during Byzantine and modern Greek history and culture.

The West idealized classical Greece and adopted the Apollonian motif, while it ignored the Dionysian. It stressed the rational and underestimated the irrational. Throughout a long Greek history, we find both the Dionysian and Apollonian dimensions, or what Sorokin refers to as swings of sensate, ideational, idealistic or mixed culture mentalities and patterns. The Dionysian and Apollonian are two sides of the same coin. They represent the Janus-headed duality of harmony vs. conflict, stability vs. change, communalism vs. individualism, rationalism vs. emotionalism, expressive vs. instrumental, external vs. internal, and sacred vs. profane aspects of society and culture. Below is a schematic presentation of the Dionysian and Apollonian orientations and ethno-cultural patterns. (See fig. 1 below)

The western Europeans who first arrived in the United States, namely the British, Scottish, Irish and Germanic ethnic and cultural groups, adopted the Apollonian and de-valued the Dionysian value orientation and cultural modalities from the classical Greeks. The new immigrants who came primarily from Southern, Central and Eastern Europe, e.g., Italians, Greeks, Jews, Slavs, Asians, brought along a Dionysian or festive way of life which manifested in their food cultures. These new immigrants and ethnic groups were more expressive and affective in their cultural patterns.

FIGURE 1. VALUE ORIENTATIONS AND ETHNO-CULTURAL PATTERNS*

Dionysian	*Apollonian*
Eastern	Western
communal	individualistic
expressive	instrumental
affective	rational
interactive	detached
subjective	objective
experiential	cognitive
ritualistic	spiritual
chthonic	Olympian
South	North

*Designed by the author.

The early Americans whose ancestors came from northwestern Europe adopted more of an Apollonian Protestant ethic which was characterized by such values as detachment, rationality, order, work, duty, individualism, seriousness. This ethic was epitomized in what is known in sociology as the "Protestant ethic." According to Max Weber, it was this Protestant ethic that gave rise to capitalism (Parsons, 1958). All subsequent generations of immigrants who followed had to adopt and internalize most of these early Apollonian Protestant values. Early Americans did not bother to learn much about the newcomers other than their Dionysian or external festive aspects of their culture. Despite the fact that ethnicity has been an important dimension of American life from the beginning, it was only since the 1960s that ethnicity has become a "household" word. However, ethnic stereotypes, racial biases, and prejudices continue to exist. When old stock Americans or early generations think of ethnicity, they think of working class ethnics in Dionysian rather than Apollonian terms.

For many early Americans ethnicity was attached to working class or new immigrants and their progenies. To most old stock Americans, Chinese, Greeks, Italians, Poles, Slavs, Arabs, or more recent immigrants such as Thais, Koreans, Vietnamese, Mexicans, ethnicity is understood in stereotypical terms, that is, through, food, music, dance, and other external or expressive manifestations of Dionysian culture. Americans use ethnicity for their Epicurean pleasures as forms of cultural diversity and multiculturalism. However, our major institutions and core values reflect Apollonian and Western European values by which all subsequent groups in the United States are judged in American society.

It is precisely for this reason that there are sub-national and ethnic nationalist movements within and across societies and cultures including the United States. For example, African American Studies or Afrocentricity, Latino or Hispanic-American Studies, and Asian Studies are the counter balance of Eurocentric culture and value orientations which are perceived along Apollonian rather than Dionysian terms. Ethnicity must encompass both elements—Dionysian and Apollonian value orientations. We must view ethnic groups not only as places of exotic food and ethnic dishes but as a convergence of both Dionysian and Apollonian dimensions of our ethno-American culture and society. We must go beyond the celebration of diversity of African-American, Hispanic-American, Asian-American, and indeed every ethnic group, along a Dionysian festive pattern only. We must incorporate a multi-ethnic-multi-cultural perspective along both the Dionysian and Apollonian dimensions in our educational system at all levels of social and intellectual consciousness. Ethnicity must be analyzed and understood as a social and cultural dynamic process. Genuine ethnicity should not be viewed only in Dionysian terms but it must include an Apollonian dimension as well. Put more succinctly, ethnicity, in its both Dionysian and Apollonian dimensions, is what gives the United States its pluralism and diversity, both essential ingredients for a healthy democracy.

ENDNOTE

[1]In his book *Assimilation in American Life* (1964), Gordon has dimensionalized the process of assimilation into various subprocesses including cultural, civic, structural, etc. One person can be assimilated in one of these subprocesses and not in others. Complete assimilation occurs when structural assimilation takes place. By structural assimilation Gordon means the acceptance of an ethnic group into the primary and secondary groups and clubs in the United States without the consideration of race, national origins or religion, etc. Despite the emphasis of multi-culturalism in the United States at present, the forces of assimilation especially among descendants of Europeans is irreversible. In fact, multi-culturalism has been promoted by African Americans, Asian Americans, and Hispanics due to the increased numbers and recent immigrants especially from Asian countries (China, India, etc.), Mexico, and other Latin American countries.

REFERENCES

Benedict, Ruth. 1934. *Patterns of Culture*. New York: Penguin Books, Inc.

Bolle, De Bal and Marcel. 1989. "Journeys to the Depth of Appearances: The Quest for an Aesthetic of Ethics." *Revue de l'Institute de Sociologie* 1-2. 193-200.

Feiner, Arthur. 1987. "Notes on the Dynamics of the Problems of Editing Psychoanalytic Journals." *Contemporary Psychoanalysis* 23, 4 (Oct.): 676-88.

Gans, Herbert. 1979. "Symbolic Ethnicity: The Future of Ethnic Groups and Cultures in America." From Herbert Gans, ed. *On The Making of Americans*. University of Pennsylvania Press.

Gasadio, Giovanni. 1990. "Dionysus and Apollo, Before and After Gutenberg." *Religioni e Societa* 5, 9 (Jan.-June): 130-38.

Hourani, Albert. 1991. *A History of the Arab Peoples*. Cambridge, MA: The Belknap Press of Harvard University Press.

Kourvetaris, Yiorgos A. and Betty Dobratz. 1987. *A Profile of Modern Greece*. Clarendon Press: Oxford England.

Krus, David and Patricia H. Kennedy. 1982. "Some Characteristics of Apollonian and Dionysian Dimensions of Economic Theories." *Psychological Reports* 50, 3(1) (June): 967-74.

Munoz, R. Eduardo. 1978. "Apollo and Dionysus, or the Controversy Between Hard Methodology and Soft Methodology in Social Research." *Revista Raraguaya de Sociologia* 15, 41 (Jan.-Apr.): 77-95.

Nietzsche, Friedrich. 1967. (Trans. by Walter Kaufmann). *The Birth of Tragedy and the Case of Wagner*. New York: Vintage Books.

Noel, Donald. 1968. "A Theory of the Origin of Ethnic Stratification." *Social Problems* 16:157-172.

Parsons, Talcott. 1958. *The Protestant Ethic and the Spirit of Capitalism (1904-1905)* (trans.). New York: Charles Scribner's Sons.

Runciman, Steven. 1991. "Rum Milleti: The Orthodox Communities Under the Ottoman Sultans," in John J. Yiannias (ed.), *The Byzantine Tradition After the Fall of Constantinople*. Charlottesville and London: University Press of Virginia.

Rutigliano, Enjo and Ralph Raschen. 1989. "Nietzsche and the Sociology of His Time: A Preliminary Recognition." *Annali di Sociologia* 5 (11): 409-25.

Silk, M. S. and J. P. Stern. 1981. *Nietzsche on Tragedy*. London: Cambridge University Press.

Sorokin, Pitirim A. 1962. *Social and Cultural Dynamics*, Vol. One. New York: The Bedminister Press.

CHAPTER 1
EARLY AND LATE GREEK IMMIGRANTS

Greece is considered a nation of diaspora. Throughout Greek history we find Greek migration and movement within and outside the Hellenic world. Following the sack of Constantinople by the Turks in 1453, many Byzantine scholars known as *logioi* (intellectuals) fled to the West and contributed to the Renaissance, including the famous painter El Greco (Dominicos Theotocopoulos), a Cretan *émigré* who settled in Toledo, Spain. More recently, the late Aristotle Onassis was a Greek refugee from Asia minor, and Maria Callas, the late world-renowned soprano, was an American-born Greek who studied in the Athens Conservatory of Music during World War II.

Early Greek immigrants came to the United States during the second phase of United States immigration and industrial capitalism (1865-1920), especially at the end of the nineteenth and beginning of the twentieth centuries (1890s to 1915). Late Greek immigrants came after World War II, especially during the 1950s and 1960s up to the mid 1970s. In this chapter an effort will be made to give a general overview of the early and late Greek immigrants. First, Greek immigration will be discussed as an aspect of the larger United States political economy of immigration; second, a brief historical look at Greece during the early Greek immigration and the impact it had on Greece and on the immigrants; third, the reasons for the internal and external migration, and finally, a profile of early and late immigrants and their ethnic institutions.

More specifically, I will try to answer a number of questions such as: What was the world of early and late Greek immigrants? When did the Greek immigrants come to the United States and why? What kinds of social and work experiences did the immigrants encounter? How did they adjust to the problems and difficulties of a strange land? In what ways were the two groups similar and in what ways were they different? By drawing some similarities and differences between the two groups, I hope to shed some light on the causes of conflict and misunderstanding between them. The problem, however, becomes more complicated and more difficult, because we have only a few empirical analyses of Greeks in America. With few exceptions most of the general studies we have are about the early Greek immigrants, and most of them are descriptive.[1]

Greek immigration to the United States is by and large a twentieth century phenomenon. The first phase represents those immigrants who came to the United States prior to the Civil War, roughly before 1860s. During this phase only a few Greeks arrived, especially those sponsored by American Protestant missionaries during and after the Greek Revolution against the Turks in the

1820s. (more about this in chapter 6). The second phase of immigration to the United States roughly commenced with the industrialization and post reconstruction period in American history. It includes the later part of the nineteenth and early twentieth centuries. This phase of Greek immigration and their progenies (second generation) represents the early Greek mass immigration to the United States vis-a-vis the late Greek immigration to the United States. As late as 1880, there were about five hundred Greek immigrants in the United States. By 1890s the number of Greek immigrants reached eighteen thousand. The numbers increased tenfold to approximately 167,000 in the first decade of the new century and would total approximately half a million by 1940 (Georgakas, 1996: 207). This phase of Greek immigration and their progenies (second generation) represents the early Greek mass immigration to the United States vis-a-vis the late Greek immigration to the United States. The third phase refers to all those who came after World War II. In sum, most of the Greek immigrants came during the last two phases of immigration to the United States. These three phases of immigration to the United States coincide with the three periods of American capitalism: commercial capitalism and the slave society (1600-1865); Industrial Capitalism (1865-1920), and the advanced industrial (multinational) capitalism (1920s-present), respectively (Feagin, 1995).

It must be noted that the second phase of immigration to the United States, the majority of these immigrants being from Southern and Eastern Europe, was characterized by intense racism and xenophobia by the earlier European immigrants and their progenies. Most of the early Europeans came to the United States from countries of Northwestern Europe. Immigrants from Southeastern Europe and Asian countries were not considered desirable by the old stock European Americans. These anti-foreign sentiments, coupled with negative stereotypes aimed at the newcomers, resulted in the passage of restrictive immigration legislation starting in 1917. In 1921 Congress first passed legislation based on nationality quotas. This discriminatory legislation culminated in the Reed Johnson Act of 1924, in which the number of entering immigrants from Southeastern European countries was based on nationality distribution of the 1890 census. The clear purpose of the 1924 Immigration Act was to restrict immigrants that came from Southern and Eastern Europe. The Greek quota was set at only 100 immigrants per year. In 1921, the last year of open immigration, 28,000 Greeks came to the United States (Moskos, (1990). In 1929, the annual Greek quota was raised to 307 which remained for most of the next three decades. Non-quota immigrants, however, averaged about 2,000 yearly between 1924 and 1930, mostly members of immediate family members (Moskos, 1990).

EARLY GREEK IMMIGRANTS AND THE WORLD THEY LEFT BEHIND

Before discussing the world of Greek immigrant experience in the United States, I would like to digress and discuss the pre-World War I, modern, social, and political-economic history of Greece and the social world from which the early Greek immigrants to the United States came. From the outset it must be understood that Greece of the 1900s was a territory smaller country than what it is at present. An extremely poor country, most of Greek's territory was still under Ottoman Turkish occupation.

Following Greek Independence and the revolutionary struggle against the Turks during the 1820s, Greece became an independent kingdom with only one third of its present territory. By 1830 only Peloponnese, central Greece, and the Cyclades islands in the Aegean Sea made up the new nation-state of modern Greece. During the post revolutionary period of the 1820s, there was a period of continuous domination of European foreign powers for influence in Greece. Indicative of this foreign intervention was the Greek political parties which were labelled French, English, and Russian. In 1864, the Ionian islands occupied by England were ceded to Greece when King George I was installed as the first King of Greece. In 1881, Thessaly was liberated from Turkey and joined Greece. Later in the Greco-Turkish war of 1897, Greece was defeated by Turkey and was forced to pay indemnity by an International Financial Control Commission. This commission was established to supervise Greece's payment of the interest on its debts. By the end of the nineteenth century a number of issues remained unresolved, most of which were: a) foreign influence vs. nationalism; b) the hereditary nature of the king vs. the elected officials; c) military vs. civilian supremacy in politics; d) country vs. city; and e) church vs. state authority (Kourvetaris and Dobratz, 1987: 4).

During the Balkan Wars (1912-1913), Greek sovereignty over the island of Crete, along with Southern Eperus and Macedonia were recognized. In July 1923 the Treaty of Lausanne resulted in Turkey receiving eastern Thrace, Impros, Tenedos, and Smyrna. Greece kept western Thrace and had its sovereignty recognized in Mytilini, Chios, and Samos (Kourvetaris and Dobratz, 1987: 44). World War I brought about a national schism of major proportions in Greek national politics. The issue was whether or not Greece should participate in the war on the side of the allies or maintain neutrality. Eleftherios Venizelos, a Cretan politician, and his Liberal party favored participation in the War. Upon King George I's assassination in 1913, Prince Constantine (who was sympathetic to the central powers because he was married to Sophia Kaiser William II's sister) who succeeded to the throne of Greece advocated neutrality.

The schism between the royalists (nationalists) and Venizelists (liberals) had a catastrophic impact on Greece. The political schism affected the Greeks of the diaspora as well as the early Greek immigrants in the United States. The decision by the Liberals to participate in the war in 1918 led to what is known as the Greco-Turkish, or Asia Minor war. Greece lost that war. The 1922 Asia Minor disaster was a watershed in modern Greek history which resulted in the uprooting of a three-millennia Hellenism in Anatolia. Over 1,300,000 Greek refugees had to be absorbed by mainland Greece because of Turkish persecution.

In short, Greece of the 1900s was, an economically, indebted nation which continuously struggled against the Ottoman Turks to liberate the rest of its territory for almost four hundred years.

REASONS OF INTERNAL AND EXTERNAL MIGRATION

Before the 1890s most external migration of Greeks was limited to eastern Mediterranean, Middle East, the Balkan countries, and Southern Russia including Egypt, Rumania, and Asia Minor (Turkey). However, at the beginning of the twentieth century Greek emigration shifted to the new world, mainly to North America (the United States and Canada) and, again in the 1950s, to North America, Australia and New Zealand.

During the first two decades of the twentieth century, about 370,000 Greeks left for overseas, about 352,000 (95 percent) of whom migrated to the United States (Psomas, 1974). However, a large number of them also returned to Greece during this period owing to adjustment problems and nostalgia for the old country. Between the 1920s and 1950s Greek transatlantic emigration subsided. Beginning in the mid-1950s, following the Greek Civil War (1946-1949) mass exodus from the countryside took place. Large numbers of people moved to the cities, such as Athens, Thessaloniki, Patrae, and so on, in what is known as internal migration.

During the 1960s researchers examined different aspects of internal and external migration in various areas of Greece. A number of studies on internal migration and urbanization were carried out by French, American, and Greek social geographers, social/cultural anthropologists, social demographers, and urban sociologists. In most of these studies the authors discussed the rural exodus and the migration of rural Greeks to urban centers, especially Athens and Thessaloniki. Also during and after the Civil War a massive portion of the rural Greek population moved overseas. The population of greater Athens, including the port city of Piraeus and surrounding municipalities and communities, increased by 118.8 per cent between 1951 and 1981. Athens grew to a large metropolis of 3,027,331 inhabitants in 1981 and accounted for almost 40 per cent of the total population of Greece. During the 1980s and 1990s the population of greater Athens remained about the same. Most migrants moved in search of employment and a better life. Indeed, the major reason for the rural depopulation of Greece was the post-World War conservative governments' inability to improve the quality of life in the periphery and to decentralize the economic, cultural, medical, educational, and political institutions of the country.

Internal and external migration often come down to the same issue: people leave in order to better themselves economically. Starting in the 1950s, however, some internal and a large number of external migrants had a different motive. They wanted to pursue higher education either as international students or professionals. Many of these migrants were sponsored by relatives to come as students in order to pursue higher education in the United States. Greek student migration was part of a larger phenomenon of international student mobility after World War II. To some extent this phenomenon continues into the late 1990s. However, most international students this time came from countries of Asia, Africa, Latin and Central America. This is also true for emigration to the United States in general.

Greek life-styles, family and kinship networks, entrepreneurial activities, neighborhood coffee-houses, groceries, bakeries, butchers' shops, and the like were replicated in big cities whether the Greeks moved to Athens or Chicago. The agrarian oligarchy declined, transferring its interests to commercial fields and politics in Athens and other big cities. After all, moving to the city meant more social mobility and better education for the Greek migrants. It has been estimated (Kayser and Thompson, 1964) that the unemployment among immigrants was not significantly different from that of the rest of the urban population. Immigrants were strongly represented in service-oriented occupations, especially those associated with tourism, small shops, and parasitic or deviant occupations (i.e. peddlers who sell their merchandise either on the street or from house to house, or also known as vendors). Also during the 1950s, 1960s, and 1970s the building trade in Athens and Thessaloniki was booming. During the 1980s and 1990s, however, it had become the most depressed areas of employment. A study of 400 randomly selected migrants to Athens and a control group of non-migrants, conducted by Tina Gioka for the National Centre of Social Research, found that migrants actually had higher occupational levels than non-migrants (Sandis, 1973). This is also consistent with Lambiri-Dimaki's (1976) finding that migrants' children more often participate in higher education than children from the urban working class. Many observers of Greek urban life have commented on the rather successful adaptation of the Greek immigrants to the city.

The people who left the village rarely returned to stay permanently. Those who went back were unable to adjust to city life, wanted to retire in the village, or were downwardly mobile. The Greek external migrants faced mostly similar problems that internal migrants faced in other countries, the most serious of these being congestion, pollution, housing shortage, unemployment, crime, family disorganization, disease, isolation, loneliness, depression, and alienation. The post-World War II governments have not stopped the depopulation of rural Greece. Their failure to improve the quality of life and create jobs in rural Greece has forced people to seek better opportunities elsewhere. If they could not find them in Greece proper, they went overseas. A recent policy of the Greek governments encourages the return of Greeks to their villages. As an incentive the Government even pays those who want to resettle in the rural areas. However, this may be too little, too late.

Since the mid-1970s, external migration from Greece has declined dramatically. Beginning in 1984, more Greeks were repatriating than leaving the country. This reversal process is rather significant because Greece has always been a country of emigration. After the 1973 oil embargo and the international economic crisis of western capitalism, there was massive unemployment in the United States and Western Europe. West Germany, for example, paid migrants to return to their countries, and thousands of Greeks did return to Greece from Germany and other Western European countries. As of 1984 there were about 166,900 Greek guest-workers in Western Europe, most of whom, (138,400) lived in West Germany (*Christian Science Monitor*, 25 Jan. 1985).

Vergopoulos (1975) argues that Greece changed decisively between the two World Wars because of two important events—the international economic crisis of 1929 and the Asia Minor débâcle of 1922, which resulted in the massive repatriation of Greek refugees. Both events, according to Vergopoulos, contributed to the national development of the Greek economy. The author singles out three basic contributions made by the Asia Minor Greek refugees: a) they provided cheap, specialized labor power; b) they diversified the internal market by introducing new businesses; and c) they inspired agrarian reform (dividing up the *chifliks*, or large lands owned by a few owners). As a result, the working class and the Communist Party emerged in Greece.

Something similar happened to the prosperous Greek communities of Egypt. Following the 1952 military coup by Egyptian officers and Nasser, the majority of Egyptian Greeks, (the most important Greek settlements abroad outside of the United States in that country) left Egypt. From the early stages of Greek migration to Egypt, Greeks formed capitalist and intellectual middleman entrepreneurial activities (Kourvetaris, 1987). However, the Greek merchants and bankers in Egypt were a tiny minority among the Greeks. According to Kalkas (1979) joint ventures between Greek and Jewish investors were frequent during the early twentieth century. A substantial number of the wealthy Egyptian Greeks gave donations to the Greek state. Then, owing to the rise of Nasserism and Pan-Arabism, most Greeks decided to leave Egypt and other Middle Eastern societies, although Egypt did not force Greeks to leave as Turkey did. Many of those who left Egypt returned to Greece, others settled in South Africa, and still others migrated to North America and Australia.

Today the largest Greek presence outside Greece proper is in North America (United States and Canada) and Australia. Although Greek transatlantic external migration to these continents is more than 100 years old, we sometimes refer to these Greek emigrants as though they arrived yesterday. We still find a smattering of Greek communities in Latin America, Africa, and the Middle East. Approximately half a million Greeks live in Australia, including their progenies who make up the third largest immigrant group after the British and the Italians in that country (Price, 1975; Papageorgopoulos, 1981). Although the presence of Greeks in Australia can be traced back to World War I, the majority of Greeks migrated there after World War II, during the 1950s and 1960s. By the early 1980s and 1990s the external migration to Australia as well as to North America had almost stopped.

The second largest external migration (both inter-European and transatlantic) occurred during the 1950s, 1960s, and the 1970s, when an estimated 1,022,000 Greeks left the country, with almost half going to West Germany and the rest to Australia, the United States, and Canada, in that order. A substantial number of these migrants were Greek students and Greek professionals in general. Most Greek immigrants to Germany and other Western European countries were considered temporary guest-workers. In the mid-1970s, owing to the energy crisis, widespread unemployment and economic recession forced many Greek migrant workers to return to Greece from Germany. Contributing also to their return, many Greek workers in West Germany faced tremendous problems of adjustment and family conflicts, especially those concerning the education of their children. However, Western Europe, and especially Germany during the 1950s and 1960s, provided, in many ways, Greek workers with more employment opportunities than Greece's industrial sector.

There are both advantages and disadvantages to external migration. The most frequently mentioned advantages are economic and occupational, i.e. immigrant remittances to the families in Greece, relief from unemployment, and educational and occupational benefits especially for the children of immigrants. Migration tends to be a safety valve for the Greek state and society. Indeed, during the 1950s Greece solved its unemployment problem through emigration, especially for the most ambitious and energetic Greeks who could not be absorbed into the economic system of the country. In short, migration overseas was a way out of economic stagnation. Among the disadvantages, the most frequently mentioned are adverse demographic consequences, i.e. the loss of manpower, including the 'brain drain' that slows the development of the country, and various socio-psychological costs including problems of adjustment, nostalgia, loss of ethnic identity, and physical separation. On balance, the costs of emigration might exceed the benefits for the nation and the individual.

Greece has a serious demographic problem. A study by a special interparty Committee of the Greek Parliament of February 11, 1993 revealed that Greece has the lowest birth rate of all other countries in the Balkans and zero population growth. Geokas (1995:4) lists the following reasons for Greece's zero population growth: 1) the extensive use of contraception, the liberal use of abortions (300,000 yearly), and sterilization as a means of family planning; 2) mediterranean anemia (800,000 to 1,000,000 afflicted in Greece), the effect of which is unknown; and 3) immigration (1954-1971 accounted for 1,439,000 leaving Greece, mainly young couples with children). Despite the return of some diaspora Greeks beginning during the energy crisis and 1970s, those who returned were not enough to make an impact. In addition to these factors, Greece has the largest number of fatalities from motor vehicles in Europe, with 4,000 deaths and 38,000 injuries per year. There are estimates that by the year 2015 the population of Greece will be further reduced by 500,000 or about 10,200,000. This is a sharp contrast to Turkey's expected population increase to about 80,000,000 people.

EARLY AND LATE GREEK IMMIGRANTS: A SOCIO-HISTORICAL PROFILE

The continued Greek emigration after World War II gave the larger Greek American community a graduated scale of ethnicity and continual doses of "Greek cultural transfusion." At one extreme of the continuum were those Greeks who were totally "Americanized," while at the other extreme were those who could hardly speak a word of English. It is only proper that one can differentiate between "early" Greek immigrants, or those who came prior to the 1920s, and the "late" Greek immigrants, or those who came in the 1950s and the 1960s. There are no exact figures for either group or the number of Greek Americans or Greek Orthodox in the United States. Based on 1980 and 1990 U.S. census statistics, Moskos (1993: 21) has calculated the generational distribution of Greek Americans in the early 1990s as follows:

First generation	200,000
(Immigrants)	
Second generation	350,000
Third generation	250,000
Fourth generation	100,000
Total	900,000

Moskos argues this number is consistent with the 1990 U.S. census, the 1975 Gallup of American religious preference, and the number of dues-paying family units of the Greek Orthodox Archdiocese.[2]

Georgakas (1996:208) believes that the overwhelming majority of early Greek Americans through to the 1940s belonged to working class. According to him, most of the history of the Greek working class has been lost. It is known, however, that most early Greek immigrants came from Peloponnese, the southern region of Greece (especially Arcadia and Laconia provinces in Southern and Central Peloponnese, respectively). Some also came from other parts of Greece and from the islands. Also, a number of Greeks came from Asia Minor. Emigration to the United States was looked upon as a vehicle of social and economic mobility, particularly for the farming and working classes. It has been reported (Fairchild, 1911:3, 35; Xenides, 1922:81; Saloutos, 1964; Kourvetaris, 1971; Moskos, 1990) that early Greek immigrants, as a rule, were poor, had limited education and skills, came primarily from agricultural communities, and consisted of young males. Included in this group was a small number of Greek school teachers, priests, journalists, and other professionals and semi-professionals who became the apostles of the ideals and values of Greek society and culture. Like most southern European immigrants, particularly Italians, early Greek immigrants did not come as families because they did not expect to stay in the United States. They intended to better their finances and return to their homeland. Despite their working-class and rural origins, however, the early Greek immigrants had a lower middle-class work ethic. They were industrious, independent, and thrifty. They had what is commonly known as "Protestant ethic" along with a sense of determination, cultural pride, ethnic consciousness, and a sense of community.

The late Greek immigrants were somewhat more educated and did not come exclusively from small agricultural communities. Many came as families, sponsored by friends and relatives who came earlier. Included in this group was a substantial number of students and professionals who came to the United States either to practice their profession or to pursue higher education in American institutions (more about this in Ch. 6). The education of the late Greeks, however, should not be exaggerated. By and large late Greek immigrants followed the same occupational patterns as the early immigrants. They followed service oriented and "middleman" occupations by becoming restaurant owners, tavern operators, grocers, ice cream and candy operators, realtors and rentiers. Early and late Greeks were over-represented in the service industry. As a rule Greek restaurants is a phenomenon of first generation (both early and late) Greek immigrants. As it was pointed out before, since the mid-1970s migration of Europeans to the United States, including Greeks, has almost ceased. It is only natural that the passing of late first generation will end the restaurant ownership among late first generation Greeks. In most instances the succession to the Greek restaurateurs will not be the children of Greek immigrants (the second generation) but other ethnic groups such as the Mexicans, Albanians, Asians or newer immigrants. Most Greek restaurateurs hire Mexicans for cooks, busboys, and kitchen labor. As a rule these migrant workers are good workers, work for less, and are dependable. It is the Greek proprietors who benefit from the cheap labor.

Both early and late Greek immigrants brought with them a lifestyle that was folk- oriented, ethnocentric, familistic, and traditional. Their provincial and traditional ways of life were a carryover from the village subculture in Greece. That subculture was maintained in the United States in the early years of immigrant life. Even today one finds a proliferation of small ethnic village fraternal societies in urban America that reflect the values and traditions of agricultural communities and regions of the country that the Greek immigrants came from. The purpose of these *gemeinshaft*-type societies, called *topika somateia*, was and still continues to be the maintenance of ethnic identity. They serve as benevolent subsocieties to maintain the group's ethnic identity and help their respective communities in the homeland. These village subcultures were transplanted to the New World and enabled the immigrant to keep in touch with their home communities, find solace and relief from urban life, and facilitate their transition and adjustment to the larger American society. They also reflected the regional diversity, localism, and individualism of the Greeks in Greece proper which was maintained in the United States even beyond the immigrant generation. Similar urban village subcultures are found among the big cities in Greece from internal migration.

Unlike the old, northwestern European immigrants who generally settled in small towns and rural America, most late Southeastern European immigrants, including the Greeks, settled in large cities where opportunities for employment and entrepreneurial activities were greater and ethnic communities flourished. These ethnic communities became the marketplace in which intraethnic, informal, social, cultural, religious, family, and business transactions took place. It must also be noted that the arrival of Greeks coincided with the industrialization and urbanization of the United States, or the second phase of industrial capitalism.

From the beginning, the early Greek male immigrant was ambivalent about his permanent settlement in the New World. His original intention was to amass his fortune and return to his place of birth. Because of indecisiveness, the scarcity of Greek women, job insecurity, the problems of social adjustment, discrimination and acceptance in the host society, the Greek male was reluctant to commit himself to marriage and to raising a family. While he was physically in America, sentimentally and emotionally he was in his land of birth, (this was also somewhat true of the late Greek immigrants). Although a substantial number of early Greek immigrants returned to Greece, the vast majority remained in America (Saloutos, 1952). Only when the Greek male felt reasonably secure in his job or business did he decide to settle down, get married, and have a family. Then he found it difficult to return to his native home in Greece. In fact, for many immigrants, marriage and family were the turning point that not only provided them with a feeling of permanence in America, but also made it more difficult, if not unthinkable, for them to return to Greece (Saloutos, 1964:85).

It must be pointed out that during the second phase of immigration, feelings of xenophobia, properly cultivated by a prejudiced press, raised questions of contamination and of lowering the standards of the Anglo-Saxon culture. Thus, Greeks along with other Southeastern Europeans, encountered problems of social discrimination because the *Herrenvolk* considered the Southeastern European immigrants to be inassimilable and inferior. As an example of the horrors of xenophobia, in Omaha, Nebraska and Salt Lake City, Utah riots and strikes resulted in the death of many immigrants, including Greeks, (Saloutos, 1964; Papanikolas, 1970; Moskos, 1990). However, the tough beginnings, coupled with problems of adjustment and ethnic prejudice, galvanized the character of the early Greek immigrants and made them more determined to master and overcome their lowly social and economic origins. Despite the success and *embourgeoisement* of thousands of Greeks, thousands of others did not succeed in America. Unfortunately, little is known about those who did not "make it" in the United States or died young, or those who never married.

Although we find considerable differences between the early and late Greek immigrants and between generations, a number of students of Greek culture and society (McNeil, 1978; Sanders, 1962; Capanidou Lauquier, 1961; Scourby, 1984) maintain that family and religion seem to be the two social institutions largely responsible for preserving the traditions, values, and ideals of modern Greek culture among the Greeks of the diaspora. However, despite the importance of these two institutions to the early and late Greek immigrants, these very institutions have been challenged by the younger Greek American generations.

Ideally, every Greek ethnic community in the United States was also a spiritual community. A Greek church signified the existence of an ethnic colony; and that every Greek was potentially a member of his/her church. The admonition of Athenogoras, Archbishop of the Greek Orthodox Church in the Americas during the 1950s, who later became the Patriarch of Constantinople, was clear. He urged the Greeks of the United States to unite around the Church.

In reality, however, and despite a considerable number of Greek Orthodox churches and Greek Orthodox priests in the United States, Canada, and South America—about 667 churches, 631 priests, a dozen bishops, and one archbishop, (*Yearbook*, 1996)—only a small number of Greek-Americans are sustaining dues-paying members. Even fewer are actively interested in church affairs. Furthermore, while Greek communities and churches were established early in the twentieth century, 1922 marked the beginning of the organized ecclesiastical life of the Greek Orthodox Archdiocese of the Americas (which includes the United States, Canada, and South America). The average Greek, both in Greece proper and in the United States, does not perceive his/her church and/or religion in institutional/organizational terms. A parish priest was closer to the Greek immigrant than the bishop, archbishop, and patriarch, that is, than the hierarchical and administrative leaders of the Greek Orthodox Church. To the Greek immigrant, a Greek church was a personalized extended family system of relationships interwoven with such events of the life cycle as births, baptisms, weddings, deaths, and religious and national holidays.

During the 1920s, the Orthodox Church, following the political developments in Greece proper, was divided along two political lines, the Royalists (supporters of the king) and the Venizelists (supporters of a Greek Republic). Although this cleavage is no longer present in the Church, it has nevertheless been replaced by cleavages along generational lines (first versus second generation, early versus late Greek immigrants, self-employed versus employed, educated versus uneducated, professionals versus small businessmen), and differences between social classes, or what Milton Gordon calls "ethclass" subcultures, (more about the ethclass hypothesis in Ch. 7). In addition, conflicts exist concerning the issues of nationality/ethnicity (as measured by Greekness and language) versus Orthodox faith and/or forms of cultural and ethnic identification in general. Most Greek Orthodox churches are bilingual and as a rule they are run by small businessmen and professionals, or the more culturally conservative Greeks. As first generation or the immigrants die out, the Greek church becomes more and more Americanized. This means that the Greek language is replaced by English and the Greek Orthodox traditions become less stringent. Greek Orthodox becomes an organizational homegrown religious identity alongside the Roman Catholic, the various Protestant denominations, and other religious identities in the United States.

When the Greek Orthodox Church was formally organized, a group of early Greek immigrants met in Atlanta, Georgia (1922) and established the American Hellenic Educational Progressive Association (AHEPA). Its original purpose was to combat ethnic prejudice and discrimination including the activities of the Ku Klux Klan. Later its scope was broadened to include educational, social, political, cultural, and benevolent activities. It endorsed a policy of "Americanization" and urged all its members to become American citizens. Although AHEPA is a secular organization, it maintains some ties with the Greek Orthodox Church in America and has become the formal linkage between the Greek and the larger American communities. A proliferation of Greek American federations and ethnic associations exist (over 163 in the United States, and this does not include the village fraternal societies) with AHEPA, by far the largest Greek American organization that boasts an estimated membership of between 20,000 and 25,000 members in America (Yearbook, 1996). Another national association includes the United Hellenic American Congress (UHAC), with its headquarters in Chicago. Its ties are primarily with the Greek Orthodox communities in the Americas. This organization is active in cultural, ethnic, and political issues affecting Greece, Cyprus, and the Greeks of the United States. In 1995, the council of Greeks abroad was established in Thessaloniki, the second largest city in Greece after Athens, the capital of Greece. The purpose of the world council, known with its Greek acronym SAE is to act as an advisor to the Greek state regarding all issues concerning the Greeks of the diaspora.

The American Hellenic Institute and Public Affairs Committee and "KRIKOS" (which means link) are two other Greek American organizations. The former is a Washington-based Greek-American Political Action Committee (PAC). For the last twelve years since its inception, the committee's main objective is to monitor legislation in the United States Congress and activities in the Executive Branch concerning foreign policy issues affecting Greece and Cyprus. KRIKOS is primarily an immigrant-Greek organization with professional and cultural link with Greece. Its main purpose is to mobilize professional and cultural resources among Greek-Americans and friends of Greece to assist Greece in any way possible for its social, economic, and scientific development. KRIKOS also draws from the larger Greek-American professional community and tries to maintain and foster professional ties and exchanges with Greek professionals in Greece. By far the most important academic professional association, however, is the Modern Greek Studies Association (MGSA). MGSA was founded by a group of academic professionals in 1968. Its membership varies and includes individuals primarily of academic professionals in social sciences and humanities. It publishes a professional journal and holds a conference every two years. Its main purpose is to promote modern Greek studies at the university level and disseminate modern Greek ideas through its publications.

Greeks of the diaspora established other ethnic institutions, federations, schools, professional societies, and ethnic mass media, which includes over 140 ethnic radio and TV stations. Among these are about 18 religious radio programs, both in the United States and Canada, 41 newspapers and magazines, both religious and secular. There is also the Greek Orthodox parochial school system of about 25 Greek American daily elementary and high schools, and an equal number of afternoon Greek school classes attached to Greek parishes, that conduct Greek instruction usually after the American public school. There are also a number of private Greek language schools (Greek Orthodox Archdiocese of North and South America, 1995). Usually most of these ethnic institutions are managed by late Greek immigrants and patronized by those who are active in the church affairs and/or other ethnic organizations. The ethnic press is often the spokesman of the businessmen of the larger Greek American community, the Greek Orthodox parishes, and to a lesser extent serves the professionals and intellectual contributions of the Greek Americans.

Three types of Greek American communities can be discerned at the present time: a predominantly post-World War II Greek community made up of late Greek immigrants and their families, a mixed Greek-American community of early and late Greek immigrants and their progenies, and a Greek-American community made up of second-, third- and subsequent generation American-born Greeks. The first two are by and large ethnic urban communities. Their members are of the working- and lower- middle-classes, with a substantial number of them engaged in small service-oriented establishments, particularly restaurants, and low white-collar occupations. The third group, which is increasingly a suburban Greek American community, is primarily of the middle- and upper-middle-classes, and its members are professionals and businessmen. They increasingly follow the patterns and lifestyles of the tripartite Catholic, Protestant, and Jewish suburban ethnoreligious groups. The majority, however, no longer identify as members of the Greek American community. They are the assimilated Greek Americans. No estimate exists of the number of those Greek Americans who do not consider themselves as members of Greek America. This group includes members of mixed marriages, those who have changed their faith and their last names.

Although most Greek churches are bilingual, in the third type of Greek community, English is gradually but steadily replacing Greek, and the priests are, by and large, American- born, second- and third-generation American Greeks and some converts. While most Greek Orthodox priests are American-born, the bishops of the Greek Orthodox Church are still foreign born, including Archbishop Iakovos who is stepping down as of July, 1996 due to age and poor health. There are about 10 dioceses in the Americas. Each diocese is administered by a bishop. The Archdiocese, the administration of the Greek Orthodox Church in the Americas, is located in New York City. Chairman of the Archdiocese is Archbishop Iakovos, who presides over the Archdiosecan council and Synod of bishops representing the 10 dioceses. In addition, there are 5 bishop assistants to the Archbishop (Greek Orthodox *Yearbook*, 1996:53-54). In the last analysis, language has become the differentiating issue between first- and second-generation Greeks. While, the Greek language is valued mostly by the late Greek immigrants, the second generation tends to value an increasingly Americanized church.

SUMMARY AND CONCLUSION

In the first chapter an effort was made to give a socio-historical overview of early and late immigrants to the United States. A brief look at Greece during the early and late Greek migration was made. Reasons for internal and external migration were also briefly discussed.

In conclusion, we can make the following observations. 1) While early Greek immigrants came, by and large, as males, late Greek immigrants came as families; 2) The majority of early and late Greek immigrants settled in cities; 3) Both groups were over-represented in service-oriented occupations. 4) The peak of early Greek emigration occurred during the closing decade of the 19th and early 20th centuries, or during the second phase of industrial capitalism. During this period we find the most intense discrimination and xenophobia against the Greeks and other Southeastern Europeans from earlier stocks of Northwestern Europeans; 5) The majority of early and late Greek immigrants came to the United States as economic immigrants. However, among late Greek immigrants a substantial number of students and professionals came to the United States; 6) Organizational life (both religious and secular) took place in the 1920s and continues to this day; 7) By mid-1970s Greek migration to the United States has almost ceased; 8) A substantial number of first generation Greeks returned to Greece but many also returned back to the United States due to their inability to make the adjustment or find jobs in Greece.

ENDNOTE

[1]See for example studies by Diamantides and Constantinou (1989) and Constantinou (1989). The former study examines the determinants of emigration from Cyprus (1946-85) and the latter looks at the dominant themes and intergenerational differences among Greek Americans. Both articles are analytical and quantitative. The former one refers to the Greek Cypriots migration and is highly quantitative.

[2]According to Moskos (1993: 20-22), the 1980 census 615,000 individuals identified as having strict Greek ancestry and another 345,000 as having some Greek ancestry. In 1975 Gallup poll of American religious preference found 670,000 self-identified Greek Orthodox in the United States. A 1990 survey found 550,000 self-identified Greek Orthodox. The archdiocese lists approximately 130,000 dues-paying family units or approximately 400,000 people. The majority of Greek-Americans identify as Greek-Orthodox. The 1990 U.S. census lists about one million and one hundred thousand Greeks in the United States who claimed or responded as having Greek ancestry.

REFERENCES

Chimbos, Peter. 1980. *The Canadian Odyssey: The Greek Experience in Canada.* Toronto, Ontario: McClelland Publishers.

Constantinou, Staveos T. 1989. "Dominant Themes and Intergenerational Differences in Ethnicity: The Greek Americans" in *Sociological Focus* Vol. 22, no. 2 (May): 99-117.

Diamantides, N. D. and S. T. Constantinou. "Modeling the Macrodynamics of International Migration: Determinants of Emigration from Cyprus, 1946-85" in *Environment and Planning* vol. 21 (1989): 927-950.

Fairchild, H. P. 1911. *Greek Immigration to the United States.* New Haven: Yale University Press.

Geokas, Michael. 1995. "A Vital Issue for Hellenism: The Demographic Problem of Greece," in *Hellenic New of America*, September 1995: 4.

Georgakas, Dan. 1996. "Greek-American Radicalism: The Twentieth Century" in Paul Buhle and Dan Georgakas "The Immigrant Left in the United States" New York: State University of New York Press.

Kourvetaris, George A. 1971a. *First and Second Generation Greeks in Chicago.* Athens, Greece: National Center of Social Research.

_____. 1971b. "First and Second Generation Greeks in Chicago: An Inquiry Into Their Stratification and Mobility Patterns," *International Review of Sociology* (now *International Review of Modern Sociology*), 1 (March): 37-47.

_____. 1973. "Brain Drain and International Migration of Scientists: The Case of Greece," *Epitheoris Koinonikon Erevnon (Review of Social Research)*, Nos. 15-16.

Malafouris, Bobby. 1948. "Greeks in America 1528—1948 (Hellenes tis Amerikis 1528-1948). New York: Privately printed.

Moskos, Charles C. 1993. "Faith, Language, and Culture" in *Project for Orthodox Renewal: Seven Studies of Key Issues Facing Orthodox Christians in America* Chicago, IL: Orthodox Christian Laity, Inc.

Papageorgopoulos, Andreas. 1981. *The Greeks in Australia*, Sydney: Alpha Books.

Plous, F. K., Jr. 1971. "Chicago's Greeks: Pride, Passion, and the Protestant Ethnic," *Midwest Sunday Magazine of the Chicago Sun Times* (April 25), pp. 22-26.

Price, Charles. 1975 (ed.). *Greeks in Australia* Canberra: Australian National University Press.

Psomas, Andreas I. 1994. "The Nation, the State, and the International System: The Case of Greece" Ph.D. dissertation. Stanford: Stanford University.

Saloutos, Theodore. 1956. *They Remember America.* Berkeley and Los Angeles: The University of California Press.

_____. 1964. *The Greeks in the United States.* Cambridge: Harvard University Press.

_____. 1976. "The Greeks in America: The New and Old." Paper presented at the Bicentennial Symposium on the Greek Experience in America, University of Chicago.

Simpson, George, and J. Milton Yinger. 1972. *Racial and Cultural Minorities: An Analysis of Prejudice and Discrimination*, 4th edition. New York: Harper and Row.

Vlachos, C. Evangelos. 1968. *The Assimilation of Greeks in the United States*. Athens, Greece: National Center of Social Research.

_____. 1975. "Greek-American Perspective: Social, Psychological and Historical." Paper presented to the Greek-American Bilingual Bicultural Education Conference, organized by HANAC, New York City.

Xenides, J. P. 1922. *The Greeks in America*. New York: George H. Doran.

CHAPTER 2
FIRST AND SECOND GENERATION GREEKS IN CHICAGO:
AN INQUIRY INTO THEIR STRATIFICATION AND
MOBILITY PATTERNS*

It is the purpose of this paper to analyze the dimensions of ethnic stratification and mobility of first and second generation Greeks in Chicago. More specifically, an effort will be made, first, to compare and analyze the dimensions of intraethnic stratification between the two early generations of Greeks in Chicago in terms of social status and political influence indices, and second, to analyze the patterns of intergenerational mobility in terms of occupational, educational, residential, and acculturation changes between the two groups.

THE CHICAGO GREEK-AMERICAN COMMUNITY

Greeks in the United States in general, and the Chicago Greeks in particular, can be designated as an ethnic community within the mosaic of multiethnic communities in the larger American society. The majority of Greek immigrants settled in big cities and established ethnic communities and institutions. From the very beginning of immigration and ethnic life, Chicago has been characterized as a social laboratory and a prototype of ethnic community life. Chicago has always been one of the most important Greek settlements and one of the oldest Greek communities in the United States. In a real sense, Greek emigration to the United States coincided with the beginning of the Chicago Greek community. By 1938, the Chicago Greek community was the largest in the United States with a population of over 60,000. At the present time, no exact figures exist, but it is estimated that the Greek-American population is between 90,0000 to 150,000 in the Chicago area.

---

* This is a condensed paper based on the author's unpublished M.A. thesis, Roosevelt University, Chicago, Illinois (1965). I am indebted to Professor Ferdinand Kolegar, Roosevelt University, for his invaluable comments and intellectual stimulation and to Professor Catherine D. Papastathopulos, Northern Illinois University, for her useful advice and criticism. I also want to thank my graduate assistant, Betty Dobratz. Originally this article appeared in the *International Review of Sociology*, 1971, vol. 1, no. 1 (March): 37-47. The present analysis is an updated version of the earlier article.

METHOD, DATA, AND SOURCES OF SAMPLE

In this inquiry, two major sources were utilized to obtain our data. a) The membership lists of two Greek parishes (St. Andrew's and St. Basil's), which represented two different levels of socioeconomic and generational characteristics, and b) the 1965 membership list of the Hellenic Professional Society of Illinois. From these two sources, one hundred couples—half from the first and half from the second generation Greeks—were selected. From the one hundred couples that were randomly selected for interviews, forty-six of the first and forty-three of the second generation actually were interviewed, during the months of February, March, and April of 1965. The interview schedule included questions on social background, socio-economic, sociodemographic, and political characteristics.

The first generation included married couples who had been in the United States for at least a chronological generation (thirty-five to forty years). The second generation included the eldest married sons who were at least thirty-five years of age. For the purpose of the present analysis, the male spouse in both generations had to be of Greek extraction that is, either their mother or father was Greek, or both parents were Greek). The sample selected were not representative of all the regions of Greece.

A five-point scale was designed to measure the three variables of social status, political influence, and acculturation. Weights from one to five were assigned to those items designed to determine one's relative social class standing, political influence, and degree of acculturation. Then, the mean score for each respondent, as well as the cumulative scores for each generation, were obtained, and compared for the two generations for each of the three variables. The higher the cumulative mean score for each of the three variables for each couple or generation, the higher was its social standing, political influence, and acculturation.

GENERATIONAL PATTERNS OF STRATIFICATION AND MOBILITY: CONCEPTS, HYPOTHESES, AND FINDINGS

In this analysis the concepts of stratification and mobility are defined as the differentiation and ranking between and within the first and second generation Greeks in terms of economic (class), social (status), and political (power) indices. More specifically, the concept of stratification was operationalized as intragenerational ethnic ranking of each generation into higher or lower social status groups of ethnic structure. Social mobility was operationalized as the more dynamic aspects of the intergenerational changes of occupational, residential, and educational indices between father and son (first and second generations).

In general, it was hypothesized that the social standing (prestige) of first generation Greeks was attenuated with the oncoming of the second generation. Thus, one would expect that first generation Greeks were more likely to achieve horizontal intra-generational mobility, whereas second generation Greeks were more likely to achieve horizontal as well as vertical mobility both between and within generations. "Horizontal" mobility refers to the direction of occupational change from one social position or occupational role to another of similar social standing, while "vertical" mobility refers to the movement from one social position to another of different social standing in both upward or downward directions.

More specifically, the following working hypotheses were investigated within the dimensions of stratification and mobility:

1. *Social Standing*: Members of the first generation found their social standing primarily from within the Greek ethnic community, whereas members of the second generation increasingly sought theirs outside of it. This hypothesis was confirmed. Social standing among the first generation Greeks of Chicago was found to be a dimension of ethnic community stratification, while among members of the second generation, it was viewed increasingly more as a dimension of the over-all system of American social stratification. Thus, the overall scale score of the second generation (3.3) was higher than that of the first generation (2.4). However, Warner's I.S.C. (Index of Status Characteristics), revealed that couples of both generations displayed lower-middle class styles of life. (See Table 2.1.)

2. *Political Influence*: It was hypothesized that political influence changed from the first generation to the second generation. Members of the first generation tended to find their influence primarily within their own ethnic community, while members of the second generation increasingly sought theirs outside of the ethnic community. The hypothesis on political influence was also confirmed. However, the overall scale scores on the indices of voting, party affiliation, and associational membership did not yield significant differences between the two generations (first generation scores of 2.9, second generation, 3.1). Although results indicated that both generations exerted little or no political influence in the larger Chicago community, certain members of the second generation Greeks recently have begun to experience a breakthrough in the municipal, county, state, and even the national levels of politics.[1]

TABLE 2.1 SOCIAL CLASS EQUIVALENTS FOR I.S.C.[*] RATINGS BETWEEN FIRST AND SECOND GENERATION GREEK COUPLES IN CHICAGO

PERCENTAGES OF SOCIAL CLASS STANDING BETWEEN FIRST AND SECOND GENERATION GREEK COUPLES

	First Generation	(N)[**]	Second Generation	(N)
Upper middle	16	(7)	42	(18)
Lower middle	76	(35)	51	(22)
Upper lower	8	(4)	7	(3)
Total	100	(46)	100	(43)

Source: Adapted from W. Lloyd Warner et al., *Social Class in America: A Manual of Procedure for the Measurement of Social Status.* New York: Harper Torchbooks, 1960, pp. 121-127. (Note: Only three out of Warner's six social class classification scheme were pertinent in the present analysis.)

[*] The I.S.C. (Index of Status Characteristics) was based upon ratings on the four sub-indices of occupation, source of income, house type, and dwelling area and multiplied by the weights of four, three, three, and two, respectively. Each of the four status characteristics was rated on a seven-point scale ranging from a rating of 1, very high status value to 7, very low status value (Warner, 1960, 1960:123).

[**] Number of cases on which percentages are based given in parentheses.

3. *Occupational Mobility*: It was hypothesized that a shift from blue collar to white collar and from entrepreneurial to professional occupations took place from the first generation to the second generation. The hypothesis on occupational mobility was also confirmed. Some of the specific findings were:

(a) First generation men tended to be proprietors of service enterprises especially in the food industry, i.e., restaurateurs, tavern operators, owners of grocery stores, etc., or were engaged in semi-skilled blue collar occupations (and service occupations) such as barbers, cooks, waiters.[2]

(b) Second generation men were found primarily in professional, white collar, and skilled blue collar occupations (see Table 2.2).

(c) The majority of spouses (two-thirds) in both generations, were found to be housewives.[3]

4. *Residential Mobility*: The growth to adulthood of the second generation was accompanied by an exodus from less desirable residential areas to more desirable ones. The hypothesis on residential mobility was not strongly

supported. An alternative hypothesis was suggested; irrespective of generation, the higher the socio-economic status of the Greek couple, the greater their spatial mobility from a less favorable residential area to a more favorable one. Greek couples were more likely to achieve intra-generational rather than inter-generational residential mobility. Some more specific findings were:

(a) Members of either generation were more likely to achieve intragenerational rather than intergenerational residential mobility.

(b) First generation couples had moved away from areas of first settlement commonly known as "Greek town" to ones more favorable and integrated.

(c) While a number of second generation couples were found to live close to first generation families, the former tended to move in greater numbers to the outskirts of Chicago and to the suburbs.

(d) Second generation couples used the Greek churches found in the suburbs as a frame of residential reference more than their fathers had before them. Thus, the higher the socioeconomic status of the couple, the greater was the tendency to live away from the Greek parish and the greater was the assimilation into the American social structure.[4]

TABLE 2.2—TYPES OF OCCUPATIONS OF FIRST AND SECOND GENERATION GREEK MEN IN PERCENTAGES

TYPE OF OCCUPATION*	FIRST GENERATION MEN (N=46) PERCENTAGES		SECOND GENERATION MEN (N=43) PERCENTAGES	
Professional	6	(3)	33	(14)
Proprietary	54	(25)	16	(7)
White Collar	2	(1)	28	(12)
Blue Collar**	34	(15)	16	(7)
Not Ascertained	4	(2)	7	(3)
Total	100	(46)	100	(43)

*Adapted from Alba Edwards, "Occupational Scale," in Edward Gross, *Work and Society* (New York: The Thomas Y. Crowell Co., 1958), p. 54 (Note: Proprietary here refers to owners and managers of small service businesses; i.e., restaurant, tavern or grocery store operators. White collar includes primarily clerical type occupations and blue collar refers to all three-skilled, semi-skilled, or unskilled workers.)

**It must be stressed here that by the late 1990's and early next century, the secondary sector (blue collar, industrial workers) will be drastically lower than 25 years ago when this research was conducted. This decline follows the sector transformation of the American economy (from primary to secondary to tertiary (service). For this reason one cannot expect to find many Greeks entering the industrial labor market. We must also keep in mind that no more Greeks came to the United States, nor many Greeks were found in the working class after the 1940s (see Georgakas, 1996).

5. *Educational Mobility*: Formal education beyond the primary level (either Greek or American) was minimum or nonexistent among first generation members, whereas second generation members increasingly pursued social class mobility through the educational facilities of higher learning. The hypothesis on educational mobility was confirmed. Educational achievement of both generations was ascertained on the basis of formal years of schooling both in Greek and American educational institutions. Table 2.3 gives the percentages of Greek and American schooling of both generations.

TABLE 2.3—GREEK AND AMERICAN SCHOOLING[*]
OF FIRST AND SECOND GENERATION
GREEK COUPLES IN PERCENTAGES

Type of Schooling	First Generation Couples (N=46)				Second Generation Couples (N=43)			
	Husband		Wife		Husband		Wife	
	Gr.	Am.	Gr.	Am.	Gr.	Am.	Gr.	Am.
Some grammar school education	60	54	76	36	50	2	77	..
Grammar school graduate	21	6	8	..	11	..	..	..
Some high school and high school graduate		..	..	..	..	30	..	46
College graduate	..	8	..	..	..	60	..	49
Not ascertained	19	32	16	64	39	8	23	5
Total	100	100	100	100	100	100	100	100

[*]Schooling in both Greek and American educational institutions was calculated in percentages for each spouse separately in both generations.

Looking at Table 2.3, one notes that by and large, first generation couples had some grammar school education only. By contrast, over fifty per cent of the second generation husbands and almost fifty per cent of their wives were college graduates.[5]

6. *Acculturation*: It was hypothesized that members of the first generation resisted acculturation, whereas members of the second generation welcomed it. The hypothesis on acculturation was confirmed. A lower acculturation score was found among members of the first generation (mean scale score, 2.03) than among the second generation (mean scale score, 3.07). However the lower acculturation score of the first generation than that of the second generation does not always mean that the former remained indifferent or completely detached from the American ways of life, particularly those pertaining to materialistic aspects of American culture. Indeed, one can argue the first generation had to become acculturated to the American way of life to avoid social isolation and alienation from his/her children.[6]

DISCUSSION AND ANALYSIS

In view of the previous findings, two questions can be asked: (1) What are the significance and implications of these findings concerning first and second generation Greeks in general? and (2) To what extent are these findings consistent with previous studies dealing with Greeks and other ethnic groups in various parts of the United States?

It has been argued in this paper that social stratification and mobility in the first generation were perceived more in terms of an ethnic economic stratification. This, in turn, means that the first generation Greeks were more concerned with their economic security than with their social status of their occupations. Economic success in the business world was viewed as an index of social standing in the ethnic community, but economic success in the eyes of one's ethnic community did not necessarily provide social acceptance in American society at large.

Early Greek immigrants, like other immigrant groups, were socially more comfortable and psychologically more secure within their own ethnic community and preferred their own distinctive modes of life. In America, says Professor Gordon, "Each ethnic group has its own network of cliques, clubs, organizations, and institutions which tend to confine the primary group contacts of its members within the ethnic enclave" (1964:110-111). In a sense, the social spaces and network of relationships of the first generation Greeks were confined within their own kinship groups. They were aware of their limitations in education. Thus, they attempted to compensate for this lack of education by working very hard for very long hours. According to Georgakas (1996: 208) "much of the history of the Greek working class, which was the dominant component Greek America through to the 1940s, has been lost." Georgakas (1996: 207-232) argues that there was a strong Greek American working class prior to 1940s which manifested itself in Greek-American radicalism among the Greeks in the early twentieth century. Greeks were members of the Industrial Workers of the World (IWW) in 1905. In 1919 Greeks were among the founders of what later became the Communist Party—USA. In addition, the Socialist Labor Party had made sufficient headway with Greek workers in New England. In 1916 it was able to launch a Greek language newspaper, *Organosis* (The Organization). Despite their meager economic and educational resources, a substantial number of them owned and managed their own places of business. They developed a style of life which was both acquisitive and frugal. Economic security per se, rather than life style, was the primary concern of the first generation. Only a few of the first generation Greeks pursued social class mobility through the avenue of educational institutions in the United States. For the majority, mobility through higher education seemed an unattainable and remote goal.

Similar observations can be made with respect to political influence of the first generation. Politics has served as a vehicle of social class mobility and power. For example, the Irish have achieved mobility and status through the channel of politics. However, among the first generation Greeks, politics and political influence as vehicles of social class mobility were almost entirely absent.

The first generation resisted acculturation and tended to be more ethnocentric for some time. It was forced to learn and adopt American ways, particularly as it came into interaction or engaged in business transactions with Americans. However, first generation Greeks were not accepted by Americans on the structural and institutional levels of the American social structure, nor did they feel the need for such acceptance. Thus, first generation Greeks actualized their dreams and aspirations and economic mobility up to a certain point. They came to the United States as unskilled workers but managed to save their earnings. It must be stressed, however, that economic mobility through business in the first generation was facilitated by the entrepreneurial or small business orientation of American society at the turn of the century and by the need for unskilled or semi-skilled labor. Of course, this was less true following World War II due to increased industrialization, bureaucratization, and specialization in the American occupational structure.

Although in many respects second generation Greeks shared similar experiences with first generation Greeks, the former were more concerned with "social acceptability" and "social status" by their peers and other Americans than with seeking acceptance from those Greeks within the Greek ethnic community.

Members of the second generation adopted only those "Greek ways" which seemed to them compatible with "American ways." They emerged as a new "cultural hybrid" with elements of both a Greek subculture and American culture. "Americanization" as a way of life exerted far greater influence upon them than "Hellenism," as the latter came to be known through the ethnic processes of family and community life. Sooner or later members of the second generation realized, as did their parents, that one of the principle avenues of getting ahead and raising their social status was to pursue an education.

While some members of the second generation followed their father's footsteps, it must be emphasized that the majority pursued social mobility through channels other than service occupations. In this respect, the second generation achieved both intragenerational and intergenerational mobility. In other words, the first generation changed from one job to another but within the same occupational category, whereas the second generation achieved both horizontal and vertical occupational upward mobility. In the last analysis, however, such changes were expected and were not unique to the Greeks alone.

A number of general studies on the Greeks and other ethnic groups in the United States have dealt with stratification and mobility patterns. In his book, *Greeks in America* (1913), Burgess gave an account of anticipated business progress of first generation Greeks and predicted the growth of a professional and business class of second generation Greeks. The author stressed the potentialities of the Greeks and their aspirations and drive for achievement. Referring to the Chicago Greeks in the early quarter of the twentieth century, the author stated, "During the short time the Greek has been in Chicago, he has already established his reputation as a shrewd businessman" (1913:131). Fairchild (1911) gave a negative account of the early Greeks in the United States. It must be stressed here that the early commentators of immigrants, including the Greeks, were Protestant missionaries with an agenda of proselytism which colored their work on the Greeks. In addition, it must be stressed that the period of early Greek immigration between the 1890s to the early 20th century was the most xenophobic and racist in American history.

Warner and Srole (1945) conducted an empirical comparative study of seven ethnic groups, the Irish, Jews, Armenians, French-Canadians, Greeks, Russians, and Poles, in which they tried to compare these ethnic groups to native or old generation Americans (Anglo-Saxons) on the basis of ethnic stratification and mobility class patterns. Some of their findings pertinent to the Greeks can be summarized as follows: a) In their first ten years of settlement, all ethnic groups except the Irish achieved higher occupational positions than residential ones. b) All ethnic groups eventually and progressively approached each other in the scale of occupational and residential indices with the exception of the Jews. c) Greeks coincided occupationally with the Irish and were below only the early Americans and the Jews. d) Residentially, Greeks were below the Jews, early Americans, Irish, and Armenians, but above the Poles, Russians, Italians, and French-Canadians. e) In terms of social class index, the Greeks were found to be low in the scale, but above the Poles and Russians (1945:40-96).

Rosen (1959) conducted a somewhat similar interethnic study of six ethnic groups and their achievement orientations. Rosen's hypothesis was that "vertical mobility rates among the ethnics are a function of their dissimilar psychological and cultural orientations toward achievement." According to Rosen, there are three main components of the "achievement orientation": a) "Achievement motivation," which provides the internal impetus to excel in situations involving standards of excellence. b) Achievement or value orientation which implements "achievement- motivation" behavior and the "desire for social status."   c) "Culturally influenced educational-occupational aspiration levels."

Equipped with this conceptual model, Rosen conducted 427 interviews with "pairs of mothers and their sons" in sixty-two communities in four states in the Northeast. They included French-Canadians, Italians, Greeks, Jews, Black Americans and White Protestants. On the basis of data provided by certain batteries of questions, Rosen (1959:60) then concluded that Greeks place great emphasis on achievement, training, and independence. The Greek child (third generation) is trained to be self-reliant and is exhorted to be a "credit to his group" in the Greek community. There are more middle-class persons among Jews, Greeks, and Protestants than among Italians, French-Canadians, and Blacks. The culture of white Protestants, Jews, and Greeks stands out as more individualistic, activistic, and future-oriented. Social class was found to be related to educational and vocational aspirations among Jews, Protestants, Greeks, and Blacks. For each social class, these groups had similar educational and vocational aspirations which also were higher than those of Italians and French-Canadians.

CONCLUSION

In this paper an effort was made to examine certain patterns of intra-generational and inter-generational mobility and stratification patterns between early first and their children (second generation) Greeks in Chicago. Social class was not expected to be stressed among the first generation for psychological rather than structural reasons even though distinctions were present. Distinctions and styles of life were blended so that the group could stay together. Social stratification and mobility became more meaningful as the

Greek community expanded, and many of the Greeks engaged in business, acquired property, and became more socially accepted within the larger American society.

This change was accelerated with the coming of age of second generation Greeks. In his book, *Greeks in America* (1964), Saloutos heralded the contemporary professional, commercial, and intellectual prominence of Greeks in the United States which he characterized as "impressive" and the beginning of an "era of respectability" for the Greeks. Saloutos aptly described the social mobility and status of Greeks in the United States with these words: "We are on the threshold of a new generation of Greeks who have carved successful niches in the business and professional world and have moved to new positions of influence. They are on the way to a new status in American society. The immigrants of yesteryear had established sobriety, industry, and integrity" (1964:378).[7] A somewhat similar observation as that of Saloutos was made by an American sociologist over a generation ago who vividly predicted and described the economic mobility of the Greek immigrant. In his words: "Once his foot is on the first step, the saving and commercial minded Greek climbs from curb to stand, from stand to store, from little store to the chain of stores to branch stores in other cities. Such are the stages of his upward path" (quoted in Xenides, 1922:81).

Although the foregoing observations were the atypical rather than the typical paths of the majority of members in both generations, these observations demonstrate the "entrepreneurial ethos" and the "quest" for a new era of "social status" and "respectability" of the Greeks in American society. First generation Greeks were more likely to view social status and mobility as dimensions of the Greek intra-ethnic system of stratification, whereas second generation Greeks tended to perceive social status and mobility from a larger frame of reference of the American social class structure.

Despite their strong ethnic identity, the first generation Greeks were not altogether detached from the American scene. As business entrepreneurs, they had to extend their horizons to Greek community affairs. They kept abreast of the non-Greek social environment through the ethnic and non-ethnic mass media. As American citizens they exercised their privilege to vote, and they were proud of their material achievement. Some became more successful than others. Those who were less fortunate projected their aspirations and dreams on to their children. As an ethnic group, the first generation Greeks achieved a relative social and economic mobility in the sense that they started from the bottom of the stratification pyramid and in a period of fifty years or so, reached a lower-middle class status. Their status almost exclusively was viewed in terms of economic or business success within the ethnic community.

By contrast, second generation Greeks had a number of advantages over members of the first generation. To begin with, the former did not experience the "culture shock" as did their parents. While both generations quite often became the targets of ethnic prejudice and discrimination, second generation Greeks did not accept second rate citizenship. They, along with members of other ethnic groups, demanded and strove for equal treatment and opportunity. Furthermore, by and large, second generation Greeks grew up in a well-knit family and ethnic subculture where some ethnic institutional forms contributed to the stability of the family, particularly those pertaining to courtship, marriage, linguistic patterns, religion, and respect for parents and elders. Of course, the ethnic cultural patterns were viewed by the second generation both as assets and liabilities for their social mobility and social acceptance in American society. Lastly, the values of aspiration, hard work, and the Greek *philotimo* (self-esteem) were implanted in the members of the second generation by their parents. Achievement and success were a pride and credit not only to their immediate families and kin, but also to the entire Greek community.

Thus, the function of social stratification and social mobility within the Greek ethnic community began to lose its appeal and became attenuated when the second generation Greek-Americans attained adulthood. Social status was transformed from an ethnocentric focus and intraethnic orientation to transcultural or along the more universalistic criteria of American social class structure. Likewise, indices of social mobility became more functional and meaningful when they were viewed in terms of the American mobility and occupational structure as a whole.

In short, achievements of the immigrants of yesteryear became the point of departure and a frame of reference for social class mobility in the second generation. From all evidence we have (more about this in subsequent chapters) the third generation Greeks in the United States continues the path of upward, vertical, social class mobility.

ENDNOTES

[1]For example, to mention only the most important political positions on the state and national levels, one must include: Vice-President of the United States Spiro Agnew (Anagnostopoulos), (Vice-president Spyros Agnew served during the Nixon administration in 1968. Like the late president Richard Nixon, Agnew was forced to resign for tax evasion.) United States Congressmen Dr. John Brademas (John Brademas lost his congressional seat in Indiana to Dan Quayle who later became vice-president during the Bush administration (1988-1992). Congressman Brademas served in Congress for a long time, and he was very supportive of the legislative agenda for the arts and humanities. Later, he became president of New York University. During the Clinton administration, he served as chairman of the Arts Council. Dr. Mike Bakalis became a comptroller for the state of Illinois. Later he ran for governor of Illinois as a Democratic candidate against James Thompson, the Republican candidate, and he lost. Subsequently, he became a dean of education of Loyola University, Chicago, and taught at Northwestern University.

In 1992 former Governor Michael Dukakis was nominated by the Democratic Party to run against Bush, but he lost. At the national level, as of 1996, we had two U.S. senators, Senator Paul Sarbanes, a democrat from Maryland who has been in the Senate for three consecutive terms. The other one is Senator Olympia Snowe, a Republican from the state of Maine who filled the position vacated by the Democratic senator and majority whip George Mitchell. In addition, we have two congressmen both in the Republican Party: Congressman Michael Bilirakis from Florida and Congressman George Gegas from Pennsylvania. With two senators and two representatives, one might argue that Greeks are technically overrepresented, at least in the Senate. We must also add that Greeks have been active in local and state politics for a long time. San Francisco, for example, had Greek mayors in the past. George Christopher served two terms as a mayor during the 1970s, and Art Agnos during the early 1990s. At least 18 individuals serve in senior positions in the Clinton Administration including an ambassador, assistant secretary for Housing, Senior advisor to the President, and other senior positions in the Clinton Administration.

[2]During the late 1990s most of the early generation (first and second) have retired or died. The patterns of occupational mobility and distribution between first and second generation of late Greek emigrants have somewhat changed. Among the late Greek emigrants and their progenies, we found more engaged in real estate, restaurants (late first generation), fewer cooks, tavern operators, and owners of small grocery stores. A number of late Greek emigrants are involved in construction (builders, entrepreneurs), gasoline operators, engineers, accountants (2nd generation), and other small and medium size businesses. We found very few Greek American factory workers. In general, even late Greek immigrants and their progenies are overrepresented in service (food) type enterprises. Most of their progenies, second and third generation, are college graduates. The most common areas of occupational specialization they choose are: business,

medicine, education, law, or client oriented occupations. (Eugene T. Rossides (ed.) *American Hellenic Who's Who 1994-1995*. Washington, D.C. AM Hellenic Institute, Inc. Pp. 243-266). In addition, one has to add thousands of hot dog, ice cream, and chestnut vendors in cities like New York and Chicago. For example, there are still hundreds, perhaps over a thousand, in New York city alone as of 1995. Added to this, we must include the popcorn vendors in Detroit. Also, we find thousands of painters, waiters, cooks, not only Greeks owned restaurant of small business but American-owned also. All these can be thought of as the quasi-small capitalists who later open their own bigger restaurants and small businesses.

[3]We found more and more Greek and Greek American wives gainfully employed outside the household. This is in sharp contrast to the early Greek immigrant wives and their daughters.

[4]This pattern of residential mobility has drastically changed in the last quarter of the century since the study was carried out. Greeks and Greek Americans have moved to suburbs of greater Metropolitan areas of Chicago and Satellite cities and municipalities of Illinois such as: Addison, Aurora, DeKalb, Wilmette, Glenview, Elgin, Belleville, Champaign, Decatur, DesPlaines, East Moline, Elmhurst, Hegewisch, Joliet, Justice, Kankakee, Niles, Oak Lawn, Olympia Fields, Palatine, Palos Heights, Palos Hills, Peoria, Rockford, Rock Island, Springfield, Waukegan, Westchester. (These cities and municipalities are where the Greek Orthodox parishes are found as compared with less than a dozen Greek Orthodox parishes found in Chicago proper: See *Yearbook of the Greek Orthodox Archdiocese of North and South America*, 1996: 125-126).

[5]Educational mobility is even greater among the late Greek immigrants and their progenies. Most restaurant owners (who, as a rule, are first generation) send their children to college. However, the majority of college graduates follow a limited occupational choice or client-money-making occupations and professions such as law, medicine, and business-type occupations.

[6]Acculturation (an anthropological concept) or what sociologists refer to as assimilation is rampant among second and third generation Greek Americans (late Greek immigrants). The assimilation of the Greek Americans is taking place at a time when American society is going through a multiculturist and diversity revolution. It is rather peculiar that the Greek Americans move away from Greek things with the exception of the Dionysian or symbolic aspects of Greek culture. One has to look at the increased number of mixed marriages among the Greek Americans, the social mobility, and the movement of the Greeks in small towns. All these are significant indices of assimilation which have been dealt with in other chapters of this volume.

[7]Moskos (1990) followed the same pattern that was begun by Saloutos to describe the embourgeoisment of Greek America.

REFERENCES

Abbott, Grace. 1909. "A Study of the Greeks in Chicago." *American Journal of Sociology*, 15 (November): 379-393.

Arnold, David O. (ed.) 1970. *The Sociology of the Subculture*. Berkeley, California: The Glendessary Press.

Bendix, Reinhard, and Seymore Lipset. 1966. *Class, Status, and Power: Social Stratification in Comparative Perspective*. New York: Free Press.

Burgess, Thomas. 1913. *Greeks in America*. Boston: Sherman French and Company.

Fairchild, H. P. 1911. *Greek Immigration to the United States*. New Heaven: Yale University Press.

Georgakas, Dan. 1996. "Greek-American Radicalism: The Twentieth Century" in *The Immigrant Left in the United States* (edited) by Paul Buhle and Dan Georgakas. New York: State University of New York, pp. 207-232.

Gordon, Milton. 1964. *Assimilation in American Life: The Role of Race, Religion and National Origin*. New York: Oxford University Press.

Huchinson, E. P. 1956. *Immigrants and Their Children: A Volume in the Census Monograph Series*. New York: John Wiley and Sons, Inc.

Ianni, Frances. 1957. "Residential and Occupational Mobility as Indices of the Acculturation of an Ethnic Group." *Social Forces*, 36 (October): 65-72.

Lipset, Seymour, and Reinhard Bendix. 1963. *Social Mobility in Industrial Society*. Berkeley and Los Angeles: University of California Press.

Mistaras, Evangeline. 1950. "A Study of First and Second Generation Greek Outmarriages in Chicago." Unpublished: A Master's Thesis in the University of Chicago Library, Department of Sociology.

Price, Charles. 1963. *Southern Europeans in Australia*. New York: Oxford University Press.

Rosen, Bernard. 1959. "Race, Ethnicity, and the Achievement Syndrome." *American Sociological Review*, 24 (February): 47-60.

Saloutos, Theodore. 1964. *The Greeks in the United States*. Cambridge: Harvard University Press.

Sanders, Irwin. 1962. *Rainbow in the Rock: The People of Rural Greece*. Cambridge: Harvard University Press.

Simirenko, Alex. 1964. *Pilgrims, Colonists, and Frontiersmen: An Ethnic Community in Transition*. Glencoe, Illinois: The Free Press.

Stycos, L. M. 1948. "The Spartan Greeks of Bridgetown." *Common Ground*, 8 (Winter, Spring, Summer): 61-70, 24-34, 72-86.

Truedley, Mary. 1949. "Formal Organization and Americanization Process, with Special Reference to the Greeks of Boston." *American Sociological Review*, 14 (February): 44-52.

Warner, Lloyd, et al. 1960. *Social Class in America: A Manual of Procedure for the Measurement of Social Status*. New York: Harper Torchbooks.

Warner, Lloyd, and L. Srole. 1945. *The Social Systems of American Ethnic Groups*. New Haven: Yale University Press.

Xenides, J. R. 1922. *The Greeks in America*. New York: George H. Duran.

CHAPTER 3
GREEK ORTHODOX AND GREEK AMERICAN ETHNIC IDENTITY*

For the last few years a number of conferences, symposia, and other scholarly activities and publications have been undertaken by different professional groups and organizations on the general theme of "Greek American Ethnicity."[1] Most of these conferences stressed the secular dimension of Greek ethnicity.

DIMENSIONS OF GREEK AMERICAN ETHNIC IDENTITY

From a religious perspective, those who came prior to the 1890s were primarily Protestant, while those who came at the turn of the century (known as the late European immigrants) were predominantly Roman Catholic, Jewish, Eastern Orthodox, Moslem, Hindu Buddhist and other non-Christian denominations. The present study is an examination of the secular and religious dimensions of ethnic identity among Greek Americans. The Greek American ethnicity is an ethnoreligious experience that is, with both a religious and secular component. The religious dimension of Greek American identity can be traced back to the Byzantine cultural tradition invariably known as Eastern or Greek Orthodox Christianity--the counterpart of Western Christianity. Bruneau (1993: 199-216) argues that the Greek Orthodox Church, through its Ecumenical Patriarchiate of Constantinople, established archdioceses in different Greek communities of the Greek diaspora. In New York, the archdiocese of North and South America was established in the 1920s. In Sydney, Australia an archdiocese was established in the 1950s. Increased Greek immigration to

---

* This is a revised and expanded version of a paper originally presented at the annual conference on "The Greek American Community: Past, Present, and Future," organized by the Greek Studies Department of the Hellenic College at Brookline, MA on October 18-21, 1990. The author would like to thank Professor Aristotle Michopoulos, Director of Greek Studies of the Hellenic College, and now the Dean of the Hellenic College. Also, I would like to thank Professor Robert Albritton of Northern Illinois University for suggestions and professional assistance for the statistical aspects of the pages. I also wish to extend my thanks to the Hellenic College and the NIU Department of Sociology for the financial support to carry out this research and attend this conference. However, the usual caveat--that the author alone accepts the responsibility for analyses and interpretations--is especially relevant here.

Africa, the United Kingdom, and Germany in the 1960s resulted in the establishment of more archdioceses. The Byzantine legacy projects a profound Greek identity within orthodoxy. It features competing models of governing which include self-controlled parishes, democratic communities, and autonomous churches. The secular component of Greek ethnicity can be traced back to the emergence of modern Greece as a new nation state in the middle of the nineteenth century. This statehood resulted in the creation of a political identity within an international system of political nation states (Tsaousis, 1983). The Greeks of the diaspora beyond the second generation, especially in Anglo Saxon countries, maintain a cultural Greek Orthodox religious identity but not a Greek political identity. While the cultural Greek Orthodox religious identity is operating in ethnocentric fashion, or *esostrophically*, the political/national secular Greek identity operates from without, or *exostrophically*. Thus a central concern becomes whether the Greek nationality and Orthodox religious identities are compatible beyond the third and subsequent generations of Greek Americans? Or are these dual identities mutually exclusive?

The early efforts to maintain Greek national identity gave way to the second transitional stage and the realization that the young were being brought up in the United States and were *Greek Americans*. The Church had become indigenous and admitting that the Greek identity was, in fact, more American than *Greek*. The Greek church has consistently tried to maintain Greek language schools in order to maintain the Greek heritage. Despite the protests of dissidents among the older generation and the newer arrivals, the Church had no alternative other than follow the Americanization and assimilation of Greek American Orthodox faithful. High intermarriage rates and mobility patterns among Greek Americans indicate an accelerated assimilation process.

In the first two generations, Greek ethnicity and Orthodox Christianity converge, but by the third and subsequent generations of Greek Americans, the secular component of Greek ethnicity alternates leaving only the institutional Greek Orthodox identity more prevalent among Greek Americans. It is the thesis of the present study that by the third generation "Greekness"--as measured by language, secular Greek traditions, and Greek values in general--give way to "Americanness." Nationality as a differentiating element of ethnic identity gives way to religion. A transformation is taking place from a sense of being Greek to a sense of being Orthodox. To many Greeks, Orthodox Christianity is still an ethnic oriented religion. Greek Orthodoxy is used to signify the ethnic differentiation of Orthodox identities. In general, we can hypothesize that as one moves from the first generation to the second, then to the third and subsequent generations, a gradual shift of Greek ethnic identity and realignment is observed. We move from an "inner-directed" Greek ethnic identity, most strongly represented by the immigrant or first generation, to an "other-directed" one in the second, third, and subsequent generations of Greeks in the diaspora (Kourvetaris, 1989:27). More and more we have to redefine our ethnic identity as a process. Concomitant to this transformation, one can observe parallel changes in the correlates of Greek American secular Greek sub-culture—a decline of Greek nationality, Greek language, family, kinship, and Greek traditions in general.

Despite the fact that there has been a growing interest in Greek American studies in the last few years, there is still a dearth of empirical studies on the Greek American ethno-religious identity. Most studies on religious identification in the United States involve Roman Catholic, Protestant, and Jewish religious identities. Only rarely do we find any studies on Eastern Orthodox or Greek Orthodox religious identity. A number of Greek American and American scholars have dealt with various aspects of the Greek American experience, including "assimilation and Greek identity" (Vlachos, 1968); "Greek American ethnicity" (Harvey and Constantinou, 1985); "Greek American ethnicity and Greek Orthodox identity" (Demos, 1989); "Greek subculture and Greek ethnicity" (Costantakos, 1982); "Greek American generational ethnicity" (Scourby, 1980); and "Greek American professionalism" (Kourvetaris, 1977, 1989). In most of these studies the authors have concluded that although there is a decline of Greek language and an increase in intermarriage among Greek Americans, Greek American ethnic identity is transformed to broader Greek subcultural forms *and* Greek Orthodox religious identity. In a study of Greek Orthodox church, Counelis (1989) argues about the "Americanization of the Greek Orthodox church as an institution," which is also the policy of the Greek Orthodox Archdiocese of North and South America. The americanization process of orthodox church as an institution is also taking place among subsequent generations of Greeks in the United States. In order to further examine the issue of Greek American identity in both its religious and secular aspects--that is to say, in its Orthodox and Greek secular nationality dimensions—a survey of a Greek American Orthodox organization in the Chicago area was undertaken in the Fall of 1990.[2]

DATA AND RESEARCH FINDINGS

The present analysis was based on data collected from a mailed questionnaire sent to all the members of an Orthodox Singles organization in 1989.[3] The first president of the Orthodox Singles made available to this author a membership list that included all 248 members as of September 8, 1989. A structured questionnaire was mailed to all members listed, of which

102 (41 per cent) were returned. Due to time and financial considerations, no effort was made to send a second reminder for greater response. In addition, eight mailed questionnaires were returned due to wrong addresses or changes in residence. Four questionnaires were received too late and were not included in the original analysis. Fifteen questions dealing with various aspects of both the religious and the secular aspects of Greek ethnic identity were included in the final questionnaire. Since there were few non-Greek Orthodox, they were excluded from the analysis.

Orthodox identity was measured in terms of questions such as the importance of faith and the rankings of various components of Orthodox faith (rituals, mysticism, icons, beliefs, doctrine, etc.). Likewise, Greek secular ethnicity was measured with questions such as the importance of Greek language, culture, nationality, history, traditions, family, food, and the like. Questions of this kind have been standard in measuring religious and secular dimensions of ethnicity. The respondents were asked to rank these various dimensions of Orthodox identity and secular ethnicity. In addition, questions on the importance of Orthodox faith vis-à-vis Greek ethnicity were correlated with various socio-demographic characteristics, including the importance of nationality, language, age and so on. (For more detailed information on the type of questions see appendix A.)

PRESENTATION OF DATA

1. *Socio-Demographic Profile.* A number of sociodemographic characteristics of Orthodox Singles is given in Table 3.1. From Table 3.1, the following observations concerning the members of the Orthodox Singles group can be made. By and large, those who returned the questionnaire were (1) professional, semi-professional, administrative, and business individuals; (2) the majority of respondents (a) were second generation Greek Americans, (b) had completed college and post graduate education, and (c) were female.

TABLE 3.1. SELECTED SOCIODEMOGRAPHIC CHARACTERISTICS
OF ORTHODOX SINGLES 1989

Sociodemographic Characteristics	Number	Percentage
Marital Status		
Single	49	48.0
Never Married	19	18.6
Divorced	29	28.4
Separated/Missing	5	4.9
Total	102	99.9
Occupation		
Professional	19	18.6
Semi-professional	24	23.5
Administrative/Technical	15	14.7
Sales	8	7.8
Business	15	14.7
White Collar	10	9.8
Blue Collar	1	1.0
Other/Missing	9	8.8
Total	101	98.9
Nationality		
Greek	81	79.4
Serbian	5	4.9
Other/Missing	16	15.7
Education		
Elementary	2	2.0
High School	11	10.8
College	44	43.1
Post Graduate	36	
Other/Missing	9	8.8
Total	102	100.0
Sex		
Male	46	45.1
Female	54	52.9
Other/Missing	2	2.0
Total	102	100.0
Generation		
First	10	9.8
Second	73	71.6
Third	12	11.8
Fourth	1	1.0
Other	6	5.9
Total	102	100.0

2. *Responses to Orthodox Identity Questions.* A number of responses to a selected number of questions on "Orthodox faith" are given in Table 3.2.

TABLE 3.2 ORTHODOX SINGLES' RESPONSES TO ORTHODOX IDENTITY

Orthodox Identity Questions	Number	Percentage
Faith*		
Orthodox	10	9.8
Eastern Orthodox	12	11.8
Greek Orthodox	72	70.6
Other	*8*	*7.8*
Total	102	100.0
Orthodox Faith**		
Very Important	64	62.7
Important	32	31.4
Somewhat Important	*6*	*5.9*
Total	102	100.0
PanOrthodox Unity***		
Yes	72	70.6
No	11	10.8
Don't Know	*19*	*18.6*
Total	102	100.0

*   If someone asked you what your faith is, how would you respond?
**   How important is your orthodox faith?
***   Are you in favor of a PanOrthodox unity in North America and other parts of the world?

Overall, the majority of respondents perceived themselves as Greek Orthodox. As expected, the Greek Orthodox faith was considered "important" and/or "very important" to over 90% of them. Also, to the question regarding PanOrthodox unity, the majority of respondents overwhelmingly favor such a unity among all Orthodox denominations.

3. *Responses to Orthodox Identity Rankings.* Since the overwhelming majority of the respondents identified themselves as Orthodox, they were further

asked to rank seven major dimensions of their Orthodox faith--ritual/rites, mysticism, theology, icons, doctrine/beliefs, Byzantine music, and Byzantine architecture. Table 3.3 gives the various rankings by the respondents of these seven dimensions of their Orthodox faith. Looking at Table 3.3 the most important dimensions of Orthodox Singles' responses to Orthodox identity were the esoteric aspects of Orthodox faith such as doctrine/beliefs, rituals/rites, and theological metaphysical questions.

    4. *Responses to Ethnic Identity Rankings.* In order to see how the respondents perceived the ethnic secular dimension of their identity, they were also asked to rank the eight dimensions of Greek secular ethnicity (namely food, language, culture, nationality, history, traditions, family, national origins) in a somewhat similar fashion as they were asked to rank their Orthodox identity. Table 3.4 shows the rankings of these eight ethnic dimensions. Almost half of the respondents, or 44 percent, ranked the Greek family as number one as an aspect of Greek ethnic identity, followed by Greek culture (30 percent), Greek history (24 percent), Greek nationality (19 percent), and language and traditions equally (about 18 percent each). Food was ranked the lowest as an aspect of Greek ethnicity.

RESPONSES OF ORTHODOX SINGLES TO MIXED ORTHODOX AND ETHNIC IDENTITY QUESTIONS.

    In order to understand whether or not the religious dimension of Orthodox Singles was stronger than their secular ethnicity (Greekness), two questions were included in the questionnaire, one on "marriage" and one on "Orthodox vs. Greek ethnicity" (for more details on both questions see questions 3 and 4 in Appendix A). Tables 3.5 and 3.6 show the responses of the Orthodox Singles to both of these questions. While most respondents would prefer both "Greek ethnicity" and "Orthodox faith" as important factors in deciding about Greek American marriage, the respondents felt that if they had to choose between the two, "Orthodox faith" would be preferable to "Greek ethnicity." This was despite the fact that the majority of the respondents perceived themselves as both Greek ethnics and Greek Orthodox.

TABLE 3.3. ORTHODOX SINGLES' RESPONSES TO ORTHODOX IDENTITY RANKINGS

DIMENSIONS OF ORTHODOX FAITH	RANKINGS BY RESPONDENTS							
	1 N (%)	2 N (%)	3 N (%)	4 N (%)	5 N (%)	6 N (%)	7 N (%)	Total N (%)
Rituals/Rites	35 (38.0)	13 (14.0)	22 (24.0)	9 (9.7)	6 (6.5)	4 (4.3)	3 (3.2)	92 (99.7)
Mysticism	15 (17.6)	8 (9.4)	11 (12.7)	10 (11.7)	19 (22.3)	11 (12.9)	11 (12.9)	85 (99.5)
Theology	34 (36.9)	23 (25.0)	14 (15.2)	5 (5.4)	7 (7.6)	6 (6.5)	3 (3.2)	92 (99.8)
Icons	12 (13.7)	5 (5.7)	16 (18.3)	23 (26.4)	19 (21.8)	9 (10.3)	3 (3.4)	87 (99.6)
Doctrine/Beliefs	37 (41.5)	27 (30.3)	3 (3.3)	14 (15.7)	5 (5.6)	3 (3.3)	4 (4.4)	89 (104.1)
Byzantine Music	13 (14.7)	7 (7.9)	13 (14.7)	12 (13.6)	11 (12.5)	18 (20.4)	14 (15.9)	88 (99.7)
Byzantine Architecture	7 (8.5)	7 (8.5)	4 (4.8)	6 (7.3)	10 (12.1)	20 (24.3)	28 (34.1)	82 (99.6)

58

TABLE 3.4. ORTHODOX SINGLES' RESPONSES TO GREEK ETHNIC IDENTITY RANKINGS

DIMENSIONS
OF ETHNIC
IDENTITY

RANKINGS

	1	2	3	4	5	6	7	8	9/Other	Total
	N/%	N/%	N/%	N/%	N/%	N/%	N/%	N/%	N/%	N/%
Food	9/8.8	8/7.8	5/4.9	11/10.8	5/4.9	18/17.6	15/14.7	13/12.7	18/17.6	102/99.8
Language	18/17.6	9/8.8	3/2.9	12/11.8	17/16.7	12/11.8	12/11.8	4/3.9	15/14.7	102/100.0
Culture	31/30.4	13/12.7	28/27.5	5/4.9	6/5.9	8/7.8	——	1/1.0	10/9.8	102/100.0
Nationality	19/18.6	8/7.8	5/4.9	15/14.7	10/9.8	8/7.8	9/8.8	5/4.9	23/22.5	102/99.8
History	24/23.5	12/11.8	11/10.8	9/8.8	15/14.7	7/6.9	11/10.8	3/2.9	10/9.8	102/100.0
Traditions	18/17.6	22/21.6	21/20.6	9/8.8	5/4.9	8/7.8	4/3.9	2/2.0	12/11.8	102/99.0
Family	45/44.1	13/12.7	8/7.8	12/11.8	7/6.9	4/3.9	4/3.9	——	9/8.8	102/99.9
National Origins	14/14.0	5/5.0	3/3.0	8/8.0	6/6.0	4/4.0	6/6.0	21/21.0	33/33.0	100/100.0

TABLE 3.5. ORTHODOX SINGLES' RESPONSES TO FACTORS

Marriage Factors	Number	Percentage
Orthodox Faith	33	32.4
Ethnicity	5	4.9
Both	41	40.2
Neither	22	21.6
Missing	*1*	*1.0*
Total	102	100.1

**TABLE 3.6. ORTHODOX SINGLES' RESPONSES TO
ORTHODOX VS. ETHNIC IDENTITY**

Ethnic vs. Orthodox	Number	Percentage
Orthodox	31	30.4
Ethnic	23	22.5
Both	46	45.1
Neither/Other	2	2.0
Total	102	100.0

Orthodox vs. Ethnic Identity. To further explore the Orthodox Singles responses to the Orthodox vs. ethnic identity issue, the question was correlated with certain selective characteristics. Tables 3.7 and 3.8 show the correlations of Orthodox vs. ethnic identity by importance of language and ethnicity (Table 3.7) and by age (Table 3.8). Looking at Table 3.7, we notice that language and nationality were ranked as first and second in importance by more respondents who identified themselves as Orthodox. As one would expect, for those who identified themselves as ethnic, both language and nationality were perceived as equal in importance. For those who identified themselves as both Orthodox and ethnic, nationality as a dimension of ethnicity was more important than language. Looking at Table 3.8, those aged 45 years or over identified themselves as Orthodox with greater frequency than those aged 25 to 45 years. Again, the majority in both age groups identified themselves as both Orthodox and Greek ethnics.

Table 3.7 ORTHODOX VS. GREEK ETHNIC IDENTITY BY IMPORTANCE OF LANGUAGE AND ETHNICITY

IDENTIFYING AS:

Persons Ranking Very Important (1st and 2nd)	Orthodox		Greek Ethnic		Both		Other		Total
	N	%	N	%	N	%	N	%	N
Language	11	42.3	7	31.8	8	21.1	1	100.0	26
Nationality	5	19.2	7	31.8	15	39.5	0	0.0	27
N	26		22		38		1		87

$$x^2 = 13.51 * p < .05$$
* (significant)

TABLE 3.8 ORTHODOX VS. ETHNIC IDENTITY BY AGE CATEGORIES

IDENTIFYING AS:

Age Categories	Orthodox		Greek Ethnic		Both		Other		Total	
	N	%	N	%	N	%	N	%	N	%
Under 25	1	0.2								
25-45	13	27.6	9	19.1	25	53.1			47	99.8
45-over	17	34.0	12	24.0	20	40.0	1	0.2	50	98.2
N	31		21		45		1			

DISCUSSION AND ANALYSIS

The present study of Greek Orthodox and Greek American ethnicity illustrates a generational continuity of both Greek Orthodox and Greek ethnic identity of the second generation. This finding is also confirmed by a number of previous Greek American studies, including those by Scourby (1980), Demos (1989), Costantakos (1982), Constantinou and Harvey (1985), and others. As one would expect with any such organization, the religious dimension of Greek ethnic identity was slightly more important to the Orthodox Singles than the secular component of their Greek American identity. Also, while the majority of second generation Greek American Orthodox Singles perceived themselves as Greek Orthodox, at the same time they favor a PanOrthodox unity.[4] The extent to which the Orthodox Singles as a group is representative of the entire Greek Orthodox American community or, for that matter, of Eastern Orthodox American experience in general, can only be suggestive from the present analysis. A number of writers have suggested that the Greek American Orthodox identity will continue beyond the second generation. However, the number of third and fourth generation respondents was too small to make any definite predictions. In addition, the Orthodox Singles organization that the analysis was based upon was, by and large, a professional and semi-professional group which cannot be construed as representative of the entire Greek American community.

Orthodox vs. Ethnic Rankings. Insofar as the rankings of the various dimensions of Orthodox and ethnic identities went, it was found that the majority of the respondents ranked as most important the more *esoteric* or spiritual aspects of Orthodox faith, such as doctrines/beliefs, theology, and rituals/rites. The more external or visible manifestations of Orthodox faith such as Byzantine music, iconography, and architecture, which are part of the Eastern Orthodox tradition, were ranked fifth and below in importance. The low rankings of the more "visible" aspects of Orthodox Christianity by the members of Orthodox Singles can be partially explained by the fact that the more educated and professionally oriented the group, the more its tendency to be more knowledgeable and appreciative of the more esoteric and spiritual aspects of the Orthodox faith.

Insofar as the rankings of the various dimensions of the secular Greek ethnicity are concerned, "Greek family," along with the broader aspects of "Greek culture" and "history," were ranked by the majority of the respondents as the first and second highest in importance among the eight dimensions of Greek ethnicity. Greek food as an indicator of Greek ethnicity was ranked last in terms of importance of Greek ethnic identity. The reason for the lowest ranking of "Greek cuisine" as a dimension of Greek ethnicity is understandable because the second generation by and large is a "status conscious" generation. Because a large number of new first generation Greek immigrants operate restaurants, Americans think of Greeks, including Greek Americans, in stereotypical terms, that is to say, as restaurateurs. To be a restaurant operator is not considered of high social status in the United States.

Language and Nationality. Those who stressed the Orthodox religious dimension of Greek ethnicity ranked language first in importance and nationality second. For those who identified themselves as Greek ethnics more than as Greek Orthodox, while both language and nationality were perceived as important, nationality was by far more important. Both language and nationality are dimensions of Greek ethnic identity. One can suggest that as the religious Orthodox identity becomes important as a component of Greek ethnic identity, one would expect nationality will decline as a dimension of Greek identity. However, since Orthodox identity is rather esoteric and a minority Christian faith, one would expect Greek ethnicity to be understood in broader Greek cultural terms rather than along Orthodox religious and/or nationality/language secular dimensions only. Americans know more about ancient Greek culture, which has much stronger roots in western civilization, than about Orthodox Byzantine identity, which has shallow roots and influence in the West in general and the United States in particular. While Greek Orthodox identity operates internally through Greek Orthodox religious communities, Greek ethnicity operates externally in the larger American society and culture. This means that while Greek Orthodox is more of an internal phenomenon, and by and large supported by the Greeks and some who are converted to Greek Orthodox, Greek American ethnicity is more external and visible, and is part of the American ethnic multiculturalism phenomenon. It is the secular dimension of Greek identity that is more visible to Americans. It is this part of Greek ethnicity that sustains the institutional continuity of Greek Orthodox faith in the United States and in other parts of the world that Greek communities exist.

SUMMARY AND CONCLUSION

In this analysis an effort was made to explore the dimensions of Greek Orthodox identity and Greek ethnicity through a survey of an Orthodox Singles organization in the Chicago area in the fall of 1990. As one would expect, the findings point to the salience of the Orthodox faith for the members of the Orthodox Singles organization. Although ethnicity was not as equally important as their faith, it was broadly perceived in subcultural terms, particularly insofar as Greek family patterns, culture, and history are concerned. Orthodox faith for this group takes precedence over nationality and Greek ethnicity in general. Greek ethnicity for this group is perceived in broader cultural terms. However, most respondents perceive themselves as both Greek ethnics and Greek Orthodox. We must further investigate the extent to which the embourgeoisement of Greek Americans accelerates the loss of Greek identity in the United States.

The findings and interpretations of this study are tentative. That ethnic transformation and ethnogenesis among ethnic groups are taking place has been documented by many students of ethnic intergroup relations. However, the extent to which such transformation is occurring beyond the second generation, and the nature of such processes, must be further investigated. For example, we must look not only at ethnic Orthodox identity among the members of third and fourth generations of professional Greek Americans, but also at ethnic Orthodox identity among members of other socioeconomic classes in this group (including, perhaps, small business operators, blue collar workers, etc.). The ethnic trends within Greek America are not unique. In general, various ethnic groups undergo similar experiences.

ENDNOTES

[1]To name the most pertinent of these conferences one has to include a) the "KRIKOS" conference--a cultural and scientific international organization which maintains links with Greece proper and the Greeks of the diaspora, held at Fordham University on October 13, 1984; b) the first Theodore Saloutos Conference on the "Greek American Experience," held at the Immigration History Research Center, University of Minnesota on May 11-13, 1989; and c) the conference on "Greek American Experience: Past, Present, and Future," held at the Hellenic College (Brookline, MA) on October 19-21, 1990.

[2]Partial results of the survey were presented at the Hellenic College conference on the "Greek American Experience: Past, Present, and Future" (1990) and in the section "Race, ethnicity, and religion" discussion panel at the American Sociological meetings held in Miami, Florida in 1993.

[3]While this was an Orthodox singles organization, the majority of its members were Greek Orthodox. Roughly one fifth were non-Greek. The reason I decided to conduct a survey of this organization was the fact that I had access to its membership because I became a member myself. The marital status of most members of the Orthodox singles fall into three categories--single, never married, or divorced. The sex ratio was about 50-50, and respondents were predominantly second generation. Since non-Greek Orthodox were very few, they were not included in the cross tabulations and analysis. For more detailed information see Table 1 sociodemographic characteristics.

Another reason for choosing this organization to examine the strength of both religious and secular dimensions of Greek ethnicity was the fact that in addition to single marital status, Orthodox identity was considered an important criterion of membership in this organization. One will expect members of this organization to have a much stronger religious rather than secular Greek identity.

[4]The first visit of a Greek Orthodox Patriarch to the United States in the summer of 1990 was significant, at least symbolically. It made all Orthodox faithful proud of their religious traditions and identity. The religious freedom following the debacle of communism in Eastern European nations for the first time since the communist takeover was perhaps an important historical event for world Orthodox Christianity, which contributed to this perception of the panOrthodox movement and the revival of Orthodoxy in Eastern Europe and former Soviet Union republics, and other parts of the world where Orthodox Christians live.

REFERENCES

Bruneau, Michel. 1993. "The Orthodox Church and the Greek Diaspora." In *Social Compass*, 40, 2 (June): 199-216.

Costantakos, Chrysie. 1982. "Greek Subculture and Greek Ethnicity." In Psomiades & Scourby, *The Greek American Community in Transition*. New York: Pella Publishing Co.

Constantinou, Stavros T. and Milton E. Harvey. 1985. "Basic Dimensional Structure and Intergenerational Differences in Greek American Ethnicity." *Sociology and Social Research*, 69, 2 (January): 234-254.

Counselis, James Steve. 1989. "Greek Orthodox Church Statistics of the United States, 1949-1989: Some Ecclesial and Social Patterns" in *Journal of the Hellenic Diaspora* vol. XVI, Nos. 1-4 (Spring-Summer-Fall-Winter): 129-139.

Demos, Vasilike. 1989. "Greek Ethnicity in Two Greek Orthodox Communities: A Study in Continuity and Change." Paper presented at the first Theodore Saloutos Conference. University of Minnesota. May 11-13, 1989.

Kourvetaris, George. 1977. "Greek American Professionals: 1820s-1970s." *Balkan Studies*, 18, 2: 285-317.

_____. 1989. "Greek American Professionals and Entrepreneurs." *Journal of the Hellenic Diaspora*, Vol. XVI, Nos. 1, 2, 3, 4 (1989):105-128.

_____. 1990. "Conflicts and Identity Crises Among Greek Americans and Greeks of the Diaspora." *International Journal of Contemporary Sociology*, 27, 3-4 (July-October): 137-153.

Saloutos, Theodore. 1973. *"The Greek Orthodox Church in the United States and Assimilation." International Migration Review* vol. 7, no. 3, pp. 395-408.

Scourby, A. 1980. "Three Generations of Greek Americans: A Study in Ethnicity," "International Migration Review," vol. 14, pp. 43-52.

Tsaousis, D. C. 1983. "Hellinismos Kai Hellinikotita" (Hellenism and Greekness). In *Hellenism and Greekness*. Athens: Kollaros and Co.

Vlachos, E. C. 1968. *The Assimilation of Greeks in the United States*. Athens: National Center of Social Research.

Appendix A

A SURVEY OF ORTHODOX AND ETHNIC IDENTITY

1.   If someone asked you what your faith is, how would you respond?

_____Orthodox _____Eastern Orthodox _____Greek Orthodox
_____Russian Orthodox _____Serbian Orthodox _____other

2.   How important is your Orthodox faith?

_____very important _____important _____somewhat important

3.   If you had to choose between your Orthodox identity and your ethnic identity
     (Greek, Russian, Serbian, etc.) which would you choose?

_____Orthodox identity _____ethnic identity _____both _____neither
_____other

4.   If you were to choose your future marriage partner, which factor or factors would
     you say will be important in your decision?

_____Orthodox faith _____ethnicity _____both _____neither

5.   Do you consider yourself:

_____Orthodox American _____Orthodox ethnic American _____simply an
American?

6.   With the demise of Communist regimes in Eastern Europe, more religious freedom
     in the Soviet Union, and the recent visit to the U.S. by the Orthodox Patriarch
     Demetrios, are you in favor of a panorthodox unity in North America and other
     parts of the world?

_____Yes _____No _____I am not sure

7.   What do you like the most in your Orthodox identity? Please rank the following
     in order of preference by placing 1 for the most likeable feature, 2 for the less
     likeable, etc.

Orthodox Faith

_____ritual/rites   _____mysticism   _____theology   _____icons
_____doctrine/beliefs   _____ Byzantine music   _____Byzantine architecture
_____other Please explain!

_____
_____
_____
_____

8. Please do the same thing for your ethnic identity as you did for your Orthodox identity. (Ranking the following features of your ethnic identity).

Ethnic Identity

_____food   _____language   _____culture   _____nationality   _____history
_____traditions   _____family   _____country of my national origins   _____other
Please explain!

_____
_____
_____
_____

9. What is your age? _____ (in years)

10. What generation American are you?

_____First generation (if you were born overseas)

_____Second generation (if you are American born of foreign parents or mixed parenthood, one foreign born and one American born)

_____Third generation (if both or one of your grandparents were born in the United States)

_____Fourth generation (if both or one of your great grandparents were born in the U.S.)

_____Other Please explain!

_____

_____

_____

11. Sex: _____Male _____Female

12. What is your marital status?

_____single _____never married _____divorced _____separated

13. What kind of work do you do for a living? Please be specific.

_____

_____

_____

14. What is your nationality?

_____Greek _____Russian _____Serbian _____Other

CHAPTER 4
PATTERNS OF GENERATIONAL SUBCULTURE AND INTERMARRIAGE OF THE GREEKS IN THE UNITED STATES[*]

Intermarriage has been called both the "final test of assimilation" (Kennedy, 1944: 331-39, 1952: 56-59; Herberg, 1955; Lopreato, 1970) and an indicator of the disposition for a person to lose his or her ethnic identification. The fusion of cultural disparities of nationality groups into an Anglo-Saxonic model is largely accomplished through intermarriage. Subsequently, the higher the rate of intermarriage, the higher the rate of assimilation. Intermarriage will be defined as that type of union in which married persons subscribe to distinctly different religious, racial, class and nationality subcultures from their own—either prior to or after marriage (Gordon, 1964: 1). Thus, we may distinguish among interfaith marriage, racial intermarriage, interclass, and interethnic marriage.[1] Generational subculture[2] is used here to refer to the cultural patterns of each of the three generations of Greeks within American society, particularly with respect to ethnic patterns of marriage, intermarriage, and styles of life.

In 1944 Kennedy (1944: 331-39, 1952: 56-59) suggested that the "single melting pot"[3] hypothesis has been replaced by the "triple melting pot" hypothesis according to which assimilation takes place within the three major religions in the United States with Roman Catholicism, Protestantism, and Judaism serving as the three fundamental bulwarks. Thus, Roman Catholics tend to marry other Roman Catholics; Protestants tend to marry other Protestants, and Jews tend to marry other Jews. Religious differences, then, function as the chief basis of differentiation in intermarriage.

It has been reported (Lopreato, 1970; Greeley, 1970; Cavan, 1970) that by and large these intrafaith marriages are interdenominational marriages particularly for Protestants and Jews. For example, Lutheran Protestants tend to marry other Lutherans, Conservative Protestants tend to marry other Conservative Protestants, or Conservative Jews tend to marry other Conservative Jews. In addition, Lenski (1961: 49) argued that "one-fifth of the now homogeneous marriages have been contracted by persons raised in different

---

[*] A version of this chapter was originally published in the *International Journal of Sociology of the Family*, 1971 Vol. 1 (May): 34-48. I would like to express my appreciation to Professor Peter Chimbos for providing me with pertinent data on Greek Canadian intermarriages (1996).

faiths." Similarly, Besanceney (1962: 3-20) found that in a larger sample, three out of five marriages involving partners raised in different faiths become homogeneous marriages through conversion of one partner or the other. Thus, whenever strict ethnic endogamy (along nationality lines) is attenuated in the subsequent generations, one would expect that religious endogamy will persist, and that future cleavages will be primarily along religious lines rather than along nationality lines. Besanceney (1965: 719) also argues that rates of ethnic intermarriage are greater than those of religious intermarriage. However, to compute the expected rate of religious intermarriage, Besanceney thinks that one must know the frequency distribution of the religious groups in the population (1965: 720).

The validity of intermarriage as an index of assimilation has been questioned by a number of writers (Marcson, 1950: 51 and 75-78; Price and Zubrycki, 1962: 58-69). Marcson, for example, argues that the significant factor in intermarriage is "class" (interclass marriage) rather than "culture," and intermarriage is more of an index of "class homogamy" rather than cultural assimilation. In other words, the greater the similarity in socio-economic status, the greater the probability of intermarriage.

The purpose of this paper is 1) to examine certain generational subcultural patterns and trends in intermarriage among three generations of Greeks in the United States, and 2) to suggest propositions for future research in this area. Initially, an effort will be made to describe and analyze some sociocultural aspects of each of the three generations of Greeks in the United States. Secondly, subcultural patterns of intermarriage will be examined in relation to the emerging patterns of assimilation among the three Greek generations. In this section of the paper, some empirical data on Greek intermarriages will be included that were collected from two midwestern middle-sized communities with small Greek populations during the summer months of 1970. Also, some data from vital statistics on marriages and divorces kept by the Greek Orthodox Archdiocese of North and South America, and the Diocese of Chicago will be used. Finally, some general conclusions and tentative propositions will be offered for further research in this area.

Due to the lack of sufficient statistical data and empirical studies concerning Greek intermarriages (with the exception, perhaps, of general current statistics compiled and kept by the Greek Orthodox Archdiocese), speculations concerning Greek intermarriages are mostly impressionistic. Thus, the analysis and discussion which follows is primarily derived from general studies on the Greeks and the author's own observations and research in the United States. Consequently, whatever propositions are advanced in this paper must be taken as tentative.

PATTERNS OF GENERATIONAL SUBCULTURE

First Generation. One can distinguish three major types of first generation Greeks with respect to marriage and family. First, there were those who returned to Greece for reasons of ill health, social adjustment, as well as for their inability to find a suitable spouse to marry. Second, there were those who remained in the United States but never married because of personal and family problems and obligations. For example, a number of Greek men sacrificed their own happiness in order to earn and save their money so that it could be sent to Greece and be used as dowries for their sisters. Finally, there were those who decided to marry, raise families, and eventually settle permanently in the United States.

To the Greek immigrant, the family was looked upon as a persisting social and cultural institution in which attitudes were formed (particularly those pertaining to sex, courtship and marital selection, language, patterns of authority, leisure activities, and food habits). Because of these considerations, many of the early Greeks journeyed back to Greece in search for a bride, had prospective brides arranged and vouched for by relatives and friends waiting for them in Greece, or simply had arranged a marriage through an exchange of photographs (Saloutos, 1964: 85). (Incidentally, similar patterns are followed by the recent Greek immigrants.)

Even in contemporary Greece, studies (Sanders, 1967; Friedl, 1962; Lambiri, 1965; Safilios-Rothschild, 1967; Bardis, 1955) have suggested that the Greek family is characterized as traditional, patriarchal, and rural with one of the most closely-knit families in the world. And despite some changes in the social structure of Greece, the family still maintains its traditional values and character. For example, cultural and societal values such as respect for the elderly, the authority of the husband, morality, honor, shame and *philotimo* (self-respect) are still maintained. The family as a social unit operates as a constraining influence against any social and moral misconduct of the children and particularly of the daughters. In addition, Sanders (1967) reported that the family unit had to be strong and cohesive in the face of the hostile world due to the fact that Greece has undergone political, social, and economic turmoil throughout its long history, both from within and from without. Thus, strong and cohesive family orientations and patterns were brought to the United States by the Greeks.

Attitudes of Greek men toward American women of other nationalities were also based on a great deal of misinformation, superficiality, and poor judgment. There were many reasons for this. In the first place, early immigrants came to know America from the bottom up. Second, due to the ethnocentric disposition, Greek men perpetuated the widely held belief in Greece that Greek women had a monopoly on virtue, homemaking, and belief in the family (Saloutos, 1964: 85). Third, many Greek men as well as other immigrants shared the belief that marriage in America was a "passing convenience" which also meant that American Women were more lax in matters of sex and marriage, and therefore, it was easier to marry exogamously since it was easier to dissolve such a marriage. If a Greek man married endogamously, dissolving the marriage was not as easy.

However, with the oncoming of the second generation (the immigrants' children), the highly ethnocentric, traditional, and folk-oriented outlook of the first generation subculture was challenged. Culture conflict between parents and children was inevitable. Of course, part of this conflict was due to generational differences.

Second Generation. The second generation (as any other generation of other ethnic groups) emerged as a product of a Greek subculture and the American culture, a new brand and cultural hybrid of Greek-American. Despite the fact that "Hellenism" and "Americanism" as ways of life are basically compatible with each other, the latter exerted a greater impact on the second generation Greeks. This generation was more concerned about social acceptability and status by their peers and other Americans than about maintaining Greek identity and Hellenism as represented by their parents in America.

Members of the second generation had many advantages over the first generation. *First* to begin with, they did not have to start from scratch as did their parents. *Second*, they grew up in a well-knit Greek family where rudiments of Greek ethnic subculture were transmitted to them, particularly those pertaining to courtship, marriage, language, religion, and respect for the authority of the father and the elderly. *Third*, the values of aspiration, hard work, the Greek philotimo (self-esteem) and family honor were implanted in them by their parents. Achievement and success were a pride and credit not only to their immediate families and kin but also to the entire Greek community.

Third Generation. Members of the third generation are the grandchildren of the first generation. This group also includes the offsprings of intermarriages as well as those of the second generation "rebels." The latter comprises those members of the second generation who left their ethnic community, Anglicized their names, and achieved structural assimilation in the American social structure.

As a rule, members of the third generation have incorporated the values, attitudes and norms of the American middle class subculture. Social class is more important to them than ethnicity. Both education and professional achievement are highly valued among members of the third generation. In an empirical and comparative study of six ethnic groups, it was found (Rosen, 1959: 47-60) that a high level of aspiration and achievement exists among members of third generation Greeks. According to Rosen, the achievement orientation of ethnic groups can be explained in terms of dissimilar psychological and cultural emphasis displayed by these groups toward achievement. The Greek child is trained to be self-reliant and is exhorted to be a "credit to his group" in the Greek community. The author argues that the cultures of white Protestants, Jews, and Greeks stand out as being more individualistic, activistic and future-oriented.

Unlike the first and second generation, members of the third generation are not preoccupied with ethnic prejudice and discrimination. Viewed in this way, they can afford to be proud of their ancestry. However, they consider themselves primarily American and only symbolically manifest an interest and liking for Greek food, music, and dancing. This Dionysian cultural "atavism" in things Greek was stimulated by the new influx of Greek immigrants following World War II and the popularized movies "Zorba the Greek" and "Never on Sunday" whose theme song became a world-wide favorite. Furthermore, such national and international developments as the military take over of Greece in 1967, the marriage of Jacqueline Kennedy to Aristotle Onassis, the Nixon-Agnew ticket in 1968 (and in 1988 the candidacy of Mike Dukakis for president of the United States), the emphasis on ethnic studies and programs, and visits to modern Greece by younger generations of Greek Americans have further awakened their interest in modern Greek ethnicity and culture. However, with the exception of the Greek Orthodox faith, one finds little or no interest among members of the third generation in maintaining the ethnic institutional aspects of Greek culture such as language, family traditions, and endogamous marriage.

The new influx of Greeks following World War II did not retard the Americanization and assimilation processes of the third generation. However, the fact of the matter is that American born Greeks (even Greeks who have been in the United States for a longer period of time) do not usually associate with the newcomers. This is especially true in the patterns of dating and marriage. For example, in dating patterns on college campuses, there is a tendency for members of ethnic groups to seek dates outside their own ethnic group. This is primarily due to the fact that dating outside of one's group does not have a constraining influence on them. It is also a matter of availability of both sexes of the same ethnic group in a college population. In general, the more ethnically oriented the Greek American, the greater the tendency to date from his or her own ethnic background. Furthermore, the more assimilated the Greek, the less likely he or she is to place importance on dating Greek young men or young women. This is also true in terms of ethnic endogamous patterns of marriage, religion, learning Greek, and the like.

As a rule, members of the third generation Greek Americans think primarily as Americans and expect to be treated as such. One can argue that while the majority of the second generation Greek Americans learned Greek in order to communicate with their immigrant parents, the third generation did not have to learn Greek to communicate with their parents (the second generation). In most cases third generation children resent learning or attending Greek afternoon classes sponsored by the church. It is because of their Greek parents that Greek American children are forced to attend Greek afternoon schools.

TRENDS OF INTERMARRIAGE

In this section of the analysis an effort is made to point out: First, to what extent both the "melting pot" and "inter- denominational" hypotheses can be expanded to the Eastern Orthodox branch of Christianity. And second, what are some general trends of intermarriage in each of the three generations of Greeks in the United States.

Eastern Orthodoxy can be considered a third branch of Christianity. Like Protestantism, Eastern Orthodoxy is also a multidenominational Christian faith that in addition to Greek includes Russian, Serbian, Rumanian, Albanian, Syrian, Bulgarian, and other ethnoreligious groups. But unlike Roman Catholicism and Protestantism, Eastern Orthodoxy derives its cultural traditions from the Christian East of Byzantium, rather than from the West. Furthermore, Eastern Orthodox denominations are distinct ethnoreligious denominational groups. Each one is autocephalous and only symbolically and historically identifies itself as a member of the Eastern Orthodox Church.

Following World War II, a movement toward the unification of all Eastern Orthodox denominations and the creation of Eastern Orthodoxy as a third Christian religion in the United States was initiated. The Russian Orthodox Church detached itself from the Russian Patriarchate and established the Orthodox church in the United States during the 1980s. In a similar move, the Greek Orthodox Archdiocese, in its biennial conference of clergy and laity (July, 1970), pronounced its intention to follow a more independent course both from the Greek Patriarchate of Constantinople to which administratively it belongs and from its affiliation with the national Church of Greece. This issue continues to plague the administrative character of the Greek orthodox church in the United States during the late 1990s.

Assuming that both the "triple melting pot" and "interdenominational" hypotheses are valid in explaining patterns of intermarriage among the three branches of Christianity in the United States or can there be another "fourth melting pot" or "interdenominational" hypothesis for explaining intermarriage among the Eastern Orthodox denominations as well? Despite the fact that there are a few empirical studies to either substantiate or refute "the fourth melting pot hypothesis," it seems to me that both the "fourth melting pot" and "interdenominational hypotheses" seem inapplicable to the Eastern Orthodox faith. This is not only true with the first generation Greeks but with the subsequent generations as well. The most important reasons which separate the Greek Orthodox ethnoreligious group from its Eastern Orthodox counterparts are not theological or doctrinal, but socio-cultural and socio-political in character. Following the end of the Cold War in 1989, however, efforts have been made to unify the Eastern Orthodox ethnoreligious denominations. This is rather unlikely to take place soon due to the power struggle among the various orthodox patriarchates and orthodox jurisdictions.

An interethnic marriage is considered an interfaith marriage for the Greeks as well. This is due to the fact that no other ethnoreligious group practices the Greek Orthodox faith. For although there are other Eastern Orthodox denominations, these are detached from the mother church and Patriarchate of Constantinople. Thus, the Eastern Orthodox faith is based primarily on "nationality" rather than on a "collective religious consciousness." Nationality, particularly among the first generation Greeks and Slavic nationalities, was considered more important than Orthodoxy. This religious ethnocentrism was also true among early European Roman Catholics and Protestant denominations. However, the difference between Roman Catholics or Protestants and those of the Eastern Orthodox faith is due to the great schism between the western and eastern branches of Christianity in the eleventh century A.D. Later, both the Protestants and Orthodox Christians were further differentiated into various denominations.

At present, some believe that the Greek Orthodox faith cannot survive in America if it is stripped of its national and cultural identification. This view is particularly held by the first generation traditionalists who argue that religion is only meaningful within the context of ethnicity in that both religion and nationality are inseparable entities for the Greeks. On the other hand, the environmentalists (members primarily of the second and third generations) believe that the Greek Orthodox faith must be detached from Greek nationality and be merged with other Eastern Orthodox denominations. The latter view is, of course, more consonant with the general trend of big religious differentiation rather than ethnic differentiation of the churches in America. Nationality, to the majority of the second and third generation members who do not speak Greek, is an abstraction and secondary to Orthodoxy. Furthermore, this view is also true with both the "fourth melting pot" and "interdenominational hypotheses" in intermarriage. In other words, members of the second and third generations and some of the first generation environmentalists are primarily interested in maintaining their religious identity rather than their ethnic or secular identity.

Both arguments are somewhat plausible. In the first place, those who argue against unification and emphasize nationality as the sustaining factor of Greek religion in America believe that as long as new Greek immigrants continue to come by the thousands to the United States, the Greeks as an ethnic group will not follow the path of other nationality groups. Greeks will still maintain their ethnic identity even though the English language replaces Greek in the church. Second, despite the fact that Greek Orthodoxy is the largest Eastern Orthodox denomination in the United States, its adherents are by and large Greek in national origin. This is not only true in the United States but in mainland Greece, Cyprus, Canada, Australia, and other parts of the world where there are Greek speaking people. Therefore, unification of the Eastern Orthodox denominations would not affect the membership of the Greek Church, except perhaps those members who have been converted to the Greek Orthodox faith due to intermarriage. Third, unification of the Eastern Orthodox denominations will face the same problems as Christian unification in general, particularly those issues dealing with economics, leadership, authority and administration of the church.

Those who favor denominational unity point out that in order for Eastern Orthodoxy to be given full status and be recognized as the fourth major religion in the United States (the third largest is Jewish; the Moslem faith is the most rapidly developing religion in the United States and indeed the world), it must first abandon its parochialism and ethnocentrism. Furthermore, the same people argue that the spirit of our age is toward ecumenicalism and Christian unity. In order to accomplish this, the Orthodox church must first move toward denominational unification. Unless the Eastern Orthodox Church moves toward unification and collective religious consciousness, one can expect that neither the "fourth melting pot" nor the "interdenominational" hypotheses can explain patterns of religious intermarriage among the Greeks and other Eastern Orthodox Christians.

Another profound reason which further complicates the "melting pot" and "interdenominational" hypotheses of intermarriage among the Eastern Orthodox ethnoreligious groups is that although Greece identifies with the West politically, socially, and culturally, ecclesiastically or religiously she, along with other Eastern European nations, shares many traditions with the Christian Byzantium. This middle-of-the-road position makes the Greek Orthodox faith a culture preserving institution in that both ethnicity and religion become inseparable entities for the Greeks. Having put forth some general notions of the "fourth melting pot" and "interdenominational" hypotheses, what are some trends of intermarriage in each of the three generations of Greeks?

First Generation. Due to the scarcity of first generation Greek women, a number of first generation Greek men married non-Greek women. However, the more tradition-bound the Greek male was, the more strongly he felt the need for a mate of his own nationality and religion. Preference for a mate of one's faith, however, did not prevent intermarriage in the first generation. Mistaras (1950) suggested that a substantial number of marriages in the first generation Chicago Greeks were inter-ethnic as well as interclass marriages. Moreover, the less assimilated the Greek spouse was to American culture, the lower his socio-economic class and the more likely he was to marry a lower class person (Mistaras, 1950). Despite the substantial number of intermarriages in the first generation, Stycos (1948: 28) reported that by 1930, first generation Greeks had the fewest exogamous marriages compared to other ethnic groups. Although intermarriage was common, it was subject to censure by the Greek Church. For instance, a religious ceremony in itself did not make a marriage valid. Both civil and religious sanctions had to be met before a marriage was valid in the Greek Orthodox Church. At present however, this is no longer true.

Although a few studies are available indicating the rate of intermarriage in the first generation, intermarriage in the first generation varied according to the social situation and the number of Greeks in the larger American community. The smaller the ethnic community of a particular minority in relation to other ethnic groups, the higher its rate of intermarriage. This was especially true in small and middle sized American communities in which a few Greeks were found. In these small communities the rate of intermarriage and assimilation were the highest among the first and subsequent generation of Greeks.

In those communities where the first generation men were compelled to marry exogamously due to the scarcity of Greek women, the non-Greek spouse was more likely to convert or simply follow her husband's faith. For example, in a study of two midwestern communities this writer found that out of 180 Greek families who were paid members of the local Greek Churches (at least one of the spouses was of Greek origin) thirty-four of these marriages were of an equal number of first and second generation intermarriages. All of the first generation intermarriages involved Greek men married to non-Greek spouses. The latter followed or were converted to their husband's faith with the exception of one. This was also true of intermarriages in the second generation where Greek men married non-Greek spouses. In a recent study of "gender boundaries" of two Greek Orthodox communities (1989: 77-93), Demos has found that "the most persistent ethnic difference between men and women is with respect of endogamy—women are more likely than men to marry within the Greek ethnic community."

In an effort to explain interfaith and/or interethnic marriages in the first generation, one can offer the following tentative propositions: (1) Ethnic identity was synonymous with religious identity for the first generation Greeks. Those Greek men who married non-Greek spouses managed to maintain their ethnic identity through the cultural institution of the Greek Orthodox Church. (This can be said of the second and to a lesser extent of the third generation intermarriages).   (2) Those non-Greek spouses who married Greek men did not, as a rule, feel a strong commitment toward their own faith.   It was easier for the former to make the adjustment to her husband's religion than vice versa. (3) Intermarriage in the first generation was also a matter of compromise and necessity of both spouses.   While the Greek male married a non-Greek female (interethnic), it was understood that his wife would follow her husband's religion.   In this way, if the couple had children, the latter had to be baptized in the Greek Orthodox Church.   While this pattern seemed the rule among first and second generation men, it is not altogether clear what the pattern was among second generation Greek women who were married to non-Greek men.

Second generation. An area in which the first generation Greek family attempted to exert its authority was that of regulating courtship and marriage of their children, the second generation.   Saloutos (1964: 313) suggested that immigrant parents thought that yielding to American patterns of courtship and marriage was equivalent to yielding to immoral behavior.   Of course, such an attitude was shared by other early immigrant groups as well.   Many Greeks and other immigrants expressed an abhorrence to the way so many marriages ended in America.   However, attitudes have changed.   Intermarriage has become more and more the norm among the Greeks rather than the exception.

Among first generation Greeks such attitudes were not without some justification.   *First*, dating among teenagers as practiced in the United States was unheard of in rural Greece (from which the majority of first generation Greek men came).   *Second*, few parents of the first generation encouraged their children, particularly their daughters, to bring their non-Greek friends to their homes, fearing that their children would marry non-Greeks.   *Third*, seeing a daughter with a boy could easily arouse suspicions even though the boy was of Greek background (Saloutos, 1964: 313).   Again these patterns of dating among the Greeks have changed.   Dating non-Greeks among the new second and subsequent generations of Greeks is widespread.   Mixed marriages are the norm and not the exception.

In the past exogamous marriage could lead to a form of social ostracism on the part of friends, relatives, and neighbors in the larger Greek American community. In Saloutos' words "a son who married outside the group could become an outcast and be stigmatized, an ungrateful errant who is setting a bad example for others. The predicament of a daughter who deviated from the ethnic matrimonial norm of endogamy was viewed as something more tragic" (1964: 313-314). Greek parents and the Greek community as a whole pointed out the advantages of marrying a girl or boy of Greek ethnic background, particularly those pertaining to family norms, morality, economic security, and the like. Furthermore, marrying endogamously was also a matter of family honor, philotimo (self-esteem), ethnic pride, and an exercise of parental authority upon the children. Likewise, parents, relatives, and friends in the Greek American community warned of the dangers of intermarriage that included such things as the loss of the children's ethnic identity (especially of the daughter), and the prospects of marrying a domineering woman who would squander the boy's money and associate with other men, and eventually take him into a divorce court (Saloutos, 1964: 313-314). Again these patterns have changed. Marrying within one's ethnic group does not guarantee the endurance of the marriage. We found as many divorces among Greek Americans as among interfaith marriages.

Comparing the divorce rates between endogamous versus exogamous marriages, Gordon (1964) found that interfaith (exogamous) marriages tend to have a higher divorce rate than intrafaith (endogamous) marriages. This is not the case among the Greek inter-Christian marriages. Table 4.1 shows the number of Greek Orthodox and Inter-Christian marriages and divorces in the United States in the last eighteen years. Looking at table 4.1, one can make the following observations: 1) Inter-Christian marriages have progressively increased and marriages between Orthodox have decreased. 2) Divorces between Orthodox couples tend to be higher than among those inter-Christian marriages. 3) The higher divorce rate among Orthodox couples is contrary to the notion that intra-faith or intra-denominational marriages are more likely to be more successful than inter-faith. Whether this is the norm, we do not know for sure. Church statistics report only those marriages (both intra-faith and inter-faith) that take place in the church.

TABLE 4.1 MARRIAGES AND DIVORCES BETWEEN ORTHODOX AND
INTER-CHRISTIAN DENOMINATIONS, 1976-1993

YEARS	MARRIAGES		DIVORCES	
	BETWEEN ORTHODOX	INTER-CHRISTIAN	BETWEEN ORTHODOX	INTER-CHRISTIAN
1976	2,537	2,201	350	201
1977	2,521	2,438	358	223
1978	2,295	2,445	419	256
1979	2,512	2,412	430	210
1980	2,009	2,660	457	306
1981	1,781	3,104	405	339
1982	1,936	3,175	442	344
1983	1,960	3,287	366	364
1984	1,821	3,322	388	336
1985	2,200	3,387	360	456
1986	1,900	3,253	363	358
1987	1,850	3,673	382	332
1988	2,001	3,710	362	357
1989	2,144	3,904	389	384
1990	2,187	3,769	402	338
1991	2,191	3,520	409	331
1992	1,922	3,530	347	417
1993	2,032	3,429	354	395
TOTAL	37,799	57,219	6,983	5,947

Source: "Vital Statistics" *Yearbook* 1995. New York: Greek Orthodox Archdiocese of North and South America.

Somewhat similar patterns of inter-Christian marriages as those for the entire Greek Orthodox Archdiocese can be observed in the Greek Orthodox Diocese of Chicago. (See Table 4.2 below.) Looking at Table 4.2 we can make the following observations: 1) Almost two-thirds of marriages in 1993 and 1994 in the Greek Orthodox Diocese of Chicago were church intermarriages. 2) Orthodox marry an equal number of Roman Catholic as they marry Orthodox. 3) Among the Protestant denominations, Lutheran, Methodist, Presbyterian, and Baptist are the most frequent denominations that Greek Orthodox members marry outside their Orthodox faith. The extent to which how many of these inter-Christian intermarriages remain Greek Orthodox or follow the other Christian faith is not known. One can speculate, however, that a substantial number of the children of these interfaith Christian marriages are raised in the Catholic faith and attend Catholic parochial schools.

The Greek parents' insistence upon their children's marrying endogamously seems to generate some latent functions for the former. (1) Greek parents, especially the mother, wanted to continue exerting influence on their children, even after the latter were married, a practice more prevalent in the extended rural type family in Greece; (2) marrying endogamously made it easier to explicitly or implicitly maintain the norms and folkways of the Greek subculture, especially those pertaining to the ethnoreligious holidays, food habits, leisure activities, kinship relationships, language patterns, and the like. Parents felt more secure and more welcome because they were unsure of being accepted if their children married exogamously. It must be noted, however, that parents' wishes were not always followed by their children. Although the children wanted to please the wishes of their parents, the difficulty or unavailability of finding a Greek spouse forced both children and parents to accept non-Greek spouses.

Somewhat similar patterns of intermarriage can be observed among the Greek Canadians. In tables 4.3, 4.4, and 4.5 below, one can notice the extent of inter-ethnic and Greek Orthodox marriages in Canada.

Looking at these three tables we can make the following observations:

1. The ethnic origin of spouses married to Greek-born Canadians in 1981 were 17.4%. Half of that number or 7.9% of female Canadians and non-female Canadians did likewise.

2. With the exception of 1991 mixed marriages, between 1989 and 1993, the majority of these marriages were mixed marriages in Canada.

3. Comparing Greek church weddings in the United States and Canada between January 1 to December 31, 1992, two-thirds of all marriages or 65.7% were considered mixed marriages.

TABLE 4.2 GREEK ORTHODOX DIOCESE OF CHICAGO

MARRIAGE SUMMARY 1994

Denomination			
ORTHODOX	215		38.39%
Roman Catholic	230		41.07%
Assembly of God	1		
Baptist	9	4	
Christian Assembly	1		
Congregationalist	1		
Episcopalian	7		
Faith Reformed	1		
Lutheran	46		
Melkite	1		
Methodist	19		
Pentecostal	1		
Presbyterian	21		
Protestant (see Memo)	4		
Reformed Christian	1		
United Church of Christ	2		
"Protestant" sub-total	115		20.54%
Inter-Church Total	341		57.02%
<u>DIOCESES TOTAL</u>	<u>560</u>		

MARRIAGE SUMMARY 1993

Denomination			
ORTHODOX	257		42.98%
Roman Catholic	245		
Ukrainian Catholic	1		41.14%
Assembly of God	1		
Baptist	15	3	
Congregational	3		
Disciples of Christ	1		
Episcopalian	1		
Lutheran	33		
Methodist	21		
Presbyterian	10		
Protestant (see memo)	2		
United Church of Christ	7		
"Protestant" sub-total	95		15.89%
Inter-Church Total	341		57.02%
<u>DIOCESE TOTAL:</u>	<u>598</u>		

Source: provided by Reverend Timothy G. Bakakos, pastor of St. Sophia Greek Orthodox Church, 1995 (The Diocese of Chicago has jurisdiction in the Mid-west states).

It must be noted that the demand for wives of Greek origin was great in the earlier years of Greek emigration because of the small ratio of females to males. Greek women of the second generation had two alternatives with regard to mate selection: (1) arranged marriage, and (2) marriage through romantic love. The former was a carry-over from Greece. Arranged marriages was a practice and still is in many parts of the world. In most instances it entails a broker or middle person, *proxenitis*, who serves as "go in between" and negotiates the marriage between the two prospective persons and families concerned. This type of marriage was looked upon as a life-time partnership not contingent upon initial romance. It was based on the notion that parents and relatives knew what was best for their children. Happiness was predicated on economic security and emotional maturity more than romantic love. Arranged marriages were thought to be synonymous with happiness for the children. The advocates of this type of marriage minimized the importance of romantic love and called for a more rational decision in marriage rather than one based primarily on the physical attractiveness of the members concerned.

TABLE 4.3 ETHNIC ORIGIN OF SPOUSES MARRIED TO GREEK BORN CANADIANS (1981)			
Gender	Spouse's Ethnic Origin		
	Canadian	Different Country	Total
Males (husbands)	10.9%	6.5%	17.4
Females (wives)	3.1%	4.8%	7.9

Source: Statistics Canada, 1981.

Note: The data do not distinguish marriages between members of two different countries of birth (e.g., husband born in Greece and wife from Greek parentage born in Egypt) that may not strictly be an inter-ethnic marriage.

TABLE 4.4 GREEK CHURCH WEDDINGS IN CANADA
(JANUARY 1, 1989 - DECEMBER 31, 1993)

Year	Greek Orthodox Marriages		Mixed Marriages	
	No.	%	No.	%
1989	443	(40.6)	548	(59.4)
1990	–		–	
1991	559	(52.0)	516	(48.0)
1992	481	(46.7)	550	(53.3)
1993	501	(47.4)	556	(52.6)
Total	1,984	46.7	2,176	53.3

Source: Greek Orthodox Diocese of Canada, Toronto, Ontario, 1995.

TABLE 4.5 GREEK CHURCH WEDDINGS IN U.S.A. AND CANADA
(JANUARY 1 - DECEMBER 31, 1992)

Type of Marriage	U.S.A.		Canada		Total	
	No.	%	No.	%	No.	%
Between Greek Orthodox	1,424	32.4	481	46.7	1,905	35.3
Mixed	2,945	67.6	550	53.3	3,495	65.7
Total	4,359	100.0	1,031	100.0	5,400	100.0

Source: Statistics of Greek Orthodox Archdiocese of North and South America, New York, 1992.

It has been suggested (Saloutos, 1964: 315-317) that arranged marriages were more prevalent among women than among men of the second generation. Stycos (1948: 31) reported that community pressure was stronger on Greek girls in that the endogamous ideals of the group had been more successfully "internalized" by the female member of the second generation. Furthermore, arranged marriages offered advantages even to shy Greek American women, and in part explains why in the earlier years it was rare to find spinsters among

Greek families (Saloutos, 1964: 315). This is not true however in more recent times. As we saw in chapter three there are many singles perhaps hundreds and thousands (both men and women) among second and third generation Greek Americans.

Younger generation American born Greeks view arranged marriages as anachronistic and a product of a semi-feudal society. It was this young Greek American male who was more likely to marry outside the Greek community. Although the better adjusted Greek American male was likely to enter into intermarriage, there is no conclusive evidence that he always did so. However, far more of the successful Greek American men married outside the Greek American group than parents and concerned compatriots desired (Saloutos, 1964: 317). In general, second generation Greek men were more likely to move away from Greek norms than second generation Greek women (Mistaras, 1950), especially those who were mobile or professionally oriented. It must be underscored that many prominent Greek Americans in politics, government, business, arts, and the professions have married non-Greek spouses. Such individuals include Brademas, Dukakis, Agnew, Dukakis' cousin Olympia (actress), Peterson, Snowe (senator from Maine), Sarbanes, Tsongas to name the most prominent Greek Americans have married non-Greek spouses.

While marriage for a second generation Greek woman meant that her parents were spared the need for providing a dowry,[4] parents always urged their children to marry into good, successful families whether the marriage was endogamous or exogamous. Parents preferred and many times insisted that their children marry endogamously. However, despite strong social pressures on the part of the relatives and the community as a whole, it was nevertheless impossible to stem the tide of intermarriage, especially by the second generation Greek men. Thus, a substantial number of marriages in the second generation can be designated as intermarriages. It appears that in most cases of intermarriage, the second generation male, rather than the female, was more likely to marry exogamously.

As with the first generation, interethnic marriages in the second generation are thought to be inter-Christian marriages as well. In most of these marriages second generation men married women of Roman Catholic or Protestant (mostly Lutheran) faith. This author contends that the non-Orthodox spouse is more likely to be converted to Greek Orthodox. Also, those converted to the Greek Orthodox faith tend to be more religiously-oriented toward their adopted faith than are their Greek Orthodox spouses.

In a pilot study of two midwestern communities in the state of Illinois involving approximately 180 couples who are paid members of their respective local parishes, results suggested that: (1) 34 intermarried couples were first or second generation; (2) 27 of the 34 couples or 79% involved both first or second generation men (16 and 11, respectively) married to non-Greek women. The remainder (7 couples) involved second generation Greek women married to non-Greek men. Of the 34 couples, all but 2 followed the Greek Orthodox faith.

Regarding the nationality of the non-Greek female spouses, no particular preference was evident by the first or second generation Greek male. Among the non-Greek members were those of German, Irish, Spanish, Swedish, Italian, Polish, or English ethnic background. The nature of interethnic marriage in the second generation varies inversely with the proportion of ethnic composition of the community. In other words, the higher the proportion of an ethnic group in the community, the less its intermarriage, and conversely, the lower the proportion, the higher its rate of intermarriage. Simply put, in communities in which only a few Greeks are found, we find a higher rate of intermarriage. Table 4.6 below reports a number of intermarriages in two midwestern communities.

TABLE 4.6—FIRST AND SECOND GENERATION
INTERMARRIAGES IN TWO MIDWESTERN COMMUNITIES[5]
(IN 1980s)

| Community | Generation[*] | | | | Generation[**] | | | |
| | Greek | | Non-Greek | | Greek | | Non-Greek | |
	H	W[***]	H	W	H	W	H	W
DeKalb	8	..	..	8	6	..	..	6
Rockford	8	..	..	8	5	7	7	5
Total	16	..	..	16	11	7	7	11
N = 34 couples.								

[*]First generation consists of sixteen couples in which all husbands are Greek and all the wives non-Greek.

[**]Second generation consists of eighteen marriages in which eleven of the Greek husbands married non-Greek wives, and seven Greek wives married non-Greek husbands.

[***](H) stands for husband and (W) stands for wife.

Furthermore, while the type of ethnic group in interethnic marriages seems less important to the second generation Greek males, one can argue that by insisting that their non-Greek spouses follow the Greek Orthodox faith, the former succeed in maintaining their Orthodox religious identity even though they are married to non-Greek and non-Orthodox spouses. Whether or not this is also true with second generation women married to non-Greek men cannot be ascertained. However, in view of the fact that second generation Greek American women more readily internalize the ideals of Greek subculture than Greek American males, one would expect that even Greek American women who are married exogamously tend to influence their non-Greek spouse and maintain their Greek Orthodox religious identity. Whether one of the members is willing to follow the other's faith depends on the extent to which one is strongly committed to his or her own faith, the presence of children in the family, and the economic, and socioeconomic class of the husband. Although there are no empirical studies to substantiate that, one can tentatively suggest that the higher the socioeconomic class of the Greek American male the more likely his non-Greek spouse will follow his Orthodox faith provided he is a committed Greek Orthodox Christian.

Another type of quasi-intermarriage in the second generation is what one might call "intercultural" marriage. To have this type of intermarriage, one of the spouses must have been born in another country or is a first generation immigrant. Although this marriage cannot be considered intermarriage in the strict sense of the word, one can nevertheless designate it as quasi-interethnic marriage. A quasi-interethnic marriage involves a second or third generation Greek American male or Greek American female spouse married to a Greek national.[6] As a rule these quasi-interethnic marriages present themselves with similar socio-psychological and cultural problems and conflicts as inter-faith and interethnic intermarriages in general. In fact, one can argue that the former may present more conflicts than one ordinarily would anticipate. One possible explanation for this is that intermarriages in the United States in general share a core of similar cultural and social characteristics that are distinctly American. This is not the case, however, with the quasi-interethnic marriages, particularly those aspects concerning family and marriage relations such as patterns of authority and decision making, husband and wife gender roles, and child and parent relationships, which in many respects are different in Greece and in the United States.

One type of the quasi-interethnic marriage includes a substantial number of Greek male students or professional Greek American men who came to the United States on a student exchange, or visitor's visa to further their education and who married second and third generation Greek American women in order to remain in the United States. The argument can be made that one more advantage that Greek American women have over Greek women born in Greece and women of other nationalities in the United States is that the American born Greek spouse is presented with a number of alternatives in mate selection. This has created resentment on the part of Greek women both in Greece and in the United States. This means Greek born women who emigrated to the United States or came as students had to compete for Greek born husbands with the Greek born American spouses.

Third Generation. If ethnicity (nationality) was the single most important characteristic in the first generation and religion in the second generation, it appears that social class or what Gordon calls "ethclass" characterize members of the third generation. Thus, the oncoming of third generation is followed by a concomitant decline of ethnoreligious factors and the increase in importance of social class and/or "ethclass" as factors in marriage. Ethclass refers to the intersection of ethnicity and class (see chapter seven on ethclass). Ethnoreligious membership is not sufficient to convince members in the third generation of the indispensability of endogamous marriage. Thus, the attenuation of either ethnic or religious identity in the third generation leads to more interclass patterns of dating and marriage.

While intermarriage in the first and second generations was looked upon as atypical behavior by the Greek community, in the third generation it is accepted both as desirable and as a form of status and social mobility. It was also unavoidable due to the fact that by the third and subsequent Greek American generations Greek ethnicity declines. Unlike the first and second generations, members of the third generation do not seem to preoccupy themselves with problems of social acceptance by their American peers. In this respect, the latter perceive themselves as American and identify as such with their peers and other Americans. As a rule, this generation is a college and professionally oriented generation. It is a status-conscious rather than ethnic-conscious generation.

One finds little data in the actual patterns of intermarriage in the third generation. A number of tentative propositions can be suggested as trends and future research possibilities in Greek American intermarriages beyond the second generation.

1.   The more assimilated a member of the third generation, the less likely he or she is to marry endogamously.

2. The more assimilated a member in the third generation, the higher his or her socio-economic status and the more likely he is to marry exogamously.

3. Men in the third generation are more likely than men in the first or second generation to leave the Greek community and marry exogamously.

4. The larger the third generation group in a given community, the less the propensity of exogamous marriages.

5. Intermarriage in the third generation varies from one community to another and from one class to another.

6. There is more intermarriage in the middle and upper middle class third generation Greek-Americans than among upper or lower extremes of an ethnic stratification system.

7. American born Greek women are more likely to marry endogomously in every generation than American born Greek men.

CONCLUSION

In this paper an effort was made to examine certain aspects of subculture and intermarriage of three generations of Greeks in the United States. As stated in the introduction, this paper was not intended to test any particular proposition but rather to suggest new ones for further research in this area. Although one finds a number of empirical studies on intermarriage, particularly those concerning interfaith and interethnic marriages among Roman Catholics, Protestants, and Jews, there are few or practically no studies of intermarriage among the Greek Orthodox and other Eastern Orthodox denominations.

Furthermore, while the concept of "generational subculture" is not a new one in the lexicon of social scientists, one finds that this concept is not utilized by family sociologists in explaining empirical findings and theories of intermarriage. With this overview of the generational subculture and intermarriage among the Greeks in the United States, some tentative propositions for further research can be offered concerning patterns of Greek American intermarriages in all three generations. These propositions, moreover, may have partial relevance to generational subcultures and intermarriages of other ethnic groups.

1. If one had to single out the most significant factor in each of the three generational subcultures among the Greeks, one would choose "nationality" in the first, "religion" in the second, and "class" in the third generation.

2. As long as there is new immigration of Greeks to the United States, intermarriage as a vehicle of assimilation will most likely affect the early generations of Greeks.

3. Unlike Roman Catholicism, Protestantism, and Judaism, one may suggest that neither the "fourth melting pot" nor the "interdenominational" hypothesis may be used in explaining future trends in Greek intermarriages in the United States.

4. Intermarriage in the third and subsequent generations is more likely to follow class, generational, "ethclass," and inter-Christian lines rather than intra-Orthodox faith marriages.

The reason for the inapplicability of the "fourth melting pot" and "Orthodox interdenominational" hypothesis is that the Orthodox (Eastern) Christian faith is a minority in the United States (about one million and a half according to 1990 United States census).

ENDNOTES

[1]An inter-ethnic marriage involves persons of the same religion and color but differing with respect to national origins and cultural background, e.g., an Irish marrying an Italian. Inter-faith marriage (mixed marriage) refers to persons identifying with a different religion prior to or after their marriage, e.g., a Catholic marrying a Protestant. Inter-class marriage (also heterogamous marriage) refers to a union in which the members come from different socioeconomic class backgrounds, especially as measured in terms of occupational, educational, and economic indices of the interested parties and families concerned. Racial intermarriage (also amalgamation or miscegenation) in which members of different races intermarry, e.g., a Caucasian and a Black. (For further discussion, see Albert Gordon, Interfaith, Interethnic, Interracial Marriage, 1964).

[2]The term generation has different meanings in different contexts. For example, it may mean interval of time between parents and children, behavioral or political patterns unique to each generation, etc. (See Dictionary of Social Sciences, 1964: 284-285).

In this paper, however, generation will be conceptualized in terms of "generational subcultures" of three generations of Greeks and Greek-Americans in the United States. First generation or first generational subculture refers to the early Greek immigrants who came to the United States about the turn of the present century;second generationrefers to the former's children; and third generation refers to the children of the second or grandchildren of the third generation.

Generational intermarriage then refers to various types of intermarriage with respect to each of the three generational subcultures of Greeks in the United States and the children of mixed marriages.

[3]The "melting pot" notion was first introduced by Israel Zangwill, a Jewish writer who wrote a drama entitled "The Melting Pot" which was produced in 1908. In that play the author portrayed the United States as a melting pot where all races and ethnic groups and their subcultures converge to produce an Anglo-Saxonic type of monoculture. Later, the concept was introduced into the lexicon of sociologists and cultural anthropologists who replaced it with such concepts as assimilation and acculturation to explain the extent to which certain ethnic groups are Americanized or have adopted the norms, attitudes, and behaviors of the predominant Anglo-American culture. For an analytical distinction, definitions, and types of assimilation, see Milton Gordon, *Assimilation in American Life*, 1964.

[4]According to the dowry system the father of the bride must provide a negotiated amount of cash or property to his future son-in-law. The dowry system is attached to the economic institution and social stratification system in general. It favors the higher socio-economic classes, for the higher the socio-economic status of the groom and his family, the greater the propensity to receive a larger dowry. It has brought tragedy to many poor families in Greece particularly those with a large number of girls.

[5]In an effort to update the data I tried to contact three medium-sized midwestern parishes; those of Rockford, Aurora, and Elgin. Of the three only the St. Sophia Greek Orthodox parish responded to my request. In a ten-year period (1986 through March, 1995) there were 53 marriages (36 of them Orthodox to non-Orthodox and 17 marriages Orthodox marrying Orthodox--seven of the 17 were conversions to the Orthodox faith). This pattern of intermarriage has continued into the late 1990s. Almost all Greek marriages are mixed marriages in both communities. This pattern is somewhat similar in most small Greek American communities.

[6]A Greek national is a person who has come to the United States as a student or as an exchange scholar and who marries an American citizen including persons of Greek origin. Under this category one can also include recent Greek immigrants who have not become naturalized citizens of the United States.

REFERENCES

Abbott, Grace.   1909.   "A Study of the Greeks in Chicago." *American Journal of Sociology* 15 (November): 379-393.

Bardis, Panos. 1955. "The Changing Family in Modern Greece." *Sociology and Social Research* 40 (October): 19-23.

_____. 1956. "Main Features of the Greek Family During the Early Twentieth Century." *Alpha Kappa Deltan* 26 (Winter, November): 17-21.

_____. 1957. "Influences on the Modern Greek Family." *Social Science* 32 (June): 155-158.

Barron, Milton L. 1946. *People Who Intermarry: Intermarriage in a New England Industrial Community*. Syracuse: Syracuse University Press.

_____. 1951. "Research on Intermarriage: A Survey of Accomplishments and Prospects." *American Journal of Sociology* 57 (November): 249-255.

Besanceney, Paul H. 1962. "Unbroken Protestant-Catholic Marriages among Whites in the Detroit Area." *American Catholic Sociological Review* 23 (1962): 3-20.

_____. 1965. "On Reporting Rates of Intermarriage." *American Journal of Sociology* 70 (May): 719.

Bossard, James H. 1939. "Nationality and Nativity as Factors in Marriage," *American Sociological Review* 4 (December): 792-798.

Burgess, Thomas. 1913. *Greeks in America*. Boston: Sherman Franch and Company.

Campbell, John, and Philip Sherrard. 1968. *Modern Greece*. London: Earnest Benn Limited.

Fairchild, Henry Pratt. 1911. *Greek Immigration to the United States*. New Haven: Yale University Press.

Friedl, Ernestine. 1962. *Vasilika: A Village in Modern Greece*. New York: Holt Company.

Glazer, Nathan, and D. P. Moynihan. 1963. *Beyond the Melting Pot*. Cambridge, Mass.: M.I.T. Press.

Gordon, Albert. 1964. *Interfaith, Interethnic, Interracial Marriage*. Boston: Beacon Press.

Gordon, Milton. 1964. *Assimilation in American Life: The Role of Race, Religion and National Origin*. New York: Oxford University Press.

Greek Orthodox Archdiocese of South and North America "Vital Statistics" in *Yearbook*, 1995. New York.

Greeley, Andrew M. 1970. "Religious Intermarriage in a Denominational Society." *American Journal of Sociology* 75 (May): 949-952.

Herberg, William. 1955. *Protestant, Catholic, Jew*. New York: Doubleday and Company.

Kennedy, Ruby J. 1944. "Single or Triple Melting Pot? Intermarriage Trends in New Haven, 1870-1940." *American Journal of Sociology* 49 (January): 331-339.

_____. 1952. "Single or Triple Melting Pot? Intermarriage in New Haven, 1870-1950." *American Journal of Sociology* 58 (July): 56-59.

Kourvetaris, George A. 1969. *First and Second Generation Greeks in Chicago: An Inquiry Into Their Stratification and Mobility Patterns*. Athens, Greece: National Center of Social Research.

Lambiri, Ioanna. 1965. *Social Change in a Greek Country Town*. Athens: Center of Planning and Economic Research.

Lenski, Gerhard. 1961. *The Religious Factor: A Sociological Study of Religion's Impact on Politics, Economics, and Family Life*. Garden City: Doubleday and Co., Inc.

Lopreato, Joseph. 1970. *Italian Americans*. New York: Random House.

Marcson, Simon. 1950. "A Theory of Intermarriage and Assimilation." *Social Forces* 29 (October): 75-78.

Mistaras, Evangeline. 1950. "A Study of First and Second Generation Greek Outmarriages in Chicago." Unpublished: A Master's Thesis in the University of Chicago Library; Department of Sociology. Chicago.

Price, C. A. and J. Zabrycki. 1962. "The Use of Intermarriage Statistics as an Index of Assimilation." *Population Studies* 16 (July): 58-59.

Rosen, Bernard. 1959. "Race, Ethnicity, and the Achievement Syndrome." *American Sociological Review* 24 (February): 47-60.

Safilios-Rothschild, Constantina. 1967. "A Comparison of Power Structure and Marital Satisfaction in Urban Greek and French Families." *Journal of Marriage and the Family* 29 (May): 345-352.

_____. 1969. "Attitudes of Greek Spouses Toward Marital Infidelity." Pp. 77-93 in Gerhard Neubeck (ed.). *Extramarital Relations*. Englewood Cliffs: Prentice-Hall.

Saloutos, Theodore. 1956. *They Remember America*. Berkeley and Los Angeles: The University of California Press.

_____. 1964. *The Greeks in the United States*. Cambridge: Harvard University Press.

Sanders, Irwin. 1962. *Rainbow in the Rock: The People of Rural Greece*. Cambridge: Harvard University Press.

_____. 1967. "Greek Society in Transition." *Balkan Studies* 8: 317-322.

Simpson, George, and J. Milton Yinger. 1965. *Racial and Cultural Minorities: An Analysis of Prejudice and Discrimination.* New Edition Revised, New York: Harper and Brothers.

Stycos J. M. 1948. "The Spartan Greeks of Bridgetown." *Common Ground* (Winter, Spring, Summer): 61-70, 24-34, 72-86.

Xenides, J. P. 1922. *The Greeks in America.* New York: George H. Doran.

CHAPTER 5
THE GREEK AMERICAN FAMILY:
A GENERATIONAL APPROACH*

THE MODERN GREEK AMERICAN FAMILY

First-Generation Greek Family

In this chapter, three generations of Greek and Greek American family patterns will be examined. The first-generation Greek family includes both the early (1900- 1920s) and late Greek immigrants (1950s to date). In analyzing the ethnic patterns of the first-generation Greek family, one should keep in mind the sociocultural and economic antecedents in Greece proper and those in the United States at both the time of early and late Greek immigration.[1]

Coming from agricultural communities in which a large and extended kinship family system was more conducive to an agrarian economy, the first-generation immigrant family in the United States followed the patterns of family similar to those in rural Greece. However, for many reasons, this did not always work out. First, the socioeconomic conditions of the immigrants and the problems of adjustment and hardships they encountered did not permit them to replicate the Greek village patterns of extended families. Second, the presence of many siblings in the immigrants' family of orientation in Greece forced them to migrate in the first place. Immigrants wanted to see their children succeed and projected their own unfulfilled aspirations onto them. The smaller the family unit, the more economic resources could be used for each child's benefit. Third, the immigrants had many obligations and promises to fulfill in their home communities such as to provide for their sisters' or nieces' dowries[2] or to pay their fathers' debts. Indeed, many never married for this reason. Fourth, the overwhelming majority of early immigrants were males with no firm decision to settle in the United States. Finally, the immigrants had to support their own families in the United States and having extended families made this more difficult. Despite all this, however, a number of early and late first-generation Greek immigrants had large families.

As noted previously, early Greeks did not come together as family units: primarily, young males migrated. Vlachos (1968) maintains that "very few females crossed the Atlantic Ocean in the early years of Greek immigration and

---

* This is a revised chapter originally published in *Ethnic Families in America: Patterns and Variations* edited by Charles H. Mindel, Robert W. Hobenstein, and Roosevelt Wright Jr., 3rd Edition, New York: Elsevier, 1996.

their small percentage increased significantly only after 1923" [quoted in Kardaras (1977)]. The scarcity of the first-generation women forced a substantial number of Greek males to marry non-Greek women (Mistaras, 1950). Evidence suggests that the resulting Greek American offspring of these Greek-non-Greek marriages who married non-Greek spouses, followed the Greek-Orthodox faith and traditions. This was true of both early and late Greek immigrants. One can observe similar patterns in subsequent generations of Greeks in the United States. However, these exogamous marriages were neither encouraged nor accepted by the more ethnocentric Greeks, especially among the early Greek immigrants. Thus the more tradition-bound the Greek male was, the more strongly he needed a mate of his own nationality and religion. Many of the early Greek males returned to Greece in search of a bride. Some had prospective brides arranged and vouched for by relatives and friends waiting for them in Greece, or they simply had arranged a marriage through an exchange of photographs (Saloutos, 1964:85). The arranged marriage should be understood in the context of the Greek kinship system where mate selection was an affair that went beyond the immediate parties concerned. It was also a matter of economics. Many early Greek male immigrants could not afford to travel to Greece searching for a bride. Furthermore, many of the prospective grooms had known their brides' families prior to coming to the United States.

In the past, the arranged marriage (*proxenió*) was more prevalent in the rural Greek family. At present, it is less often practiced. More and more mate selection is left to the individual. Sanders (1967:8) distinguished three major types of marital selection in Greek agricultural communities: marriage arranged by parents, marriage with parental consent, and marriage by the future couple themselves. The *proxenió* highlights the importance of marriage and of the family as an enduring, interdependent, social institution. Marriage was to be taken seriously. It was not simply the union of two independent individuals, but it was and still is considered to be a fundamental union of two families. In the past, romantic love was not a prerequisite in the arranged Greek marriage, unlike today where romantic love and physical attraction play a more decisive role. The institution of the dowry system also played its part within the arranged marriage and mate selection.

In the past, marriage and family ties were viewed as permanent responsibilities. First-generation Greeks would take care of their parents. Today, the situation has changed. There seems to exist an erosion of family ties. Tensions developed between generations, one that tried to maintain old-country values in the new world and the other that strives to be accepted fully as Americans. Today's generation see to consciously reject the old Greek traditions. Marriage and motherhood, the most revered institutions in the past, are no longer the only options for Greek American women. The 1975 revised Greek Constitution, Article 4, paragraph 2 states that: "Greek men and women have the same obligations and rights." No longer is the Greek husband the sole head of the household; rather, both husband and wife decide on family matters. In many respects, the patterns of the rural Greek family were continued in urban United States, but they had to be adjusted to the existing conditions and could not be exactly replicated in the United States.

Another important dimension of Greek American family organization involved the structural gender role differences and decision making processes traditionally vested in different family statuses and occupied by different members of the immediate family. Thus, one can speak of father versus mother, male versus female, husband versus wife relationships and gender roles. The majority of fiction and nonfiction writers (Bardis, 1955, 1956; Safilios-Rothschild, 1967b; Vlachos, 1968; Saloutos, 1964; Petrakis, 1966; Chamales, 1959; Stephanides, 1972; Koty, 1958; Lambiri-Dimaki, 1965; Capanidou Lauquier, 1961 Moskos, 1990; Scourby, 1984) have suggested that the early Greek family, both in the United States and Greece, was a male-dominated, patriarchal, and close-knit social unit. In most of these writings the Greek father is portrayed as an imposing figure whose authority over the rest of the family members, particularly the wife, was absolute. The Greek wife was depicted as a submissive and powerless creature whose major role was homemaking and catering to the rest of the family. Scourby, for example, argues that the "overall image that emerges of Greek women through the eyes of novelist, therapist, the ethnographer, and the social scientist is that of good wife, good mother, and good housekeeper whose needs are always subservient to those of her husband and children" (1984:130). This image of the Greek husband's authority and gender-roles was a carryover from Greece, but they were not unique to the Greeks alone. However, one can argue that these gender roles were contingent upon the social-economic conditions and prevailing ethos in male-female relationships in the United States and Greece.

That there is an "ideal" and "real" dimension culturally and socially prescribed for every gender role and family member is well documented. However, one finds the tendency among students of the sociology of marriage and the family to describe normative/ideal patterns of gender-role differentiation as real facts. Most studies tend to deemphasize the conflict and pathology of the Greek family. With the exception of some studies[3] conducted by Safilios-Rothschild (1967 a & b) and those conducted by Friedl (1967) and Campbell (1964) in Greece proper, no systematic studies have been conducted on the gender role differentiation and authority relationships in the Greek family at the level of role performance and conflict in the United States. The Greek women's role was confined primarily in the private domain--including the home, church, and relatives—not in the public domain.

A more realistic analysis of role differentiation in the Greek family would entail a network of role complementarity rather than strict differentiation on the basis of widely held beliefs of male-dominated (instrumental) versus female-subordinate (expressive) roles. In other words, in most cases a Greek husband/father could assume both expressive and instrumental roles simultaneously whenever the primary group (family) interests were served and family contingencies demanded it. The early Greek immigrant father, as a rule, was older than his wife. Most first-generation Greek men took an active role in the household chores including shopping, cooking, and so forth. Some of these roles were learned in restaurants, owned and managed by Greek immigrant men. Ideally, the Greek father was considered the head and authority figure of the family unit, and he expected respect and cooperation from his wife and children. In reality, however, his authority was contingent upon his ability to prove himself and be a good provider for his family, a compassionate husband, and an understanding father. Masculinity alone, based on arbitrary exercise of authority without considerations of fairness, family unity, and common good, could not sustain the first-generation immigrant family. While he was primarily a provider for the entire family and had to work incredibly long hours outside the home, he helped whenever he could in the household chores, in the discipline and socialization of his children. These norms have changed both in the contemporary Greek family in Greece proper and the late Greek immigrant family. At present Greek women work outside the home and men do more chores in the house.

The discrepancy between the "ideal" and "real" aspects of husband-wife and mother-father gender roles is also evident if one examines what Friedl (1967) and Campbell (1964) refer to as the "public" versus "private" domains of behavior in the rural family in Greece. In the public/social sphere, both Greek husbands and Greek wives put on a façade and behave according to the prevailing societal and cultural norms. These norms depict Greek husbands-fathers as if they were the true masters and dominant figures within the family unit. The Greek wives-mothers, however, are expected to behave in a modest and submissive manner, particularly in public places when their husbands are present. However, in a more private family setting, husbands-fathers and wives-mothers roles change considerably and behave more naturally. What seems to the outsider to be the unequivocal dominance exercised by the husband over the wife is in reality significantly different in more informal family settings. In many instances, the Greek wife-mother was the most dominant figure in the

Greek immigrant family. Her presence and influence was felt not only in the family but in the larger ethnic community affairs. To a Greek immigrant husband who left his parents at a young age, his wife was more than the sociological sex-role partner. She was the wife, the adviser, the partner, the companion, and the homemaker. She also assisted her husband in the business and the family decision-making. Wives-mothers usually exercised their influence in the family decision-making through the process of socialization of the children, because the Greek father had to work long hours away from the home. Children were thus more attached to the mother, rather than the father, particularly in the formative years of immigrant life. Later, it was the wife-mother who had to approve or disapprove of her daughter's marriage, and then she would convince her husband. Furthermore, it has been reported by Tavuchis (1972) that among his "respondents and a large unknown proportion of second-generation Greek Americans, the father emerges as a shadowy, distant figure throughout childhood and adolescence but his sociological presence was always felt." In addition, the relatively higher status and freedom enjoyed by the American women vis-á-vis Greek women in Greece benefited the Greek women more than the Greek men in the United States.

Greek immigrant women have played an important role not only in the family but in the Church and Greek American community in general. Moskos (1990) argues that the arrival of Greek women contributed greatly to the cohesion of the Greek American family and indeed the Greek American community and the Church at large. As a rule, early Greek immigrant women—married and unmarried—did not work outside the house. This contrasts sharply with post-world War II Greek immigrant women who, by and large, worked outside the house either in the family restaurant or in some other capacity as seamstresses, beauticians, and factory workers.

As a rule, early Greek brides were younger and became widowers at a younger age. In addition to being mothers, they assumed other family roles including heads of families, mothers, fathers, business women, match-makers, and so forth. The late Greek immigrant brides, however, were not that different in age from their prospective husbands.

As in the American family in general, one of the primary functions of the Greek family is procreation. A family without children was, and still is, thought to be incomplete. It is not by accident that the formal ideology of the Greek Orthodox Church (and other religions, for that matter) encourages procreation within a marital context. The birth of a child is not only an affair of the family but of the Church as well. Motherhood is highly esteemed in the Greek Orthodox faith. Those couples who have children are looked upon by the Orthodox Church as fortunate and blessed. Doumanis (1983), in her study of mothering among two dozen rural and Athenian Greek working class mothers who did not work outside the home, found that motherhood still has been the only means by which a woman can achieve full adult status in Greek society. Mothering, she observed, is a more individual and alienating experience in the modern Greek metropolis than it is in the collectivistic and emotionally supportive village setting.

Childless couples were, and still are, made uncomfortable in the Greek American community, especially the husband.   Not having children was suspicious and impinged on the Greek male image.   In many instances the childless immigrant family or the old bachelor uncle would support a nephew or niece, but adoption of Greek or non-Greek children was not an accepted practice.

It has been reported (Stephanides, 1972; Tavuchis, 1968) that first-generation Greek parents tended to overprotect their children, even to the extent of wanting to find marriage partners for them. This should be interpreted in the context of the traditional ideal norms of a family and kinship system. In most instances this was part of the arranged marriage practice in Greece which continued in the immigrant family. Parents underwent personal sacrifices for their children and therefore expected their children to meet their high expectations even after they reached maturity. Ideally, first-generation Greek parents worked and strived to give their children happiness, love, and material comforts. In return, children were expected to respect their parents, develop a sense of responsibility and self-reliance, and become a credit to their family unit and the larger ethnic and American communities.

Like their immigrant parents, the children had a minimum of leisure time. They were exposed to the vicissitudes of life at a tender age and were socialized to postpone their immediate gratifications for a future goal. For a majority of the Greek parents that goal was to see their children happily married, maintain certain ethnic traditions, and move up on the social and economic ladder through the avenue of education, business, and commerce outside the Greek ethnic community.

In general, the Greek immigrant family was adult- rather than child-centered. The child had to learn to respect his/her parents and the elderly. It has also been reported (Vlachos, 1968; Capanidou and Lauquier, 1961) that there was a differential preference for boys in the immigrant family. One can argue, however, that this preferential treatment was not as pronounced in the United States as it was in Greece because: 1) There was no dowry system in the United States as such other than the usual gifts from relatives or friends of the couple. 2) Girls maintained the Greek traditional norms and ideals more readily than boys. 3) Girls were more attached to their parents, particularly to the mother. 4) Above all, it was the daughter, not the son, who would look after her elderly parents even after she was married.

Despite many similar experiences between the early and late first-generation Greek families, they displayed the following differences, which created many conflicts between them and their progenies: 1) In contrast to the earlier, the late immigrant arrived when there was a more equal number of males and females in their age groups. 2) In contrast to the earlier, the later first-generation Greek women (both married and nonmarried), particularly from blue collar and working classes, were gainfully employed outside the household. 3) Late Greek immigrant families more than early Greek families visit Greece via cheap charter flights, which was not the case in the early Greek American families. 4) The late Greek immigrants were less integrated in the Greek ethnic (church) community than were the second-and third-generation (children of the early arrivals). 5) In contrast to the earlier, the late Greek immigrant families tended to be more educated, more diverse in social class background, less religious, less conservative, more materially and exogamously oriented, more likely to divorce, less traditional, more business-oriented, and more ethnically oriented through Greek language and nationality identification rather than Orthodox religious identification. Some of these differences and conflicts stem from generational, age, class, regional, and cultural differences in general. Despite many contrasts between the two groups of the first-generation Greek family, both groups share a work ethic, strong ethnic family ties, the drive to compete for material success, ethnic pride, and a sense of ethnic community.

Gender roles are rapidly changing in Greece toward a more egalitarian or shared familial and occupational responsibility among men and women. The position of women has been improved. For the first time Greek rural women and wives receive some form of social security after 60 years of age. The 1976-1982 family law bill, for example, reflects the gradual liberalization of the traditional gender roles which gave men greater power over women. According to the new law both spouses have equal rights and equal responsibilities. No longer is a woman's role restricted to the domestic domain and the man's to the public domain. Women can pursue their own interests. Schooling is also more co-educational.

These changes in gender roles have been going on in American families and marriages for the last 30 years or so. One would expect that the first generation late Greek immigrant family is not immune to these changes going on both in Greece and the United States. In a comparative study of the Greek Immigrant family in the United States and Canada, Tastsoglou and Stubos (1992) have found that "prior to the 1940s, immigrant Greeks assumed a more traditional institutional form characterized by more conservative values of kinship and extended family characteristic of rural life in Greece. Subsequent waves of Greek immigrants after World War II became more Americanized and were characterized by increased distancing from the kinship group, greater emphasis on interfamily and interpersonal relations, equalitarian marital relationships, greater marital autonomy for children and decreasing interfamily financial obligations."

In general, while many ethnic patterns were replicated in the first generation Greek American family, many changes occurred. These changes reflected the ongoing gender role re-definition and debate both in Greece proper and the United States.

Second-Generation Greek American Family

The second-generation Greek American family is that social unit in which both parents are American-born of Greek extraction or mixed parenthood (one parent Greek from Greece and the other either non-Greek or American-born Greek). As in other ethnic groups, the second-generation Greek American family is a transitional family. Children are born and raised in two social worlds or subcultures. One is particularistic, with an ethnic subculture made up of the Greek immigrant parents and relatives, immigrant priests (especially for the early second generation Greek American progenies), school teachers, Greek religious and national holidays, and Greek peers. These agents of socialization transmitted similar experiences and attempted to socialize the children to traditional norms and values of the Greek subculture. The other is a more universalistic world made up of American public schools, non-Greek peers and friends, and institutional norms and values of the dominant American society and culture. The second generation emerged as a product of a Greek subculture on one hand and an American culture and society on the other, a sociocultural hybrid with a dual identity. An identity crisis and/or generational conflict were common phenomena of the second generation.

In many respects, members of the second generation (both early and late) shared similar experiences and lifestyles with their immigrant parents throughout their formative and adolescent years. However, pressures from within and from outside the family unit made them somewhat ambivalent and marginal. They were torn between two ways of life. The emphasis on family ties, the Greek language, and the Greek Church shaped their attitudes and behavior (Saloutos, 1964:311). These early attitudes and behaviors changed, however, as the children came of age, went to public schools, began to work, moved away from the original settlement, were married, and started a family. However, it must be pointed out that the influence of the first-generation (immigrant) family on the second generation was not uniform in all Greek American families throughout the United States. Not all Greek-American families shared symmetrical ethnic family experiences in the United States. For example, in small towns and communities where fewer Greek American families were found, the process of assimilation and convergence (including intermarriage) with the rest of the population was greater than in larger cities with larger numbers of Greek ethnic communities.

Three types of family lifestyles seem to be prevalent among the second-generation Greeks (Vlachos, 1968:150-151). From a somewhat different perspective these family lifestyles appear to be phases along a continuum of assimilation-acculturation. One type represents a complete abandonment of the traditional Greek way of life. A substantial number in this group Anglicized their names and moved away from the Greek community, some changed their religion, and many minimized their interaction with their foreign-born parents and relatives. This group was more concerned with social status and acceptance by their peers and other Americans. They were not interested in adopting the norms of Greek culture as represented to them by their parents and relatives in the United States. They wanted to become "assimilated" as soon as possible. In many respects, this type of second-generation family passed for an American family, and it was rather atypical. It was more prevalent in small towns and suburbs with dispersed Greek ethnic populations.

A second type of the second-generation Greek family illustrates "cultural atavism," an inward retrogressive orientation and identification with what was perceived to be, by second-generation Greeks, ethnic Greek lifestyles. Ideally this type of family was economically, culturally, socially, and psychologically tied up with the Greek community and its ethnic institutions. This Greek American type of family was usually working-class or blue-collar. It was found close to original Greek immigrant colonies. Many of these families could be described as "stables" or downwardly mobile working-class ethnic families.

A third type of second-generation Greek American family was marginal at the structural, cultural, and social-psychological levels. Norms and values were of a "hybrid" nature. Social interaction and networks of social relationships were neither genuinely American nor Greek. The family was likely to move out of the original settlement, and its members were less likely to engage in primary-group interaction with members of the first- generation Greeks outside the immediate intergenerational kinship group. In most instances, this type of family accommodated living between two worlds by taking what it considered the best of each. This family appeared to be more representative of the majority of the second-generation Greeks, a contention supported by the existing literature on the second-generation Greek Americans (Moskos, 1990; Scourby, 1983; Kourvetaris, 1996).

To these three types we must add a fourth where ethnicity and class intersect, what Gordon (1964) referred to as "ethclass." In a study of ethclass (Kourvetaris and Dobratz, 1976), it was found that second- and third-generation Greek Americans follow ethclass rather than ethnicity or class alone in patterns of interpersonal and primary group relations including marriage. Thus, if a second-generation male/female marries with his/her ethnic group (religious), the tendency is that he/she will marry within his/her social class in the Greek American community. This type of ethclass marriage is also prevalent in the first generation. It is more characteristic, however, in the second-generation Greek American family.

As in other ethnic groups, second-generation Greek Americans had certain advantages over the first generation. First, they did not have to start from scratch as their parents did. Second, they grew up in a fairly close knit Greek family in which rudiments of Greek ethnic subculture were transmitted to them, particularly those pertaining to courtship, marriage, language, religion, and respect for mother, father, and the elderly. Third, the values of aspiration, hard work, the Greek *philotimo*, or love for honor, were implanted in them by their parents. Achievement and success were a credit not only to their immediate families and kin but also to the entire Greek community. It is within this frame of reference that the organization of the second-generation Greek American family emerged in the United States. Although first- and second-generation families actually shared many of these advantages, they contributed markedly to the mobility of the second generation.

Several writers (Saloutos, 1964; Sanders, 1962, 1967; Friedl, 1962; Vlachos, 1968) have reported that Greeks traditionally display a high degree of family cohesion and extended kinship relationships within and across generational lines. It has also been reported (Rosen, 1959; Handlin and Handlin, 1956; Kourvetaris, 1971a, b; Tavuchis, 1972; Chock, 1969; Moskos, 1990) that this intergenerational kinship system is coupled with a strong ideological commitment to social mobility and achievement in the American social structure. Tavuchis (1972), in his study of 50 second-generation male family heads, found an elaborate system of kinship and ethnic ties coupled with strong intergenerational patterns of vertical class mobility.

Unlike other social scientists, particularly family sociologists who have lamented the weakening of kinship bonds and the demise of family as a viable institution, Tavuchis found no evidence of family disintegration among the second-generation Greeks. In fact, Tavuchis argues that the stronger the kinship ties, the more highly mobile its members were found to be: "Differential class mobility was not found to be a detriment to close ties with parents, siblings, and affines. . . ." Tavuchis (1972:296-297) refers to five mechanisms that in his judgment prevented potential strains: a strong commitment to kinship values, a close propinquity to relatives, extra class criteria of ranking, identification with successful kinsmen, and gross status differences neutralizing insidious distinctions. However, during a conference (1980s) on the Greek American family organization sponsored by the Greek Orthodox Ladies Philoptochos Society, the participants lamented the erosion of family ties, the rejection of traditions, the increasing divorce rate in the Greek American family, and the loss of faith among the young Greek Americans.

Although Tavuchis' finding was not unique among Greek Americans, it is somewhat contrary to the prevailing notion among sociologists who believe that extended kinship relationships are a detriment to intergenerational social mobility. A somewhat similar finding has been reported by Kardaras (1977) who found no relationship between different types of modernity (marital, sexual, and educational) and structural/ psychological assimilation. The second generation were found to be conservative or traditional in one dimension and modern in another. Somewhat surprisingly, the higher the social class among the second generation, the greater the tendency to espouse a more traditional (conservative) view in gender roles.

The structure of authority relations is a source of tension in Greek American family life. The assertive or over-confident Greek woman is seen as a threat to the authority of the father. The long absence of the first-generation father from the home made it difficult for the son to identify with him. According to Scourby (1984:128), the father's absence enabled the son to identify not with his individuality and self-reliance but, inaccurately, with his authoritarianism alone. And the son's exposure to the equalitarian model in the United States only magnified the father's authoritarianism and thus created a conflict between dependency and independence.

Themes of stress and cultural conflict between first and second generation Greeks are found in a number of novels written by second generation writers. *Going Naked in the World* is a moving account of the frustrations Tom Chamales encountered as a member of a traditional authoritarian family of the 1940s. Elia Kazan's *The Arrangement* portrays a Greek- American with an unyielding father. In *Lion At My Heart*, Harry Mark Petrakis describes the painful conflict between the patriarchal father and his sons and the subsequent despair and disillusionment experienced by the father (mentioned in Scourby, 1984). Although fictional accounts provide us with insights into human and family relationships, they are not a substitute for a vigorous sociological analysis of intergenerational and family conflicts.

Three trends of authority relations seem to be prevalent in the emerging literature on the second-generation Greek-American family:

1. The "quasi-patriarchal" model, or a trend toward lessening the patriarchal orientation in which ultimate authority in decision-making no longer is exercised by the father (Tavuchis, 1972);

2. The "equalitarian" model in which the father shares his status and authority with his wife (Capanidou Lauquier, 1961:225; Kardaras, 1977); and

3. The "patriarchal" model (Vlachos, 1969:162) in which the father is still the ultimate authority with final responsibility for providing for his family and for the discipline of his children, partly because that is a father's duty and partly because he is a man and men are economic providers (Chock, 1969:38).

Gender roles of the siblings are also viewed in normative terms by most Greek writers. As a rule, they do not describe actual role performances. For example, the traditional Greek cultural norms and ideals of filial piety and respect for one's parents and the elderly persist in the second-generation Greek American family. Unlike the case of the first generation, the father is not perceived as a fearful and distant person, but the father-son relationship is one of mutual understanding and respect (Tavuchis, 1972; Chock, 1969; Lauquier, 1961; Moskos, 1980). According to Chock, "Greek children are expected to love their parents, to respect them and to assume some care for them if they need it in their old age." Despite the respect between first and second generation, as a rule, second-generation Greeks do not live in the same household with their parents and in-laws. More and more immigrant generations (especially widows) live alone or are placed in homes for the aged. The immigrant family, particularly the father, has a sense of pride that does not accept living with one's children, especially not a son-in-law. This is even more true of the second-generation family in a mixed marriage.

As in the first generation, both parents in the second generation share in the responsibility for the care, education, and well-being of their children. Second-generation families tend to have fewer children than the first generation. However, many second-generation parents tend to spoil their children. Second-generation Greek women are inclined to take a greater interest in the Greek Orthodox Church and religion rather than in the Greek language schools. Scourby (1984:131) argues that women more than men identified as "Greek Orthodox" or "Greek American" reaffirming their positive response to the church. They are also less critical of the church. As in the first generation, second-generation families show respect for their parents and the elderly. Grandparents (*pappou* and *yiayia*) are important figures in the Greek American family.

The Women's Liberation movement of the 1960s has changed many gender roles in the second generation. Safilios-Rothschild, Costantakos, and Kardaras (1976) and Kardaras (1977) have found that both husbands and wives in the upper-class, second-generation families in the Detroit metropolitan area share somewhat similar views on marriage and the family. Thus, both husbands and wives are against a double standard on sexual matters, disapprove of infidelity and extramarital relations, and approve of divorce on grounds of abuse. They also believe that they should have the right both to initiate and refuse sexual activity. Although we do not know the extent to which these findings are uniform among all second-generation Greek American families, one can suggest that "ethclass" and "generation" are more important variables in explaining ethnic family patterns than ethnicity, class, or generation taken singularly.

Greek Americans, regardless of generation, tend to be conservative on civil rights and economic issues. Moskos (1990) contends "the conservativism of the Greek Americans is an attitude of mind rather than a body of ideas—a distaste for confrontation politics and a suspicion of collective action for social improvement." Greek Americans, Moskos argues, "search not for a better world, but for a better life."[4] The conservative ethos of Greek Americans reflects the individualistic orientations of the Greek entrepreneur, the influence of the Greek Orthodox Church, emphasis on the cohesiveness of the family, and the rural origins of the early Greek immigrants, the majority of whom came from the southern part of Greece (Peloponneses). One can also conclude that second-generation Greek American families tend more often to be church-goers on Sunday than first generation (especially the late Greek immigrants). Being a member of a denomination is part of the American civic culture and religion. In short, Greek American families maintain an ethnic identification through their membership in the Greek Orthodox Church and some ethnically oriented organizations such as AHEPA (American Hellenic Educational Progressive Association) or a professional ethnic association such as medical, educational, legal and so on.

Third Generation Greek American Family

The third-generation family consists of grandchildren of the first generation or the children of the second-generation Greek family in America. This group also includes the offspring of intermarriages of second-generation couples. By the third generation, there is a significant decrease in Greek ethnic identification (as measured by language and Greek family norms); but some vestiges of ethnic social behavior remain, particularly those pertaining to politics (Humphrey and Brock, 1972), Greek religion, and the Dionysian aspects of modern Greek culture (Kourvetaris, 1971c; 1995).

As a rule, members of the third generation have incorporated the values, attitudes, and norms of the American middle- and upper-middle-class subcultures. Social class and lifestyle are more important to them than ethnicity and religion. Despite the lack of empirical studies, both education and professional achievement seem to be highly valued among members of the third generation. In an empirical and comparative study of six ethnic groups, it was found (Rosen, 1959:47-60) that a high level of aspiration and achievement exists among members of third-generation Greeks. Rosen argued that white Protestants, Jews, and Greeks stand out as being more individualistic, activistic, and future-oriented than Italians, Blacks, and French Canadians.

Unlike the first and second generations, members of the third generation are not preoccupied with ethnic prejudice and social discrimination. Viewing their world this way, they can afford to be proud of their ancestry. However, they consider themselves primarily American and only symbolically manifest an interest in and liking for Greek food, music, and dancing. This Dionysian cultural atavism in things Greek was stimulated by the new influx of Greek immigrants following World War II and the popular movies, *Zorba the Greek* and *Never on Sunday*, whose theme songs became worldwide favorites. Furthermore, the marriage of Jacqueline Kennedy to Aristotle Onassis, the Nixon-Agnew ticket in 1968 and 1972, the democratic candidacy of Mike Doukakis for president of the United States in 1988, the resurgence of ethnic studies and programs, and summer excursions to Greece have further awakened their interest in modern Greek ethnicity and ethnic culture. In addition, the new influx of post-World War II Greek immigrants brought a new awareness of Greek ethnic identity. However, one finds little or no interest among members of the third generation in maintaining the ethnic institutional aspects of Greek culture, such as language, family traditions, and endogamous marriage—with the exception of the Americanized form of the Greek Orthodox Church.

It has been argued by some Greek American writers that the new influx of Greeks following World War II would retard the Americanization and assimilation processes of the third generation. However, American born Greeks (even post-World War II Greeks who have been in America for a longer period of time) do not usually associate with the newcomers. This is primarily because dating within one's own group has a constraining influence. Greek American women are no different from other American women—especially when they date non-Greeks. When Greek American women date Greek American men, they tend to be more serious about marriage, especially if they are members of the same community. There is also a matter of availability of both sexes of the same ethnic group, especially in a college population. In general, the more ethnically oriented the Greek man or woman, the greater the tendency to date someone with similar ethnic background. Furthermore, the more assimilated the Greek, the less likely he/she is to place importance on dating Greek women/men. This is also true in terms of ethnic endogamous patterns of marriage.

If ethnicity (nationality) is the single most important characteristic in the first generation and religion in the second generation, it appears that an awareness of social class characterizes the third generation (Kourvetaris, 1971a, b). Thus, the oncoming of the third generation brings a concomitant decline in ethnoreligious concerns and an increasing emphasis on the importance of social class as a factor in marriage. However, those who maintain their ethnic (nationality/religiosity) identification tend to date and marry within their class segment of their ethnic group (ethclass). In a recent study, Safilios-Rothschild, Costantakos, and Kardaras (1976), found ethnic generation and class to be the most differentiating variables between traditional Greek culture and third-generation Greek Americans. For example, the higher the social class, the more removed is a Greek American woman from her Greek cultural heritage and gender role restrictions. As a rule, the third generation is a college-oriented generation. It is a status- and class-conscious generation rather than an ethnic-conscious generation.

At the same time, while intermarriage in the first and second generations was not an accepted norm in the Greek American family, by the third generation it is not only accepted but, in some Greek American communities, it is the norm rather than the exception. It has been estimated that one in five Greeks entered a mixed marriage by 1926 [Saloutos (1973) quoted in Moskos (1980)]. By the 1960s, intermarriages accounted for three out of ten church marriages; by the mid-1970s, it was about half (Moskos, 1980: 73). In some communities it is even higher. In the vital statistics kept by the Registry Department of the Greek Orthodox Archdiocese of North and South America (Yearbook, 1986: 102-103), there is a steady increase of mixed marriages. While up to 1979, there was an equal number of mixed marriages and marriages between Greek Orthodox, from 1980 to 1984 there were more mixed marriages than orthodox marriages. In some areas, mixed marriages reached a ratio of 2 (mixed) to 1 (Greek ethnic). Even the Archbishop, in a speech delivered to the Academy of Athens, acknowledged that intermarriage is inevitable, and in some communities has reached 65% and higher.

By the same token, we find an increase in the divorce rate among Greek American families. While in the first generation divorce was rare, the third generation matches the divorce pattern of the American family at large more and more. In a 1980 conference on the Greek Orthodox family, sponsored by the Greek Orthodox Philoptohos Society (a charitable and benevolent Greek Orthodox institution) and held in San Francisco, dealt with a number of changing realities and issues (including divorce, abortion, gender roles, cults, and ethnic and religious identity) faced by Greek-American families in the 1980s. They reported an increased number of divorces and mixed marriages.

Scourby (1984) argues that traditional role expectations continue to be the norm across generations, particularly with respect to attitudes toward the institutional Greek Orthodox Church, ethnic identity, and views toward gender roles and intermarriage. In her study of 76 Greek-born students drawn from three generations of college students from four colleges of the New York metropolitan area, Scourby (1984) found that a) females of all three generations were more favorable toward traditional adherence to the ethnic church than males; b) males showed a weaker attachment to their ethnic identity, were more likely to favor exogomy, and displayed a more assimilative attitude for getting ahead in American society; c) American-born students perceived the church as the locus of identity in a pluralist society whereas the first generation was identified with nationality.

CHANGE AND ADAPTATION

The movement from the lifestyles of early first-generation Greek family to those of the third generation is accompanied by an attenuation of the old world family ideals and norms (as exemplified in the first- generation Greek family) and new values more symmetrical with those of the American middle-class family (as exemplified in the third-generation Greek family). "Greekness" (nationality) as a form of ethnic identification in the first generation gives way to the "orthodoxy" (religion) in the second generation, which in turn gives way to "class" lifestyles (behavioral identification) by the third generation. A study by Constantinou and Harvey (1985) of a Greek community in Akron, Ohio found a two dimensional structure underlying Greek-American ethnicity. One they called *externalities* (that which pulls the Greek-American toward the place of origin), and the other, *internalities* (that which binds Greek-Americans together as a community). While they found a variation across generations, use of the Greek language was found to be on the decrease. They found the first generation to be the most cohesive, tending to identify with the ancestral home, insofar as preserving the Greek language goes. By contrast, the second generation was found to be the least cohesive of the three due to its transitional nature. The third generation was found to be less cohesive than the first but showed signs of ethnic revival. The authors concluded that no single factor is adequate to define ethnic identity. They examined 17 ethnically related factors including Greek language, Greek cooking, church membership, family, Greek press, and endogamy as the most important dimensions of ethnic identity. This author suggests that by the third generation the "Greekness" of the first generation has been transformed into philhellenism (friend of Greece). (More about this in chapter 12.) This generational transformation might be genuinely conceptualized as following roughly five processes and/or phases of acculturation initially suggested in part by Park (1950): the *initial* contact, the *conflict*, the *accommodation*, *assimilation*, and the *pluralist* phases.

THE INITIAL CONTACT PHASE

In the first decades of Greek immigrant life in America, the organization of the Old World family was still fairly intact. As a result of pressures from within and outside the family structure, the Old World ideal was challenged. Some of the most salient factors were the physical/ecological separation from the parental and kinship system and village subculture in Greece. The urgency of the immigrant's physical survival and social-psychological adjustment to a different sociocultural and urban ecological environment was real. The separation of work and residence, and the exposure of the immigrant's children to the lifestyles of the American community and public schools, which in many ways meant ethnic prejudice and social discrimination against those ethnic groups and families, were contributing factors that made the first generation culturally different from the dominant Anglo-Saxon group. All these made the first-generation immigrant family extremely ethnocentric and highly cohesive as in the Old World. In this phase of initial contact, the immigrant family was socially and culturally insulated in the Greek colony and did not seriously feel the pressures of American society. Despite its many problems, the first-generation Greek family was stabilized by its strong desire to return to Greece. It drew social and psychological support from the family unit, the family and kinship system, the Church, and the Greek community in general. However, this initial phase gave way both to the conflict and accommodation phases with the coming of the second generation.

THE CONFLICT PHASE

With the oncoming of the second generation, the highly ethnocentric, traditional, and folk-oriented outlook of the first-generation subculture was challenged. Although cultural conflict between parents and children was not inevitable, in many instances it did take place. Out of this generational conflict, three major subtypes of first-generation Greeks emerged: the ethnic subculturalists, the social assimilationists, and the convergent type (in some respects ethnic pluralists and in other respects social assimilationists).

The ethnic subculturalists were faced with major difficulties in carrying out their intent to socialize their children in Greek ways of life. These difficulties and their fear of losing control over their children were intensified when the children came into contact with the larger American society. This was evident particularly when they entered public schools, began working, dating and came of marital age. The Greek immigrant's exaggerated fear of losing control over his/her children was further aggravated by the Greek Orthodox Church and the family kinfolk. Furthermore, it stemmed from the inability of the immigrant himself/herself to adjust more readily to the subtler, nonmaterial aspects of American culture, and thus be able to understand his/her children. This group, usually found in cities with large Greek colonies, proved unyielding. They insisted on preserving their ethnic institutions, particularly those pertaining to religion, language, endogamous marriage, and a close-knit family. They attempted to convince their children of the mystique of the Greek ancestry, warned them against the dangers of intermarriage, and made an effort to instill in them a sense of ethnic pride and consciousness. According to Papajohn and Spiegel, clinical studies of mentally disturbed second-generation Greek American children indicated that these children came from families where an extremely traditionalist Greek form of child rearing was attempted. In fact, those immigrant parents who were more open to American influences were more successful in passing Greek ethnicity than those parents who tried to resist totally all American encroachment [quoted in Moskos (1990)].

Dunkas and Nikelly (1978), in their study of 60 maladjusted first-generation Greek women who had emigrated from Greece, found that Greek married women were more attached to their mothers than their husbands, which the authors called the "Persephone Syndrome." This dependency bond remains between the mother and the daughter. The Greek female, compared with the Greek male, was especially vulnerable to this "dependency hang-up." According to Scourby (1984:135), as a result of the dependency of the daughter on the mother, the daughter is incapable of developing her own self-identity: "The mother keeps her daughter's ego confounded with her own." Scourby further writes, "The ego-boundary weakness compels the daughter to define herself in terms of others, a pattern in keeping with the relational system that has characterized Greek family life." According to Scourby, both the Greek subculture and American culture tend to reinforce these daughter-mother dependency roles. The dependent daughter, when married, becomes the dependent wife, and then the dependent mother. In this way, the cycle continues.

The social assimilationists (known also as environmentalists) believed that their children must grow up as Americans but wanted them to retain membership in the Greek Orthodox Church, maintain their Greek name, and learn some Greek (Saloutos, 1964:312). This group felt that the assimilation process could not be stopped but only temporarily delayed. They were more realistic, experienced less conflict with their children, and were more aware that powerful social and cultural forces operate in the American social structure that exert an unprecedented influence on their children pulling them toward Anglo conformity and Americanization. This assimilation process has been challenged by the ethnic resurgence of the 1960s and early 1970s. This is especially true among Greek-born, post-World War II, Greek immigrants, students, and professionals. The lack of support in American foreign policy for the Greek national issues such as Cyprus, the Greek minority in Northern Eperus, Albania, the name of the former Yugoslavian of the Republic of Macedonia (FYROM), and other similar issues has alienated many Greeks and Greek Americans from the policies of the U.S. Government. Cyprus became the catalyst for ethnic solidarity and consciousness, especially for the new first-generation Greek immigrants and some second-generation (especially Greek-American politicians who expect financial contributions and support from Greek businessmen).

The social assimilationist process began roughly during the second decade that the first-generation family lived in America, especially when the first-generation immigrant family abandoned its intent to return to Greece. It was during this period that both the institutional structure of the Greek Orthodox Church, and the largest ethnic association, AHEPA, launched an all-out effort to organize the Greeks in America, to facilitate the transition and Americanization processes, and to maintain the ethnic institutions of church and family, which in many ways became complementary to each other. Nationality gradually was giving way to religion, particularly during the 1920s when Greeks, along with other southern and eastern European immigrants, were targets of prejudice and discrimination. Second-generation Greeks were discovering that to be of Greek ancestry did not necessarily indicate particularly high social status. This phase gave way to the new realization that religious identity was preferable to ethnic or national identity, and a new intergenerational relationship emerged. While the first generation (both early and late) perceived both religion and ethnicity as inseparable, many in the second and subsequent generations saw them more and more as separate and independent of each other phenomena.

A number of the first generation, especially the more educated (both early and late), followed a mixed approach; it was a compromise between the two polar opposites. This was compatible with the pluralist ideology of ethnic groups in the United States, which replaced the Americanization and assimilation models. It started in the 1940s, but was more evident during the 1950s and 1960s with the influx of new immigrants. The ethnic resurgence of the 1960s gave a new impetus to ethnic consciousness in American society. The post World War Greek ethnic renaissance was also reinforced by the defeat of the Italian forces by the Greeks in October 1940. It gave a shot in the arm to the second-generation Greeks in America and a new ethnic pride and consciousness flourished. This pride, along with the rise of a professional and commercial class of second-generation Greeks and the arrival of post-World War II Greeks, contributed to a new status for Greeks in America. It must be stressed that conflict between the first and second generations was always there, but both groups worked out a *modus operandi* and followed a pattern of accommodation.

THE ACCOMMODATION PHASE

An effort was made to broaden the base for continued and meaningful interaction between the two generations. On the one hand, the first generation realized that they had to modify the Old World family lifestyles for the sake of retaining the affection of their children and maintaining the unity of the family. On the other hand, the second generation came to the realization that complete repudiation of the parents' way of life would hurt their parents and leave them isolated. Both generations searched for points of compatibility, mutual levels of tolerance, complementarity of lifestyles, individuality, and family unity.

This period of accommodation between first- and second-generation family units led to a more stable form of family relationships. The parents came to realize that life in the United States was to be permanent. They also recognized that social and economic status and success could come to their offspring as the latter became more and more socialized into the dominant Anglo-American culture. A parallel effort was made on the part of the second generation to resocialize their parents to their own generational values and lifestyles. The inter-dependence between parents and children gave way to the dependence of parents on their children as interpreters and informants on the American scene (especially those whose English were not proficient). This dependence led to the conscious and unconscious willingness on the part of the parents to sacrifice certain norms and ideals of the Old World family for the sake of their own happiness and that of their children. Finally, it was a matter of realism and convenience.

As the first generation was dying out, both the conflict and accommodation phases between the first and second generations gave rise to new forms of social and generational change. By the late 1950s and 1960s the coming of the third generation Greek American was caught between an ongoing process of assimilation, *embourgeoisement*, and the ethnic resurgence spearheaded primarily by African Americans and later by Chicanos or Mexican Americans. Added to these ethnic movements was the new Greek immigration of the mid-1960s and early 1970s, which brought a new cultural transfusion and a new ethnicity to Greek Americans. It is my contention that neither the rise of ethnic/racial consciousness in the United States nor the late Greek immigration arrested the Americanization process of the third generation Greek Americans. By the late 1950s and early 1960s, by and large, second- and third-generation and subsequent generations of Greeks had entered the American middle and the upper-middle-class lifestyles. While "ethnicity" had been there all along, it was giving way to class and ethclass lifestyles and patterns of behavior.

Most of the third- and later-generation Greek Americans, hedonistic as most American youth, retained mostly the Dionysian aspects of Greek culture, and had very little knowledge and understanding of the contemporary Apollonian aspects of the Greek culture. Greek cuisine, dancing, and music were more appealing to them than the abstract and remote notions of *philotimo* (honor, generosity), *philoxenia* (hospitality), Greekness (ethnicity), nationality, the Greek language, literature, family traditions, history, and the like. The Greek American youth, like American youth in general, were disenchanted with the institutional forms of religion. During the 1960s the Greek American youth complained that they could not understand the almost mystical and highly ritualistic practice of Orthodox Christianity cited in Biblical Greek. Many turned to more socially minded religions or were converted through intermarriage to other religions. However, during the 1980s and 1990s, there appears to be a rebirth of religious spirituality and Orthodox identity.

ASSIMILATION OR PLURALISM?

By the third and subsequent generations, the Greek American family's lifestyle becomes more and more symmetrical with that of the larger American middle class family. This, however, does not mean that all vestiges of ethnic subcultural lifestyles are lost. The Greek American maintains some of its unique ethnic features. For example, Greek names, the Orthodox faith, ethnic food, trips to Greece, some intergenerational family ties, and to some extent, some endogamous marriages remain. Assimilation, a multidimensional process in itself, does not have to be complete. It has been suggested (Kourvetaris, 1971c) that Greek Americans maintain their ethnic identity through their religion. As the subsequent generations of Greek Americans grow remote from the original generation, emphasis on Greek nationality and language is replaced by religion for those who support the organization of the Greek Orthodox Church in the United States. The Greek American family lifestyle is both assimilative and pluralistic. It is a blending, but not necessarily a perfect or equal blending, of two cultures.

One can tentatively suggest that as one moves away from the first generation to the second and subsequent generations, there is an increasing rate of intermarriage (this includes interethnic, interreligious, and interclass marriages). The first generation tends to be the most endogamous, the third the least, and the second is in between. By the third generation, intermarriage is more likely to follow class lines. Ethnicity, defined in most cases by nationality, religion, language or a combination of the three, declines as one moves from the first to second and to subsequent generations (Kourvetaris, 1990; Demos, 1988).

The gradual transformation from the Greek rural traditional (first-generation immigrant, both early and late) family to the Greek American urban middle class is somewhat coterminous with those changes brought about by urbanization and internal migration processes in Greece proper. Since the 1920s, and especially the 1940s, these processes have been accelerated. By the third generation, even Greeks in Greece have changed family lifestyles and norms from those found in the traditional rural family to those more symmetrical with the contemporary middle-class urban Athenian family (Safilios-Rothschild, 1967a). The differences lie in linguistic, national, and cultural areas, but the values and norms are similar to Greek-American ones. In short, unless Greek immigration continues, the Greek American family in America by third and subsequent generations will retain mostly the organizational and institutional aspects of Greek American subculture, particularly religion, family, and the success ethic, but not the more subtle aspects of Greek culture and ethnicity. Generational family ties will be attenuated, but Greeks will not lose respect for those institutions that sustained them throughout their long history, particularly religion and family.

In conclusion, the Greek-American family is progressively moving away from the ethnic patterns of the old world and becoming more of a homegrown phenomenon. It is undergoing the same changes as the American middle class family at large. The divorce rate and pathology of the American family have affected the Greek-American family as well. The divorce rate, unheard of in the first-generation immigrant family, has become a common occurrence by second and third generations. Parental respect, family traditions, and cooperation among the members of the family unit, all typical of the first generation, have been undermined by the decline of the father's authority. The erosion of family solidarity and the growing individualism within American families have also affected the Greek American family. Extra-family agencies and organizations, including state laws, have taken over many family functions. The American family, including the Greek-American, feels the pressures and demands of a consumerist psychology which has challenged the stability and cohesiveness of the Greek-American family.

ENDNOTES

[1]The Greek embassy estimates the Greek American population to be 2,000,000 while the Greek Archdiocese estimates it to be about 3,000,000. The 1980 U.S. census of foreign-born Greeks reports that 1.5% of the population is mostly concentrated in the Northeast and Northcentral with 2.4%, respectively; one percent is found in the South and 0.5% in the western states. Most foreign-born Greeks, estimated at 210,998 persons, live in urban and suburban areas. Insofar as selected ancestry groups of U.S. population, the U.S. census reports Greek ancestry at about 615,882, most of them found in NE and NC regions. Moskos (1982) estimates that there were about 1,250,000 Greek-Americans in 1980 distributed among first, second, third, and fourth generations.

[2]The dowry system was an extension of the arranged marriage system whereby the bride's family had to provide their future son-in-law a negotiated amount of cash or property in exchange for marrying their daughter. The dowry system has long been a part of the economic stratification and social status systems in general which views marriage as a vehicle of class mobility or immobility for the parties concerned and favors the higher socioeconomic classes. For example, the higher the socioeconomic class or social status of the groom, the greater the amount of expected dowry. In the past, the dowry system has brought tragedy to many poor families in Greece, particularly to those with large numbers of girls. Since 1975, by law, the institution of dowry has been abolished. However, in many parts of Greece it is still practiced on a voluntary and informal basis. While in the United States the institutionalized form of dowry as practiced in Greece in the past was discontinued among Greeks, nevertheless, vestiges of this practice continue to exist in informal ways in terms of gifts and elaborate wedding ceremonies provided by the bride's parents. The dowry system was more prevalent in the rural and southern parts of Greece.

[3]On the contemporary Athenian urban family, for example, see studies by Safilios-Rothschild (1965, 1967a, b, 1969a, b, 1971-1972) whose repertoire of topics is extensive and includes, among others, research on fertility and marital satisfaction; social class and family; deviance and mental illness; morality, courtship, and love in Greek folklore, and sex roles. Also see the study by Vassiliou and Vassiliou (1966) on social attitudes, stereotypes, and mental health in the Greek family.

On the rural and semi-urban Greek family see studies by Lambiri-Dimaki (1965) on dowry and the impact of industrial employment on the position of women in a Greek country town. Also, see studies by Friedl (1962) on dowry, kinship, and the position of women in rural Greece. In addition, Bardis (1955, 1956, 1967), Campbell (1964), and Sanders (1962, 1967) have also written on various aspects of the rural Greek family.

[4]For the *embourgeoisement*, success, and struggle of Greeks in America, see Moskos (1980). The book is a second-generation view of Greeks and Greek Americans. It somewhat exaggerates the success and *embourgeoisement* thesis and underemphasizes the

failure and problems. Moskos draws primarily from English writings and not from Greek sources written by the Greek immigrants.

REFERENCES

Bardis, Panos. 1955. "The Changing Family in Modern Greece," *Sociology* of *Social Research*, 40 (October): 19-23.

_____. 1956. "Main Features of the Greek Family During the Early Twentieth Century," *Alpha Kappa Delta*, 26 (Winter, November): 17-21.

_____. 1957. "Influences on the Modern Greek Family," *Social Science*, 32 (June): 155-158.

Campbell, J. K. 1964. *Honor, Family, and Patronage*. Oxford: Clarendon Press.

Campisi, J. Paul. 1948. "Ethnic Family Patterns: The Italian Family in the United States," *American Journal of Sociology*, 53 (May): 443-449.

Capanidou Lauquier, H. 1961. "Cultural Change Among Three Generations of Greeks," *American Catholic Review* (now *Sociological Analysis*), 22 (Fall): 223-232.

Chamales, Tom T. 1959. *Go Naked in the World*. New York: Scribner.

Chock, P. Phyllis. 1969. "Greek-American Ethnicity," unpublished Ph.D. Dissertation in the University of Chicago Library, Department of Anthropology, Chicago, IL.

Constantinou, Stavros T. and Milton E. Harvey. 1985. "Basic Dimensional Structure and Intergenerational Differences in Greek American Ethnicity." *Sociology and Social Research* vol. 69, no. 2 (Jan): 241-246.

Cutsumbis, N. Michael. 1970. *A Bibliographic Guide to Materials on Greeks in the United States 1890-1968*. New York: Center for Migration Studies.

Demos, Vasilike. 1988. "Ethnic Mother Tongue Maintenance Among Greek Orthodox Americans" *International Journal of Sociology of Language*, 69:59-71.

Doumanis, Mariella. 1983. *Mothering in Greece: From Collectivism to Individualism*. London: Academic Press Passim.

Dunkas, Nicholas and Arthur G. Nikelly. 1978. "The Persephone Syndrome," *Social Psychiatry*, 7: 211-16.

Fairchild, H. P. 1911. *Greek Immigration to the United States*. New Haven: Yale University Press.

Friedl, Ernestine. 1962. *Vasilika: A Village in Modern Greece*. New York: Holt.

_____. 1967. "The Position of Women: Appearance and Reality," *Anthropological Quarterly*, 40 (July): 97-108.

Gordon, Milton. 1964. *Assimilation in American Life: The Role of Race, Religion and National Origin*. New York: Oxford University Press.

Greek Orthodox Archdiocese of North and South America. 1986 *Yearbook*. New York pp. 102-103, 156-167.

Handlin, F. Oscar, and Mary F. Handlin.1956. "Ethnic Factors in Social Mobility," *Explorations in Entrepreneurial History*, 9 (October): 4-5.

Humphrey, R. Craig, and Helen T. Brock. 1972. "Assimilation, Ethnicity, and Voting Behavior Among Greek-Americans in a Metropolitan Area," paper presented at the 1972 Annual Meeting of the Southern Sociological Society, April 5-8, New Orleans.

Kardaras, Basil P. 1977. "A Study of the Marital and Familial Options of the Second Generation Greek-Americans in the Detroit Metropolitan Area," M.A. thesis, Department of Sociology, Wayne State University, Detroit, MI.

Kazan, Elia. 1968. *The Arrangement*. New York: Avon Books.

Koty, John. 1958. "Greece," in Arnold M. Rose (ed.), *The Institutions of Advanced Societies*. Minneapolis: University of Minnesota Press, pp. 330-383.

Kourvetaris, George A. 1971a. *First and Second Generation Greeks in Chicago*. Athens, Greece: National Center of Social Research.

_____. 1971b. "First and Second Generation Greeks in Chicago: An Inquiry Into Their Stratification and Mobility Patterns," *International Review of Sociology* (now *International Review of Modern Sociology*), 1 (March): 37-47.

_____. 1971c. "Patterns of Generational Subculture and Intermarriage of the Greeks in the United States," *International Journal of Sociology of the Family*, 1 (May): 34-48.

_____. 1973. "Brain Drain and International Migration of Scientists: The Case of Greece," *Epitheoris Koinonikon Erevnon (Review of Social Research)*, Nos. 15-16.

_____. 1977. "Greek-American Professionals: 1820s-1970s," *Balkan Studies*, 18:285-323.

_____. "Ethnic Conflicts and Identity Crises Among the Greeks in the Diaspora with Emphasis on the Greeks in the United States: An Exploratory Analysis." A paper presented at the KRIKOS Annual Conference held at Fordham Univ. New York, October 13, 1984.

_____. 1990. "Conflicts and Identity Crises Among Greek Americans and Greeks of the Diaspora" in *International Journal of Contemporary Sociology*. vol. 27 3-4 (July-October): 137-153.

Kourvetaris, George A., and Betty A. Dobratz. 1976. "An Empirical Test of Gordon's Ethclass Hypothesis Among Three Ethnoreligious Groups," *Sociology and Social Research*, 61 (October): 39-53.

Kyriazis, Elpis (Chairman). 1982. "Focus Greek Orthodox Family" at the Philoptochos Biennial Convention, July 4-9, 1982.

Lagos, Mary. 1962. "A Greek Family in American Society," unpublished eight page transcript, Franklin and Marshall College, Lancaster, PA.

Lambiri-Dimaki, Ioanna. 1965. *Social Change in a Greek Country Town*. Athens: Center of Planning and Economic Research.

McNeill, William. 1978. *The Metamorphosis of Greece Since WWII*. Chicago: University of Chicago Press.

Mistaras, Evangeline. 1950. "A Study of First and Second Generation Greek Outmarriages in Chicago," unpublished Masters Thesis in the University of Chicago Library, Department of Sociology. Chicago, IL.

Moskos, Charles C., Jr. 1982. "Greek American Studies," in Harry J. Psomiades and Alice Scourby, *The Greek American Community in Transition*. New York: Pella Publishing Co., pp. 17-19.

_____. 1980. *Greek Americans: Struggle and Success*. Englewood Cliffs, NJ: Prentice-Hall.

Papajohn, C. John. "The Relation of Intergenerational Value Orientation Change and Mental Health in An American Ethnic Group," a manuscript in the Florence Heller Graduate School for Advanced Studies in Social Welfare, Brandeis University.

Papanikolas, Z. Helen. 1970. *Toil and Rage in a New Land: The Greek Immigrants in Utah*. Salt Lake City: Utah State Historical Society.

Park, Robert E. 1950. *Race and Culture*. Glencoe, IL: The Free Press.

Petrakis, Harry Mark. 1966. *A Dream of Kings*. New York: McKay.

_____. 1959. *Lion at my Heart*. Boston: Little Brown, An Atlantic Monthly Press Book.

Plous, F. K., Jr. 1971. "Chicago's Greeks: Pride, Passion, and the Protestant Ethnic," *Midwest Sunday Magazine of the Chicago Sun Times* (April 25), pp. 22-26.

Rosen, Bernard. 1959. "Race, Ethnicity, and the Achievement Syndrome," *American Sociological Review*, 24 (February): 47-60.

Safilios-Rothschild, Constantina. 1965. "Mortality, Courtship, and Love in Greek Folklore," *Southern Folklore Quarterly*, 29, (December): 297-308.

_____. 1967a. "Class Position and Success Stereotypes in Greek and American Cultures," *Social Forces*, 45 (March): 374-383.

_____. 1967b. "A Comparison of Power Structure and Marital Satisfaction in Urban Greek and French Families," *Journal of Marriage and the Family*, 29 (May): 345-352.

_____. 1969a. "Patterns of Familial Power and Influence," *Sociological Focus*, 2 (Spring): 7-19.

_____. 1969b. "Family Sociology or Wives' Family Sociology? A Cross-Cultural Examination of Decision-Making," *Journal of Marriage and the Family*, 31 (May): 290-301.

_____. 1971-1972. "The Options of Greek Men and Women," *Sociological Focus*, 5 (Winter): 71-83.

Safilios-Rothschild, Constantina, Chrysie Constantakos, and Basil P. Kardaras. 1976. "The Greek-American Woman," paper presented at the Greek Experience in America Symposium 1976 at the University of Chicago, October 29-31.

Saloutos, Theodore. 1956. *They Remember America*. Berkeley and Los Angeles: The University of California Press.

_____. 1964. *The Greeks in the United States*. Cambridge: Harvard University Press.

Sanders, Irwin. 1962. *Rainbow in the Rock: The People of Rural Greece*. Cambridge: Harvard University Press.

_____. 1967. "Greek Society in Transition," *Balkan Studies*, 8: 317-332.

Scourby, Alice. 1984. *The Greek-Americans*. Boston: Twayne Publishers pp. 133-151.

Seder, L. Doris. 1966. "The Influence of Cultural Identification on Family Behavior," Ph.D. dissertation in Brandeis University Library, Department of Social Work, Boston, MA.

Simpson, George, and J. Milton Yinger. 1972. *Racial and Cultural Minorities: An Analysis of Prejudice and Discrimination*, 4th edition. New York: Harper and Row.

Stephanides, C. Marios. 1972. "Educational Background, Personality Characteristics, and Value Attitudes Towards Education and Other Ethnic Groups Among the Greeks in Detroit," Ph.D. dissertation in Wayne State University Library, Department of Sociology, Detroit, MI.

Stycos, J. M.   1948.   "The Spartan Greeks of Bridgetown," *Common Ground* (Winter, Spring, Summer), pp. 61-70, 24-34, 72-86.

Tastsoglou, Evangelica and George Stubos. 1992. "The Pioneer Greek Immigrant in the United States and Canada (1880s-1920s): Survival Strategies of a Traditional Family" *Ethnic Groups*. 93, 3 175-189.

_____. "The Greek Immigrant Family in the United States and Canada: The Transition From an "Institutional" to a "Relational" Form (1945-1970)" *International Migration*. 30, 2 (June): 155-174.

Tavuchis, Nicholas, 1968. "An Exploratory Study of Kinship and Mobility Among Second Generation Greek-Americans," Ph.D. dissertation in Columbia University Library, Department of Political Science, New York, NY.

_____. 1972. *Family and Mobility Among Greek-Americans*. Athens, Greece: National Centre of Social Research.

Terlexis, Pantazis, 1979. "Metanastefsi Kai Epanapatrismos: 1 Prosklisi to 1980" (Immigration and Repatriation), *Review of Social Sciences* (in Greek), July-September.

U.S. Department of Commerce. 1983. *Bureau of the Census. General Social and Economic Characteristics* vol. 1, part 1 (Dec.)

Vassiliou, George, and Vasso Vassiliou. 1966. "A transactional Approach to Mental Health," Contribution to the International Research Conference on Evaluation of Community Mental Health Programs of N.I.M.H.

Vlachos, C. Evangelos. 1968. *The Assimilation of Greeks in the United States*. Athens, Greece: National Center of Social Research.

_____. 1969. *Modern Greek Society: Continuity and Change*. Special Monograph Series No. 1, Department of Sociology and Anthropology, Colorado State University.

Xenides, J. P. 1922. *The Greeks in America*. New York: George H. Doran.

CHAPTER 6
GREEK-AMERICAN ENTREPRENEURS AND PROFESSIONALS*

Occupations and professions are considered of strategic importance in contemporary societies. They are among the main mediators between the individual and society. In a significant way, they enable us to understand the nature of society, its social institutions, and the individual. Historically, certain professional and occupational groups have played vanguard roles in spearheading societal change or have blocked change. From the perspective of stratification and social class, the individual's occupation and/or profession is the single best indicator of socioeconomic class.

The study of occupations and professions among ethnic and racial minorities in the United States has been of sustaining interest to social scientists. The sociological literature is replete with descriptions of the differences in economic performance among American ethnic and racial groups. Ethnic differences in occupational distribution and concentration are essential for the study of social organization in general, mobility and ethnic stratification in particular. To mention a few of the most pertinent studies, one may include Lipset and Ladd (1971) on Jewish-American academics; Greeley (1972) on American-Roman Catholic professionals; Featherman (1971) on ethnic achievement, Petersen (1971) on Japanese-American professionals; Edwards (1959) on Black-American professionals; Kuvlesky et al. (with Thomas, 1971 and with Patella, 1971) on Black-American and Mexican-American occupational aspirations. In addition, the United States Census (1973) reports the occupational/professional orientations of at least two dozen first and second generation ethnic and racial minorities. While one finds some general and

*I would like to express my gratitude to the following individuals for helping locate or provide information on Greek-American professionals: Ms. Helen Z. Papanikolas, University of Utah (Libraries); George E. Perry of the Library of Congress; Mr. A. M. Angelides, Minister Counsellor in the Embassy of Cyprus; Professor N. Choulis of West Virginia University; and Mr. James F. Greene. Deputy Commissioner of Immigration and Naturalization Service. It must be stressed, however, that the author alone accepts the responsibility for the interpretations. Parts of this chapter were originally published in the *Balkan Studies*, Vol. 18, No. 2, 1977, and parts were published in the *Journal of the Hellenic Diaspora*, Vol. 16, Nos. 1-4, 1989. Also, information was taken from a variety of sources including *Who's Who* in Greek America.

special studies on a number of ethnic/racial professionals, there is little or nothing on Greek-American professionals. Furthermore, although one can speak of a visible and energetic entrepreneurial class of Greek-Americans, it is doubtful that many Americans will recognize the existence of an emerging and viable class of Greek-American professionals.

An analysis of Greek-American professionals, or of any professionals for that matter, entails a conceptual refinement of what sociologists mean by professions/professionals and related concepts. The concepts of profession and/or professional is one of the most elusive and abused concepts in the lexicon of social science. "Profession" originally meant the act of professing that was associated with the vows of religious order. Gradually it has come to mean "the occupation which one professes to be skilled in and to follow a vocation in which professed knowledge of some branch of learning is used in its application to the affairs of others, or in the practice of an art based upon it" (Hughes, 1963). Professionals then profess to know better in this respective professions than others and their clients. More cogently, a profession is typified by a career which involves a lifelong commitment. It entails a succession and/or sequence of discrete stages through which a professional moves in a hierarchical fashion. A profession, then, is that occupation which requires extensive training; it is more specialized, demanding and costly and prepares the individual for a life-long career. A profession is more than a job or an occupation. It is an enduring and continuous career that is sharply differentiated from a non-profession.

The professional claim to esoteric and specialized knowledge gives the individual an exclusive right to practice his or her vocation, while at the same time it disqualifies the non-professional from exercising that right. A professional claim to knowledge generates a fiduciary role relationship in which a client has to trust the professional's judgement, and the professional has to abide by a code of ethics defining the perimeters of professional-client relationships.

Despite the efforts by many occupational sociologists to clarify the conceptual distinction between occupations and professions, one of the most perennial issues in the literature involves the differentiation between profession and non-profession. Although no overall conceptual/theoretical framework exists for the study of professions, Ritzer et al. (1974) have identified three major models in the sociological study of professions: the structuralist, the processual, and the power perspectives.

The Structuralist Model. Known also as structuralist-functionalist and/or attribute approach, it has been suggested mainly by scholars of the Ivy League schools including Greenwood (1957), Gross (1958), Goode (1960), Hall (1969), and Hughes (1963), among others. The structuralists tend to view professions as possessing certain "core characteristics" that differentiate them from all other occupations. However, no consensus exists among the structuralists as to what these attributes are. Greenwood (1957:44), for example, lists systematic theory, authority, community sanction, an ethical code and a culture as differentiating attributes of professions from non-professions. Goode (1960:903) stresses "a prolonged specialized training in a body of abstract knowledge and a collectivity or service orientation". Hall (1969) distinguishes between structural and attitudinal attributes of professionalism. A structural attribute is an integral part of the profession, e.g., graduate or professional school, while an attitudinal attribute refers to the belief a professional holds toward his profession and his role in society, i.e., belief in service to the public or belief in self-regulation. Hall contends that professionalism and professionalization are conceptually and empirically distinct. It is his contention that structural and attitudinal aspects of professionalism do not necessarily vary together. Some more established professions have rather weakly developed professional attitudes or vice-versa. This structuralist model has been criticized as the least useful approach because its emphasis is on the product rather than on the process of professionalization (Vollmer and Mills, 1966). Friedson (1970a) criticizes it as a self-serving approach while Bucher and Strauss (1961) find it rather pretentious for assuming that professions are a homogeneous group of independent practitioners. Ritzer et al. (1974) argue that a profession is more of an organizational concept while professionalism refers to attitudes and behavior of individual professionals.

The Processual Model. Also known as the historical and/or professionalization process, this model focuses on a developmental sequence. Those who adopt this model are typically interested in how professions emerge, develop, and legitimate in society. This approach is usually associated with the University of Chicago and supported by Wilensky (1964) and Vollmer and Mills (1966), among others. Wilensky (1964), for example, identified five steps in the process of professionalization: establishment of a full time occupation, the establishment of training schools, formation of professional associations, political agitation for legal recognition and exclusiveness, and development of internal rules and code of ethics.

Power Model. While the structural and processual approaches are analytically distinct and both have vied for hegemony within the sociology of professions, another model is the so-called power perspective. Friedson (1970a, 1970b, and 1973) suggests that the political clout of an occupation to win recognition as a profession is the single defining power characteristic of a profession. Friedson illustrates this power perspective in his study of medicine as a profession. Friedson's view examines not whether one has a claim to knowledge but how that knowledge comes to be utilized, evaluated, and controlled (1973:28). Ritzer et al. (1974) argue that indeed if one accepts the power perspective for becoming a profession, then it is essential for a would-be profession to develop an ideology (a belief system) and try to convince others of the profession's exclusive right to a particular domain of knowledge.

More recently, Abbott (1988) examines professions as an interdependent system. The author argues that in such a system each profession undergoes various kinds of jurisdiction. It is the history of jurisdictional disputes which is the determining factor of the legitimation and exclusivity of professions. The author argues that jurisdiction provides the link between an occupation and its work. Abbott discusses both the internal and external cultural and social forces bearing on the system of professions by looking at the histories of three contested jurisdictions—those of information, law, and psychotherapy.

Types of Professions. A professional possesses an exclusive right which allows the practice of his or her vocation, while at the same time disqualifies the non-professional from that practice. We can distinguish: a) consulting or client-dependent professions (e.g., lawyers, doctors, accountants, or all those professionals who provide services to various clients by using their expertise and specialized knowledge to solve practical or specific problems); and b) scientific or colleague-dependent professions (i.e., biologists, medical researchers, chemists, or academic professionals in general). The latter group includes academics who produce or create knowledge by carrying out basic research in universities and research institutes. Saunders (1933) has classified professions into five major types: 1) old established professions (religion, law, medicine, higher education); 2) new professions (chemists, engineers, natural and social scientists); 3) semi-professions (nursing, pharmacy, optometry, social work, school teaching); 4) would-be professions (sales engineers, business counselors, funeral directors, etc.); and 5) marginal professions (medical and lab technicians). The study of occupations and professions is also related to the study of occupational achievement and class mobility. A number of studies and general works have documented intergenerational Greek-American mobility between first and second generations and between Greek-Americans and other American ethnic groups. Some of these issues will be dealt with later in this chapter or subsequent chapters in the reader.

Other writers distinguish professions into "emergent professions," "professions in transition", and "professions in process." These professional types, Pavalko (1971) maintains, represent dimensions of the professionalization process, or the extent to which certain occupations change their position on one or more dimensions of the occupation-profession continuum. Wilensky (1964), in his study of the temporal sequence of professionalization of a number of occupations, has proposed a fourfold classification: "established professions" (law, medicine, architecture); "professions in process" (or marginal professions), e.g., librarian, nursing, optometry, pharmacy; "the new professions" (city management, city planning, hospital administration), and finally, the "doubtful category of professions" (including advertising and funeral directors).

The concept of entrepreneur has different meanings. In economics, it is used to denote risk-taking in founding a new business. Entrepreneurship also refers to small enterprises or family-owned small businesses (e.g., restaurants). The concept also refers to all those who display an independent mind, foresight, creativity, and boldness in initiating or founding not only business but also social movements, voluntary associations, and public agencies. Entrepreneurs are not limited to business enterprises only; we can apply this concept to all types of occupations and professions, including scientific ones (e.g., professional entrepreneurs). The United States Census code book, 1980 Census Technical Documentation Part II (1982: 224-225), also defines self-employed workers as:

> Persons who work for profit or fee in their own incorporated business, profession, or trade, or who operate a farm. Included here are the owner-operators of large stores and manufacturing establishments as well as small merchants, independent craft-persons and professionals, farmers, peddlers, and other persons who conduct enterprises on their own. Persons whose own business is incorporated are counted as employees of their corporation and are tabulated in the "private wage and salary workers" category.

Who are the Greek-American professionals and entrepreneurs? What kinds of professions are Greek-Americans more likely to enter? Who are the Greek-American entrepreneurs? What kinds of enterprises do they engage in?[1] As we pointed out before, we have very few empirical studies on Greek-American professionals and entrepreneurs. In this paper, I will argue that Greek-American entrepreneurs, like Greek-American professionals, have not succeeded in penetrating the corporate structure of the United States, except in a few cases. We have hundreds, perhaps thousands, of restaurant establishments individually- or family-owned but very few McDonalds, Burger Kings, or other corporate or franchise-type and/or hotel establishments on the national or international level. Likewise, we have a few thousand Greek-American professionals concentrated in a few professions, but they are not a diverse and organized group, nor have they established a tradition of Greek-American professionalism. Greek-Americans are known in America as restaurant operators and not as professionals.

Greek-Americans have made some inroads and progress in the professions and small businesses more as individuals or family-oriented enterprises than as organized and institutional professionals and corporate entrepreneurs. This is due, in part, to the fact that the very nature of professional occupations and entrepreneurial activity in which Greeks usually engage reflects the "dominant American ideology" of individual opportunity and success. This individualistic orientation almost exclusively finds the individual responsible for his or her socioeconomic mobility in the American class structure. Greek-Americans have embraced this dominant ideology.

The foregoing discussion serves as a conceptual prolegomenon to the analysis of Greek-American professionals proper. In the present paper the emphasis will be primarily on the established professions and only secondarily on other types of professions. More concretely, an effort will be made 1) to delineate the socio-historical antecedents of contemporary Greek-American professionals and 2) to investigate the contemporary Greek-American professionals with respect to a number of socio-demographic and professional variables.

For the purpose of this analysis, the terms "profession" and "professional" will be used interchangeably. A "Greek professional" will include a rather small aggregate of first and second generation Greek-Americans[2] who possess at least two structural and/or organizational/institutional characteristics: one, the possession of a graduate or professional degree from an accredited college or university (e.g., M.A./M.S., Ph.D., M.D., LL.D., J.D., or M.D.S.) and two, an organizational/institutional affiliation (i.e., college or university, hospital, law office, and the like).

THE GREEK IMMIGRANT EXPERIENCE: OLD AND NEW

In this section, an effort will be made to discuss briefly the Greek immigrant experience as entrepreneurs and professionals, both among old and new immigrants. Is there an ethnic pattern of entrepreneurial and professional activities among the early and late Greek immigrants? Were the early and late Greek immigrants any different from other immigrant groups? We can only highlight some of the trends and patterns of Greek immigrant entrepreneurs and professionals.[3]

Greek entrepreneurs. A number of social scientists ask why certain immigrant groups engage in entrepreneurial activities while others pursue occupations in agriculture, industry, government, and/or politics. There are basically three prevailing explanations in the literature of inter-ethnic variations in entrepreneurship. First, there is the so-called "reactive version of cultural theory" (Light, 1972). According to this explanation, certain immigrant groups experience discrimination in the host society. To combat discrimination, these immigrant groups release latent facilitators which promote entrepreneurship. These facilitators emerge not from "the ethnic cultural baggage" of a particular group but rather from the existing minority situation in the dominant society. Confronted with systematic discrimination and exclusion in the general labor market, ethnic members take a collective or family, rather than individualistic, approach to establishing and managing a business. Light (1972) argued that the early Chinese and Japanese entrepreneurs before WWII utilized intra-ethnic resources such as "rotating credit association," trust, informal ethnic associations, and ethnic solidarity to establish and manage businesses. This approach is more applicable to first-generation immigrant groups, which experience not only discrimination in the market and workplace but find themselves in cultural shock and react to it by releasing certain facilitators such as mutual aid based on kinship ties, regional ties from back home, etc. This might apply to the early and late or first generation Greeks in part, but not to the second and third generations. The Greeks have a cultural tradition of entrepreneurship going back to the nineteenth century in the Middle East, Eastern Mediterranean, and Southeastern Europe (Kourvetaris, 1987).

Another perspective on ethnic entrepreneurial activities is known in the literature as the "middleman economic minority hypothesis." According to this view, certain minorities occupy a middle-rank position in the economic stratification system of the host societies. A number of scholars—Blalock (1967: 79), Bonacich (1973: 77), Bonacich and Modell (1980:83)—argue that certain ethnic minorities occupy "middle" positions or find their economic niches as go-betweens between elites and workers, or as small business people positioned between producers and consumers. According to Bonacich and Modell (1980), these groups function as buffers between elites and the masses, "playing the roles of rent collectors and shopkeepers to the subordinate population while distributing the products of the elite and/or exacting tribute for them." Middleman minorities are not primary producers, but facilitators who help the flow of goods and services through the economy (Portes and Bach, 1985). Choi (1988: 7) singles out three major aspects of the middleman minority hypothesis: a) the immigrants' position as buffers between elites and masses; b) "middleman economic roles" to help the flow of goods and services through the economy; and c) an old middle class or petit bourgeoisie between the capitalist class and the working class. Entrepreneurs concentrate on small self-employed businesses. Ethnic business becomes an extended form of family and kinship relationships. Some concentrate in retail trade and commerce or service-oriented industries (restaurants, taverns, groceries). Most of these enterprises are found in the peripheral sectors of the economy. Other immigrants enter professions such as medicine, dentistry, law, or accounting, in the core or high-tier sectors of the economy (Bonacich and Modell, 1980: 17). Both early and late Greek immigrants engaged in middleman economic enterprises as restaurateurs, grocers, confectioners, tavern-owners, shoeshine operators, florists, and theater-owners. The second generation did not, as a rule, follow these middleman minority enterprises. By and large they entered white-collar, professional and semi-professional, and managerial-type occupations.

There is a third explanation of entrepreneurial activities, "the ethnic enclave hypothesis." According to this hypothesis, middleman minorities develop ethnic economic and business enclave communities as economic niches that complement the general more dominant economic structure of society (e.g., the Cubans in Miami, the Koreans in Los Angeles, the Chinese in San Francisco, or the Greeks in Tarpon Springs or at Halsted (among early), Western, and Lawrence Streets in Chicago among late Greek immigrants). These enclave ethnic business communities cater to customers inside and outside the ethnic communities. Ethnic enclave economic communities provide a frame of reference and an economic base for subsequent generations of immigrants. Most ethnic groups followed this pattern of entrepreneurship, including the Greeks. As new arrivals of immigrants came to the United States, they found these ethnic enclave communities to be a starting-point for subsequent mobility and incorporation into the American economic system. Both the ethnic enclave and middleman minority explanations recognize the importance of racial and ethnic stratification and economic incorporation in niches (Feagin, 1989: 40). Ethnic enclaves, unlike "colonies" of internal colonialism, do not relegate newcomers to a permanent position of inferiority and exploitation. The internal colonialism thesis is more applicable to African Americans (Blauner, 1972). Many sociologists are critical of the internal colonialism and split labor market viewpoints which try to explain economic conditions of all non-European minorities. In general, ethnic enclave economies require a substantial inflow of immigrants with business capabilities, available capital, and a large pool of low-wage labor (Feagin, 1989: 40).

In order to discuss the professional and entrepreneurial orientation of Greek-Americans, one has to not only look at the differences between Greek-American generations within the Greek-American experience but also compare Greek-American professionals with other ethnic professional and entrepreneurial groups. The present analysis is primarily of Greek-American professionals and entrepreneurs within the Greek American community and experience in America and only secondarily an effort to draw comparisons with other ethnic groups.

Greek-American Entrepreneurs. First-generation Greek entrepreneurs have followed the same occupational patterns for most of the twentieth century. They are heavily concentrated in service-type entrepreneurial activities.[4] The majority of restaurant owners are first-generation Greeks (both old and new Greeks follow similar patterns). This, however, does not mean that Greeks did not go into other entrepreneurial activities. A large number of new Greek immigrants, for example, went into real estate. The 1989, 1990, and 1994-95 *Hellenic Who's Who in Professions and Businesses* do not include the entire occupational distribution of Greek-Americans. They tend to favor all those Greek-Americans who are easily identified among various institutions and organizations, e.g., universities, corporations, government, law firms, etc. The majority of small-business people, such as restaurateurs, are not contained in the *Hellenic Who's Who*. As individual entrepreneurs, Greek immigrants followed what Useem (1980) calls family capitalism, which was the dominant form of capitalism in the nineteenth and early twentieth centuries. While there has been a decline of family capitalism in American society, the new immigrants—whether Greek, Korean, or Chinese—tend to enter this kind of business. First-generation Greeks did not have the skills or money to go into managerial forms of capitalism. Greeks have not succeeded in moving into other forms of more organized capitalism—namely, managerial and institutional corporate capitalism. This individualistic capitalist orientation reflects the character of the peasant background and farming classes of rural Greece. The first-generation Greeks brought these rural patterns to America. The first generation also established an economic base which was used by the second and subsequent generations. The absence of managerial-type capitalism in the first generation hindered the ascent of the second generation into the managerial, and indeed the corporate, capitalism of the United States. The concentration of the first generation in small entrepreneurial activities, especially service-oriented occupations, is not unique among Greeks. Similar patterns are followed by the majority of new immigrants as they enter American society. Italians, Jews, Greeks and now the new Asian immigrants (Koreans, Chinese, Vietnamese, Indians) are engaged in small businesses. Like earlier immigrants, Koreans, for example, are engaged in small businesses. Surveys of metropolitan New York and Atlanta found that 34 percent of all Korean families are engaged in the management of small businesses. By comparison, only about seven percent of the general population is self-employed, with even a lower percentage for blacks (2.4 percent) and Hispanics (3.8 percent) (In-Jin Yoon, 1988: 1).

Second and subsequent generations as a rule did not follow the entrepreneurial orientation of their parents. They did not follow the family capitalist model of entrepreneurship. Some followed a managerial or institutional form of capitalism, which was more characteristic of American occupational structures and American capitalist development in general. Even for the second generation, it was difficult to move into this type of capitalism because of a lack of a frame of reference. The extent to which second and subsequent generations of Greeks have penetrated the institutional and corporate world is not known for sure. One thing is certain, however: Greek-Americans are not found in the top positions of corporate America. In 1988, *Fortune* magazine listed only one Greek-American as a multi-millionaire. In Dye's book *Who Is Running America* (1995), no Greek-American is found in any of the twelve elite sectors of American society.[5] In my analysis of the *Who's Who in Professions and Businesses* among the Greeks, it was found that the second generation pursues more executive positions in the corporate world than the first generation. However, the type of executive positions pursued and the ranking of the corporations have not been among the leading corporations in the United States (maybe with a few exceptions).

To what extent do these ethnic entrepreneurial perspectives explain the propensity of Greeks for entrepreneurial activities? To put it differently, what is the appropriateness of each of these explanations for the Greek experience in America? In general, these explanations are more appropriate for the early and late Greek immigrant or the first generation. The ethnic enclave economic communities were more reminiscent of the 1960s and 1970s of the late Greek immigrants which had their counterparts in the 1920s and 1930s of early Greek immigrants. Greek immigrants have embraced an entrepreneurial ideology. Entrepreneurial ideology is linked to dominant American economic ideology. Along with many other ethnic Americans, Greek-Americans have accepted what Huber and Form (1974) have labeled the "dominant stratification ideology." This ideology is also called the "logic of opportunity syllogism" (Klugel and Smith, 1986: 5). It provides a deductive argument that justifies inequality of economic outcomes in the American stratification system. The basic assumption in the "opportunity or dominant" economic hypothesis is that opportunity for economic advancement is based on hard work, and that this opportunity is plentiful. From this premise, two deductions follow (Kluegel and Smith, 1986: 5):

a)   Individuals (*not* society) are responsible for their economic fate. This is also in accordance with economic entrepreneurial or classical laissez-faire economic liberalism in that individual economic outcomes are directly proportional to individual outputs (talent and effort). From this follows

b) The second deduction, namely that the resulting unequal distribution of economic rewards in American society is, in the aggregate, equitable and fair.

The attitudes of Americans in general and of Greeks in particular toward inequality are shaped by their respective positions in the stratification system, which include such factors as education, income, economic and social status, and similar socioeconomic variables. Indeed, like many other ethnic Americans, especially the late immigrants from southeastern and central Europe (Polish, Italian, Greek, and Slavic minorities), Greeks tend to oppose policies which support social welfare for the poor and the underclass. These late European immigrants feel that they've "made it" in America on their own without relying on any government handouts.

One can argue that ethnic Greeks who voted for Michael Dukakis, especially Greek entrepreneurs, voted against their own economic interests. However, in the case of Dukakis's presidential candidacy, ethnicity took precedence over economic considerations. The Democratic Party in the 1988 elections, and Dukakis in particular, represented "social liberalism," which is somewhat contrary to the dominant economic ideology of the "economic opportunity hypothesis." Within the American social and political structure, there are two contradictory but coexistent trends. First, there is the dominant economic ideology of equal opportunity and social mobility which disposes people toward a more conservative evaluation of welfare and distributive economic or social programs. In this instance, one would expect Greeks to be more conservative economically due to their entrepreneurial orientation.

The other trend is toward social liberalism, an acceptance of social and political equality with such groups as blacks, Hispanics, and women, but without the bases of economic inequality being challenged. During the 1960s, many white ethnic Americans changed their social and racial beliefs. Surveys have shown marked reductions in traditional racial prejudice, such as overt racial bigotry or denial of equal rights to blacks and other minorities. In the case of Greeks, Christakis (1987) argues that they are successful in business because they adopt a work ethic similar to the one Weber talked about for Protestants, which demands deferring immediate satisfaction for a future goal. Greek children are socialized early in life, both by the family and the Greek community, to value work and success. Entrepreneurship preceded Greek-American entry into the professions. Entrepreneurs are mostly associated with the first-generation Greek immigrants, both old and new. Greeks have been engaged in entrepreneurial activities on a smaller scale for a long time. They are heavily represented in the service industries (restaurants). We find thousands of Greek restaurateurs not only in the United States but in Canada, Australia, and other parts of the world. Greeks and food service became almost synonymous.

Generally, in big cities and small towns across the United States, Greeks become proprietors or managers of small restaurant businesses. The pattern of business ownership followed pretty much the same course: fruit or vegetable peddlers became owners of groceries; flower vendors moved on to florist shops; bootblacks moved into their own shoe repair, hat blocking, or dry cleaning establishments and confection and sweet shops became a Greek monopoly (Moskos, 1990). Other Greeks went into business in a variety of retail, wholesale, and manufacturing enterprises. Many Greeks became wealthy in real estate and stock market speculation.

Another area of business in some Greeks prospered was movie theaters. The Pantages theater chain controlled about 80 movie houses in the 1920s. The three Skouras brothers brought even greater Greek-American prominence to the movie and entertainment industry. By 1926, the Skouras brothers controlled 37 theaters in St. Louis alone. During the 1930s, the brothers had a chain of over 400 theaters. They became major figures in the motion picture industry in Hollywood itself. Eventually, Spyros Skouras became president of 20th Century Fox.

Rassogianis (1982) examines the various businesses of the Chicago Greeks during the period of 1900-1930. Some of the most important businesses discussed were shoeshine parlors, which were the most popular and profitable. Most of these shoeshine parlor owners operated in the best downtown Chicago locations. They were extremely successful and many of them operated chains of shoeshine parlors throughout the city. The Greek shoeshine parlor owners and the boys working in these establishments surpassed the Italians and blacks. Later, after World War I, shoeshine business began to decline. In order to remedy this, Greek owners introduced shoe repairing, cleaning and pressing of clothes and hats, and they sold items ordinarily sold in drug stores such as tobacco.

The majority of the boys working in these shoeshine parlors were recruited through the notorious *padrone* system. The "labor boss" wrote to friends and relatives in Greece targeting poor boys from the rural mountain villages of the Peloponnesos. These shrewd and ambitious padrone "godfather figures" promised these kids "the world" but in reality lured them into an exploitative system. The earnings of those who worked in the Chicago parlors ranged from $80 to $250 a year, with the average being between $100-$200 (quoted in Rassogianis, 1982: 35). Their counterparts in smaller, less populated cities averaged about $100 a year. In almost all of the shops, money made by the boys from tips was turned over to the owner immediately after a shine or at the end of the day. The owner used the tips to cover the wages and daily expenses of the workers. By the 1920s, the padrone system began to decline along with the shoeshine business.

The next line of business was the confectionery. Confectioners started as peddlers of candy and gradually opened candy and ice cream shops. By 1925, thousands of ice cream parlors and candy shops were in existence in most metropolitan areas of the country (Rassogianis, 1982: 44). One of the largest and most popular of the confectionery chains in Chicago was DeMets Candy Stores. In addition, the Greeks established candy-manufacturing businesses which supplied stores. By the early 1920s, the Greeks of Chicago dominated all phases of the candy business. Foremost among the candy manufacturers were the Gallomis brothers.

The next lines of business were restaurants and chains of restaurants. The first restaurants were those serving Greek cuisine. In the early years, most Greeks operated moveable lunch wagons selling hot dogs, sandwiches, and tamales to factory workers. The traveling lunch wagons later became permanently sited businesses. These early restaurants were owned by families. By 1923, there were 1,035 Greek-owned restaurants. One of the leading enterprises was John Raklios's chain of restaurants. He established his own company.

Another field in which Greeks were successful was the fruit business. By 1921, the Greeks of Chicago owned 90 retail fruit stores, 26 fruit and vegetable stores, and 80 wholesale fruit businesses (Rassogianis, 1982: 70). By 1925, the retail fruit stores rose to 388, with 18 wholesale fruit stores. Floral businesstable for some Greeks. In 1923, there were about 13 Greek-owned flower shops in Chicago and 175 in New York.

Many recent Greek immigrants have followed in the path of their predecessors, going into the food service business. Greek restaurant establishments increased dramatically with the arrival of the new Greek immigrants in the 1950s and 1960s. Lovell-Trʌy's study (1981) of Greeks in Connecticut in the pizza business has shown an ethnic pattern of economic enterprise different from that followed by Italians in the same business. According to the author, the Greeks tend to establish their pizza businesses in those towns without Greek populations while Italians tend to establish theirs in towns with Italian populations. Lovell-Troy has also shown the persistence of ethnic characteristics of enterprises among Greek immigrants over a 70-year period. Greek immigrants have been heavily concentrated in the restaurant business as owners and employees since the beginning of the twentieth century. However, national occupational data for 1970 indicates a reduction in the percentage of Greeks opening their own restaurants in comparison to previous years. For example, in the national occupational data in 1950, there were about 32 percent Greek-foreign born males who concentrated as managers, officials, and proprietors (except farmers category); by 1970, there were only half, or 16 percent, in the same category. Since Greek immigration had almost stopped by the mid-1970s and 1980s, and since Greek restaurants are a first-generation phenomenon, it is reasonable to assume that the traditional Greek pattern of restaurant entrepreneurship is rapidly declining. The extent to which second-generation children of late Greek immigrants followed the patterns of their fathers is not known. If we accept the proposition that the children of early Greek immigrants as a rule did not follow their fathers' entrepreneurial activities, it can be argued that the same will happen with the children of the late Greek immigrants. Indeed, there are indications that the second generation of late Greek immigrants are by and large college-bound.

GREEK-AMERICAN PROFESSIONALS: A CAPSULE SOCIO-HISTORICAL PROFILE

Greek-American Professionals. In terms of professionals, we have the same phenomenon. There are several thousand Greek-American professionals, but only a few Greek-Americans in elite universities, foundations, research institutes, top hospitals, prestigious law firms, or top positions in communications and the media. We have no major Grammy Award winners, no National Book Award winners. There are no major Greek-American symphony orchestra or music directors. We find no Nobel Prize winners. There are no Pulitzer Prize winners in journalism or letters (fiction, drama, history, biography or autobiography, poetry, etc.). We have no award winners in sports or athletics, except perhaps for Greg Louganis, who is not of Greek extraction but was adopted by a Greek-American family.

Thalia Cheronis Selz discusses Greek-Americans in the visual arts. However, very few Greeks went into the arts due to the fact that Greeks chose a small number of occupations and professions which offered more financial security. Scourby (1984) briefly discusses two dozen first- and second-generation painters and artists, she characterizes as "outside the mainstream."[6] In addition, Karanikas (*Hellenic Letters*, 1985: 200-205) briefly discusses two dozen or so first- and second-generation prose writers.[7]

Drawing primarily from an article written by Peter Marudas, "Greek-American Involvement in Contemporary Politics" (also in *Greek-American Community in Transition*, edited by Harry Psomiades), Scourby (1984: 100-108) discusses the role of Greek-Americans in politics.[8] With the exception of a dozen or so elected and appointed high positions of Greek-Americans, there is no real political power among Greek-Americans. Most of these appointments were from the Democratic Party and a few from the Republican Party. There is a tendency to exaggerate the so-called Greek lobby, which became even more exaggerated during the Cyprus crisis.

19th Century Greek-American Professionals. Historically, a number of Greek and American authors (Burgess, 1913; Canoutas, 1918; Malafouris, 1948; Dendias, 1919; Kourvetaris, 1977) reported the existence of a few dozen Greek-American professionals in the United States during the 19th century. Canoutas (1918), for example, differentiated between three major sources of Greek immigrants to the United States in the 19th century: One, Greek orphans of the Greek Revolution of 1821 and those who survived the massacre of Chios by the Turks in 1822. Second, those who came to the United States as merchants and sailors. Third, those who arrived at the end of the 19th century and the beginning of the 20th century.

It has been reported (Burgess, 1913; Canoutas, 1918; Dendias, 1919; Malafouris, 1948) that a number of Greek orphans of the Greek Revolution of 1821 were brought to the United States by American missionaries and sponsored by either American philhellenes or the missionaries themselves. These orphans became the proto-Greek-American professionals in the United States. While some of the orphans maintained their ethnic identity, returned to Greece after their studies, and thus became the first unofficial ambassadors of the United States to Greece the majority became assimilated by changing their faith (from Orthodox Christian to Protestant) and their names. Exact figures for the number of Greek orphans brought to the United States, those who came by other means, and those who studied in institutions of higher learning are not known. It has been estimated (Kastanis, cited in Malafouris, 1948:48-19) that about 40 Greek male youngsters were brought to the United States by American missionaries and American philhellenes following the Greek Revolution of 1821.

Canoutas (1918) maintained that in the 19th century most Greeks, other areas from which many, including the orphans, came from the Greek islands of the Aegean Sea, such as Chios. Other areas from which many Greeks arrived to the United States included Asia Minor, Epirus, and Macedonia. Many of the early Greek-American professionals studied at Yale, Amherst, Princeton, Hartford Seminary, Kenyon of Ohio, Eastern of Pennsylvania, and Knoxville of Tennessee colleges, and excelled in a number of professions including theology, politics, classics, medicine, military (navy), and the sciences. Canoutas (1918:96-97) also maintains that many Greeks in the 19th century studied Protestant theology but not all of them later followed that profession.

Greek-American Professionals: 1900-1940's. While Greek immigrants came sporadically to the United States in the 19th century, the preponderance of Greek immigration to the United States began at the turn of the 20th century. While most European immigration to the United States has declined, Greek immigration, excluding the interwar years, has declined only in the mid-1970s. Continued Greek immigration has given to the larger Greek-American community "a graduate scale of ethnicity" with sustained doses of "Greek cultural transfusion." At one extreme of the continuum are those Greeks who are totally "Americanized," while at the other are those who can hardly speak a word of English.

The overwhelming majority of the "early immigrants" in the United States, including the Greeks, were from the working class. Like most "early immigrants" Greeks as a rule were poor, had limited education and skills, and came primarily from agricultural communities. In addition, Greeks (like Italians) did not come as families because they did not expect to stay in the United States. By contrast, the post World War II Greek immigrants tend to be more educated, do not come exclusively from small agricultural communities, and many come as families sponsored or invited by relatives and friends among the "early" Greek immigrants.

Included in both groups were a small number of Greek professionals, semi-professionals, ethnic literati, and ethnic apostles. The latter particularly became the purveyors of ethnic ideals and values of Greek culture and society. It has been reported (Burgess, 1913; Canoutas, 1918; Dendias, 1919; Malafouris, 1948; Kourvetaris, 1971a and 1975) that the majority of Greek professionals in the first quarter of the 20th century were doctors. (This is a profession whose skills do not demand high proficiency of the English language as for instance practicing law demands). Burgess (1913) estimated that there were about 40 or 50 Greek doctors throughout the United States at the turn of the century but that only half of them were licensed. Most of these early Greek doctors received their training in Greece and had no other choice but practice among their co-ethnics (a phenomenon which continues to some extent even today).

Later, however, Canoutas (1918) and Dendias (1919), both Greek authors, estimated that about 100 or so Greek doctors were in the United States. Added to that number were many Greek students who studied medicine in the first quarter of the 20th century. Malafouris (1948) reports that these were approximately two dozen Greek doctors, most of them established in major U.S. cities, between the 1890s and 1920s. In contrast to Burgess, Malafouris cites that Greek physicians in the 1890s and 1920s were, for the most part, born in Greece, but studied medicine in the United States.[9]

The next largest professional groups[10] were lawyers, dentists, pharmacists, and chemists (in that order) which altogether did not exceed 70 to 100 professionals. In addition, around the turn of the century there were a few dozen other Greek professionals in literature, philosophy, classics, sociology, and mechanical and electrical engineering. Added to that number there were about 30-60 students enrolled in American colleges by 1913. Burgess (1913) reported that very few of the lawyers were admitted to the Bar because of the language barrier. Most of the lawyers received their degree from the University of Athens.

Canoutas (1918), however, predicted that by the 1920's the number of Greek professionals would be doubled and tripled, due to the fact that many hundreds of Greek students already attended a number of universities including the Universities of Boston, Cambridge, California, and Pennsylvania. Dendias (1919) also reported that many Greek students attended Amherst, Yale, Harvard, Cornell, Washington, and Maryland Universities. Vavoudis (1925), on the other hand, estimated about 100 graduates from American universities by the 1920's.

CONTEMPORARY GREEK-AMERICAN PROFESSIONALS

Writing at the turn of the century, Burgess (1913) predicted the coming of the professional and business class of the Greek immigrant. Fifty years later, Saloutos (1964), a second generation Greek-American professor of history, describes the advent of professional, commercial, and intellectual prominence of the Greek which he characterized as impressive or the coming of "the era of respectability for the Greek in America". In Saloutos' words, there is "the emergence of a new generation of Greek-Americans to positions of influence. Greek-Americans are on the way to a new status in American society. The immigrants of yesteryear had established sobriety, industry, and integrity". While generalizations such as those mentioned by Burgess and Saloutos are often found in the literature, no empirical study has attempted to investigate a number of pertinent questions concerning Greek-American professionals. Thus this part of the analysis will seek to report the findings of a survey on the contemporary Greek-American professionals with emphasis on academics.

There is an emerging and viable Greek-American professional class. Furthermore, it will be argued that the emergence of Greek-American professionals is both a rather post World War II phenomenon, and a product, by and large, of the so-called Greek "brain-drain," that is, the immigration of Greek scientists, engineers, doctors, and professionals in general and Greek students (potential professionals), who came to the United States on student visas especially in the 1950's. Put another way, this part of the analysis will consist of 1) a report and discussion of survey findings of selective demographic characteristics of the Greek-American professionals in general (i.e., sources of recruitment, place of birth, location of Greek-American professionals, education, area of competence and nature of institutional affiliation), and 2) a report of survey findings and discussion of Greek-American academics only with respect to a number of selective socio-demographic variables.

Sources of Greek-American Professional Recruitment. Three major categories of Greek-American professional recruitment may be distinguished that can invariably be seen as sources of international migration of Greek scientists and professionals, also known as Greek "brain drain". These categories are the actual, the potential, and the hidden,"[11] which are also applicable to other nations with a similar problem of brain drain. (This area of recruitment and brain drain will be dealt with more extensively in Chapter Ten.)

The "actual" includes all those professionals, technical and kindred workers (including scientists, engineers and doctors) who, after completing their professional training, decide to migrate to more advanced countries, particularly to the United States, Canada, Western Europe, and Australia, and only secondarily to Third World countries that are less developed or equally developed (as that of Greece) in Asia, Africa, and Latin America. It has been estimated (Coutsoumaris, 1968:169) that between 1957-1961, Greece lost to the United States alone over one fifth of all her professionals with first degrees in engineering. Coutsoumaris believes that the total loss is even greater than this if one adds those who left for the other advanced countries of Western Europe and Canada, and even those who migrated to the less advanced countries of the Third World.

The next, and indeed major, source of Greek brain drain includes Greek students[12] who are granted immigrant or non-immigrant visas by foreign consulates to pursue their education abroad. Coutsoumaris (1968:169) estimated, for example, that Greece has an annual average of over 8,000 Greek students abroad, 10% of whom are in graduate and 80% in undergraduate schools. This number represents about 15% of the total student body enrolled in institutions of higher learning in Greece. Despite the fact that no empirical studies have been conducted to determine the percentages of Greek students who received undergraduate and graduate degrees from foreign universities, and the number of them who settle in the host country or repatriate upon the completion of their studies, it is safe to speculate that a substantial number of them do manage to graduate, but the majority remain abroad after graduation, particularly those studying in the United States and Canada.

GREEK-AMERICAN ACADEMICS

With the exception of a hundred or so Greek-American academics by the 1940s, Greek-American academic professionals are a rather recent phenomenon. Saloutos (1964:324) contends that the professions which mostly appealed to second generation Greeks were law, medicine, and, to a lesser degree, dentistry. These were the professions that counted more in Greece and also in the United States. Later, teaching and engineering acquired more appeal Saloutos contends. Thus, despite the number of professional and cultural societies in the 1920's and 1930's, and some student associations, by the 1940s and early 1950s the Greek-American professionals amounted to a few hundred, or perhaps even a thousand, in contrast to the many thousands of Greek-Americans and their progenies in the United States. Malafouris (1948), in his survey of Greek-Americans, specifically lists about 38 or so academics total--13 in humanities, 10 in social sciences, 7 in natural sciences, 4 other miscellaneous, and 4 mentioned in the text (2 each in medicine and chemistry).

One of the most learned Greek men of letters in the United States was Professor Aristides Phoutridis, who was a summa cum laude from Harvard and a recipient of many scholarships. Professor Phoutridis was a founder and pioneer in the establishment of the first Greek student association "Helikon"[13] in 1911 in Boston, where he lived for a number of years. He taught at Yale and translated part of Palamas' (the most celebrated modern Greek poet) poetry into English. His premature death, however, at the age of 35 deprived Greece and Greek-Americans of one of its brilliant sons.

Other prominent men of science in medicine were noted by Malafouris (1948). Dr. George Papanikolaou (M.D.), for example, stands out as the most illustrious among the Greek-American medical scientists. While professor of anatomy at Cornell University he discovered what is commonly known as the "Pap" smear test for detecting cancer of the uterus. Dr. Polyvios Koryllos (M.D.), professor of medicine at the University of Athens and Yale, was another medical scientist famous for his contributions in the diagnoses of tuberculosis patients. In chemistry, Professors Nicholas Mitropoulos of the University of Chicago and Pythagoras Sfaellos of New York University both took part in the scientific research of atomic energy. The former was also present at the atomic test in New Mexico.

Despite a sporadic number of Greek academics, including a few illustrious scientists and scholars, one can argue that by 1940 there was no genuine professional class of Greek-American academics. Instead, we had a smattering of Greek-American academics scattered in a number of American colleges and universities. It is suggested by this author that due to the demands of their work, geographic dispersion (away from Greek-American communities), and small numbers, Greek-American academics were isolated from each other and from their ethnic communities. This double isolation can be termed "double marginality."[14] This problem continues in the present, especially for those who are located away from large Greek-American ethnic communities and find themselves in colleges or universities which are located in small towns where, for the most part, few or no other Greek-American professionals live.

Socio-Demographic and Professional Characteristics. This part of the analysis includes findings on contemporary Greek-American academics or all those currently teaching in and/or affiliated with institutions of higher learning in the United States.

Place of Birth. Of the 993 academics for whom place of birth was determined, 56% were born in the United States and 44% in Greece.

Region. The regions where Greek-American academics are located follow the general pattern of Greek-American professionals and/or the geographic distribution of Greek-Americans in general. Most Greek-American academics are found in the Northeast followed by the Midwest, South, and West respectively.

Formal Education. Of 1,610 academics for whom the type of degree was determined, 80% had Ph.D.'s or equivalent, 18% M.S.'s or M.A.'s, and only 2% B.A.'s or B.S.'s.

Academic Institutions. The majority of Greek-American academics, 68%, teach at universities. Of the remaining 32%, 25% and 7% teach at four and two year colleges, respectively.

Areas of Competence. Physical sciences, humanities, social sciences, health specialties, engineering, education, fine arts, biological sciences, and business are the disciplines and professions in which most Greek-American academics are found, in the order mentioned above.

Quality of Graduate Faculty.[15] Only 295 graduate faculty members were rated according to their specialty. In all other cases, either the department was not rated, the university or both were not rated, or the academic was not in a school which awarded graduate degrees in a particular area. Among those rated, 53% were distinguished, 22% strong, and 25% good.

Effectiveness of Graduate Faculty. Only 281 graduate programs were rated in which graduate faculty were teaching. Of those rated, 49% were good, 26% strong, and 25% distinguished.

Undergraduate Rating.[16] The undergraduate rating includes those in 4 year colleges and universities. The mean score was 636 with a range of 641 points.

SOCIAL-PROFESSIONAL CORRELATES AND GREEK-AMERICAN ACADEMICS

The relationship between Greek-American academics and socio-demographic and professional background variables was also examined. Variables in the analysis of socio-demographic background included place of birth and region where academics are located. The analysis of professional background variables included degree, academic institution, quality, and effectiveness of graduate faculty and program, and undergraduate rating of the college or university (the latter two might be called the caliber variables).

Region. Whether one was born in Greece or in the United States did not greatly affect the location of Greek-American academics. However, those born in the United States were more likely to be located in the Midwest than those born in Greece: 28% versus 20%, respectively. The reverse was somewhat true for those academics located in the South. Twenty-five per cent were born in Greece and 19% in the United States. Of those located in the West, 17% were born in the United States and 15% in Greece.

Education[17]. For those Greek-American academics whose type of degree could be determined, it was found that those born in Greece tend to have attained higher formal education than those born in the United States. This is reflected in the percentage of Ph.D.'s or equivalent held by those born in Greece and the United States: 83% and 66%, respectively. Conversely, the percentage of M.S. or M.A. degrees held by the American born Greek academics vis-à-vis those born in Greece is 31% and 15%, respectively. The relationship was found to be statistically significant at the .001 level.

Academic Institution. A greater majority of those born in Greece, compared to those born in the United States, taught at universities: 75% and 64%, respectively. Conversely, those born in the United States were more likely to teach at 2 year and then some at 4 year colleges than their counterparts born in Greece. This relationship was also found to be significant at .001 level and is also consistent with the previous finding of formal education and place or birth.

Quality of Graduate Faculty. While the relationship between quality of graduate faculty and place of birth was not found to be statistically significant, nevertheless the relationship shows that there is a slight tendency for those born in Greece to be located at universities with higher graduate faculty ratings.

Effectiveness of Graduate Program. As with the relationship mentioned previously between quality of faculty and place of birth, this relationship too was not found to be significant. However, there was a slight tendency of those academics born in Greece to be located more frequently at departments with distinguished programs than those born in the United States.

Undergraduate Rating. The undergraduate mean score of those born in Greece was higher than those born in the United States: 623 and 608, respectively. However, there were data on rating for 1,260 people, but data for place of birth included only 253 born in the United States and 204 born in Greece. The overall mean rating for both those who had place of birth data and those who did not was higher than for either those born in the United States or in Greece.

SUMMARY AND CONCLUSION

In this analysis, an effort was made to delineate the patterns of professional and entrepreneurial orientations of Greek-Americans. Both the early and late Greek immigrants and their descendants were briefly discussed. The historical patterns of Greek entrepreneurial activities of early and late Greek immigrants and their descendants were examined. A number of writers have suggested that Greek immigrants have followed consistent patterns of occupational choice. Early Greeks were predominantly in service-oriented occupations, e.g., restaurants. Other types of entrepreneurial activities in which Greeks engaged were liquor and candy stores, shoeshine parlors, theaters, real estate, the fur industry (primarily in New York), florist shops, vegetable shops, ice cream shops, and similar types of small entrepreneurial activities. Late Greek immigrants followed similar patterns of occupational and entrepreneurial activities. Among the late Greek immigrants, one must add pizza, construction, real estate, tourism/travel, publishing, and radio/mass media types of businesses.

Greek entrepreneurs followed a family-type capitalist orientation. While the family type orientation of Greek American capitalism remains dominant, one can argue there is a growing minority of corporations, including utilities like LILCO TV in New York (i.e., sports, weather). Greeks are found in such programs as *Star Trek*, the *Commish*, or *Friends*. In addition, the quartermaster for the Gulf War was a Greek American general. However, with the exception of a few executive positions in corporate America, we find few Greek-Americans occupying top positions in American social and political structures. Currently, Greek-Americans of the second generation are not part of the inner circle and/or power elite of the American corporate, political, military, educational, civic, media, and celebrity worlds. So, while Greeks have "made it" economically and have achieved a comfortable middle-class status in America, few have achieved preeminence in any top positions in American society. There is no established professional, intellectual, or political tradition among the Greek Orthodox in America. On the contrary, it seems to me that Catholic and Jewish ethnic groups, the majority of which have been in the United States as long as the Greeks, have established more viable and dynamic ethnic and professional institutions/organizations, e.g., universities, hospitals, and intellectual and professional group life in general. While the Greeks made money as individuals and families, they did not succeed in establishing enduring institutions, with the exception perhaps of the Greek Orthodox Church in the Americas.

Looking at the more contemporary profile of Greek-American professionals, we can make the following general observations. 1) For both generations, medicine is an important area of professional choice, but the first generation has a larger number of doctors in both absolute numbers and percentages. Greeks go into medicine not as medical or academic researchers but as medical practitioners, in order to make more money. There are more doctors of the first generation than second generation. 2) Sciences, especially physics and engineering, are by far the occupational choices for the first generation rather than the second one. This is also a trend in American society as a whole. Foreign students specialize in engineering and natural sciences more than American students.[18] 3) Engineering and physics are to the first generation as corporate executives are to the second generation, with both categories very similar in absolute numbers and percentages. 4) In the area of business, greater numbers are found in non-service-oriented enterprises in the second generation. 5) In terms of Ph.D.s, the first generation exceeds that of the second generation in the number of Ph.D.s. This is consistent with the findings of Kourvetaris (1977). It seems that there are more academics among the first than second generation. However, there are more in the second generation who hold M.A.s or M.S.s. 6) Lawyers are by far greater in number among the second generation than the first generation. This was expected due to language problems for the first generation. This was also true of earlier periods of Greek immigrants.

In comparing the socioeconomic profiles of a number of urban ethnic groups, Katzman (1969: 351-366) found a recurring pattern: the groups with the highest education and higher income, employment rates, and occupational status tend to come from Northwestern Europe. Most of them are of Protestant origin, including descendants from Britain, English Canada, Scandinavia, and Germany. On the other end of the socioeconomic spectrum, we find Catholic groups: Puerto Ricans, Mexicans, Italians, Poles, Czechs, and French Canadians. This is the Weberian Protestant ethic and the rise of capitalism at work. The Greek-American, it seems to me, is closer to the Protestant model than the Catholic model. One can argue that Greek-American professionals and entrepreneurs are found more on the lower tiers of the professional, semi-professional, and entrepreneurial- (service-) oriented occupations. To reiterate, Greek-American economic power is found in individuals and families, not in corporations. However, the real economic and political power in the United States is located in the corporate world, rather than in the entrepreneurial and professional one that Greek-Americans are engaged in.

In the professional world, Greek-Americans have pursued those professions and occupations that bring them quick money (professional entrepreneurs) rather than professions in the arts, social sciences, or humanities. We have a few thousand professionals in medicine, law, business, education, and engineering, but one tries in vain to identify a dozen outstanding legal scholars, academic heavyweights, medical researchers, outstanding authors, journalists, and intellectuals in general.

I believe it is time for Greeks in America to branch out into other areas of professional and intellectual endeavor which are not primarily pecuniary and entrepreneurial in nature. Greek-Americans must go beyond the "gyros" and "opa" syndrome and the lucrative professions and pursue more intellectual, political, and scholarly pursuits if they expect to have an impact in the decision- and rule-making in America in the twenty-first century.

ENDNOTES

[1] For the present analysis, two types of data were used. For the immigrant experience (both the old and new Greek professionals and entrepreneurs), a review of published general and specific material, and my own published work on the topics, were used. For contemporary Greek American professionals and entrepreneurs, the main source of data was the 1989 *Hellenic Who's Who in the Professions and Business* and some material and information on the Greeks from the United States Census.

[2] First generation includes all those born in Greece or overseas while their progenies or those born in the United States of Greek or mixed parenthood are the second generation. Third generation will include the children of the second generation and so on.

[3] For more extensive historical analyses of the Greek immigrant experience as entrepreneurs and professionals, see Lovell-Troy (1981), Rassogianis (1982), Saloutos (1964), Scourby (1984), Moskos (1980), Kourvetaris (1971, 1977, 1987), Malafouris (1948), Canoutas (1918), Dendias (1919), and Burgess (1913).

[4] The concentration of Greeks in a few professions is not unique. Jews, Italians, Poles, and other ethnic groups follow similar patterns. In his study of ethnic groups and the practice of medicine, Lieberson (1958) found that Jews were overrepresented in medicine in Chicago. In 1958, for example, Jews comprised roughly seven percent of Chicago's population but made up about 30 percent of Chicago's physicians (Lieberson, 1958: 42). Heavy concentration of Jews in the professions and business was also found in Providence, Rhode Island. Nine out of ten employed Jewish males were found in white-collar occupations. The largest occupational category of Jewish males was found in the managers and proprietors category, forty-one percent as compared to eleven percent in the total population, and twenty-one percent in professions as compared to 9.2 percent in the general population (Goldstein, 1968: 78).

[5] In his book, *Who's Running America*, Dye divides the American elites into twelve sectors: 1) industrial corporations; 2) utilities, transportation and communication; 3) banking; 4) insurance; 5) investment; 6) mass media; 7) law; 8) education; 9) foundations; 10) civic and cultural organizations; 11) government; and 12) military. Altogether, there are about 7,314 positions which make up the elite structure running America. There is no Greek American on the list.

[6] Scourby includes artists Cavacos (1903), Xerocostas (1904), Tsavalas (1911), Lucas Samaras, Chryssa, Stephen Antonakos, Basil Marros and John Vassos (1919), Kimon Nicolaides (1891), George Constant, Polygnotos Vagis (in sculpture), Nassos Daphnis (1920), Constantine Pougialis Wm. Baziotes (1944), Tom Botis, Louis Trakas, Dimitri Hadgi and Theodore Stamos, Kristodimos Kaldis, and Vagis. The most prolific

artist in the postwar period was Stamos. He has participated in exhibits abroad. In Stamos's words, "The Greeks here are pretty dead, even with all their cultural organizations. It's a strange thing to say but the Greeks in Greece are more advanced. Here art is more accessible, but the Greek middle class, doctors, lawyers don't buy anything, don't support art," quoted in Scourby (1984: 111). Most of these artists came from Greece. In her monograph *Greek Americans in the Visual Arts, 1910-1995* Thalia Chironis-Selz (1966) lists a dozen or so Greek Americans in the visual arts. The most important of these in terms of name recognition are: William Baziotes and Theodoros Stamos (painters), Chryssa and Lucas Samaras (sculptors), and Peter Voulkos (sculptor-ceramist).

[7] In his article, "Greek American Prose Writers," Professor Emeritus Alexander Karanikas mentions four prose writers of the first generation: 1) Demetra Vaka, who wrote more than fifteen novels and other works, many of which describe life in Turkey and the Near East. 2) Theano Papazoglou-Margaris (born in Constantinople), whose short stories describe the sorrows and problems of Greek immigrants. Her collection of short stories, *The Chronicle of halsted Street* (1962) won a prize from the Greek government. 3) Elia Kazan, one of the most popular prose writers (also born in Turkey), stage and film director. 4) Nicholas Gage, who is more of a journalist and became known for his book *Eleni*, in which he describes his mother's assassination during the Civil War. Others among the first generation include Demetrios Michalaros, Stratis Haviaras (poetry), Nikos Rozakos (journalist), Dino Siotis (poetry), Konstantinos Lards, and Olga Broumas. Among the second generation Greek American writers Karanikas includes Roxanne Cotsakis, Ariadne Thompson, Tom Chamales, Thomas Doulis, George Theotokas, Daphne Athas, H. L. Mantzouranes, Charles E. Jarvis, Harry Mark Petrakis (the most ethnic-oriented writer of Greek Americans), Jim Dilles, Dean Brelis, George Christy, Theodore Vrettos, George N. Rumanes, Athena G. Dallas-Damis. We must include John Cassavetes (an actor) who died in 1988. he received an academy award nomination for best supporting actor in 1968. Also George Tsakiris, who became famous in *West Side Story* in the 1960s, and Telly Savalas, who became known from the *Kojak* TV series.

[8] A few of these political appointments include: George Vournas (AHEPA leader), active in Democratic politics; Tom Pappas, as oil industrialist who was influential in Republican politics during the Eisenhower administration and was accused of having supported the military dictatorship during the late 1960s and early 1970s; Dean Alfange, who ran for governor of New York in 1942 as an American Labor Party candidate; Michael Manatos, who was appointed by President Kennedy as administrative assistant to the White House; Peter Peterson, former president of Bell and Howell, held the Cabinet post of Secretary of Commerce in the Nixon administration; John Nassikas was appointed chairman of the Federal Power Commission; Eugene R. Rossides served as an assistant secretary of the treasury in the Nixon administration; Charles Maliotis, a businessman and Greek-American benefactor, was a close friend of the Kennedys and

Tip O'Neil; Bill Collins of Minneapolis was a close friend and supporter of Hubert Humphrey; Angelo Geocaris was a Chicagoan who spearheaded the campaign for Senator Paul Douglas of Illinois; William Helis, the New Orleans oil tycoon, had considerable political influence. According to Marudas (quoted in Scourby), since 1966 eight Greek Americans have been elected to the House of Representatives and two Senators, Paul Sarbanes and Paul Tsongas, (Tsongas later resigned for health reasons) two were elected as governors (Agnew became vice-president under Nixon and later resigned in disgrace) and Dukakis of Massachusetts was the Democratic presidential nominee in the 1988 national elections and lost to Bush. In addition, there were six mayors. Almost all of these political appointments and elected officials were second generation. Most elected Greek Americans were elected not by Greeks but by a broad ethnic base. With a few exceptions, the majority of them did not in the past and do not now strongly identify with the Greek-American community. More recently, Mr. Sotirhos, a second-generation Greek-American, was appointed ambassador to Greece.

[9] Among the 336 Greeks in *Who's Who* in Business reported by Malafouris (1948), about 13 could be classified as first generation Greek-American professionals. In addition, Vavoudis (1925) mentions another four doctors who were active with the Greek Students' Association "Helikon."

[10] During the first quarter of the 20th century about one dozen or so lawyers, three engineers, one chemist, and one sculptor were mentioned by name in Malafouris (1948), Vavoudis (1925), and Burgess (1911). In an informal discussion with the president of the Greek American Lawyers Association in Chicago as of nov. 11, 1995, I was told that there are 175 dues paying members. According to him there are about 600 Greek American lawyers in the Chicago area.

[11] Hidden "brain drain" includes all those scientists and other professionals who, while working in their respective countries, might be employed by more lucrative foreign companies and/or research institutes that have branches or have investment in various countries. For the purpose of this report and because it was not possible to collect any data on this source of Greek brain drain, the subsequent analysis will be based on the actual and potential sources of Greek brain drain only.

[12] In most instances Greek students studying abroad have finished their secondary education or have graduated from an institution of higher education in Greece. If the Greek student completed both his undergraduate and graduate studies abroad, it is not clear whether or not one can classify him even as a potential source of Greek brain drain.

[13] Greek-Americans over the years established many fraternal, benevolent, professional, and students' associations. Only the more pertinent in this study will be mentioned. The Greek students' association "Helikon" was founded in Boston by students and faculty of Harvard in 1911. Aristidis Phoutridis became its first president. Between 1912 and 1913 the association numbered about 30 to 60 Greek students. The "Helikon" is now in its 64th year of existence.

Later during the 1930's and 1940's similar efforts were made in other cities and universities. In New York, for example, Greek students' associations were established at Columbia University (1924), New York University, Hunter College (1937), Intercollegiate Federation of Hellenic Societies, Fordham University, Long Island University, College of Brooklyn, and others.

Greek students' associations were established at the University of California at Berkeley, University of Indiana, University of Pennsylvania, Temple University, San Francisco, University of Illinois, Northwestern University, University of Toledo in Ohio, Bryn Mawr College, Wayne University of Detroit, Washington University at St. Louis, Missouri, University of Michigan at Ann Arbor, Syracuse University, Cornell University, and elsewhere.

Various professional societies were established during the 1920's and 1930's, some of which are still in existence, e.g., the Hellenic Professional Society of Illinois; the Pythagoreans of Detroit; the Greek Women's University Club of Illinois. In addition, one finds professional associations of specific professions (especially established ones). One of the most important ones that is organized at national and international levels is the Modern Greek Studies Association (MGSA) founded in 1968 with about 300 members (mostly academics in the humanities and social sciences). A recent issue of its Bulletin (Vol. 5, No. 1, June 1973) included a useful bibliographic documentation of more than 200 Ph.D. dissertations and 130 M.A. theses on Modern Greece, mainly written in the last 10 years or so. Also, the Democritos Society with over 100 members is primarily for natural scientists, engineers, medical scientists and the like.

[14] The concept of marginality refers to those individuals who find themselves in two cultures, one particularistic (ethnic subculture) and one more general (dominant Anglo-Saxon culture) but they are full-fledged members of neither. Members of first and second generation (ethnic groups) are in this instance marginal. "Double marginality" is suggested by this author to refer to two types of marginality present among Greek-American academics and other Greek-American professionals in general, one stemming from within its own ethnic community and the other from the American professional community at large. One is internal and the other external. In their internal marginality Greek-American professionals find themselves by and large detached from their ethnic communities, while in their external marginality they are interethnically perceived to be of little avail in the overall United States occupational and ethnic power structures. Although this thesis cannot be substantiated with the existing data, it is offered here as a heuristic hypothesis.

[15] For an assessment of quality of American graduate faculty and effectiveness of graduate programs see Kenneth D. Roose and Charles J. Anderson, *A Rating of Graduate Programs*, published by the American Council on Education (1970). This report is an updated version of the original study by Allan M. Carter in 1964 entitled an *Assessment of Quality in Graduate Education*, and published in 1966 by the same council as above.

[16] The undergraduate rating was based on the book *College Rater* with a composite index of 700 numerically ranked colleges and universities by Allentown, Pa. (1967). Major criteria for evaluating schools included such items as SAT/ACT scores of recently enrolled freshmen, proportion of faculty with doctorate, faculty salaries, etc.

[17] Whether those born in Greece attained their higher education there prior to coming to the United States or were educated in the United States was not ascertained. It has been suggested (Kourvetaris, 1973), however, that the majority of academics born in Greece attained their higher education in the United States.

[18] In a personal communication from friends who work at Argonne National Laboratory, Fermi Laboratory, and AT&T in the Chicago metropolitan area, the following has been communicated to me: At Argonne National Laboratory, Argonne, Illinois, there are eight Greeks with Ph.D.s and one M.S. Eight of them were born in Greece and one in the United States (Dr. Costas Tzanos, personal communication). From Fermi Laboratory, western suburbs of Chicago (6 Ph.D.s in high-energy physics, 5 born in Greece and one born in the United States) and 6 Greek students working on the M.S. or Ph.D. in experimental physics or high energy physics. (Dr. Nikos Geogaris, personal communication.) At AT&T Chicago (Mr. John Bratis, personal communication), 8 had M.S. degrees, 3 Ph.D.s, and 2 B.A.s and B.S.s. Seven of them were born in Greece, one in Cyprus, and the remainder in the United States. Five of them were electrical engineers, one in mechanical engineering, one in physics, one in math, and the rest in liberal arts, journalism, and other disciplines.

REFERENCES

American Hellenic Who's Who. 1989, 1990. edited by Eugene T. Rossides, Washington, D. C.: American Hellenic Institute, Inc.

Blalock, Hubert M. Jr. 1967. *Toward A Theory of Minority Group Relations*. New York: Wiley.

Blauner, Robert. 1972. *Racial Oppression in America*. New York: Harper and Row.

Bonacich, Edna. 1973. "A Theory of Middleman Minorities," *American Sociological Review* 38 (October): 583-94.

Bonacich, Edna and John Model. 1980. *The Economic Basis of Ethnic Solidarity.* Berkeley: University of California Press.

Bucher, Rue and Anselm Strauss. "Professions in Process," American Journal of Sociology, 66 (January 1961): 325-361.

Burgess, Thomas. 1913. "Greeks in America and Boston." Sherman, French and Company.

Canoutas, Seraphin, O. 1918. *Hellenism in America*, New York: Kosmos Press.

Carr-Saunders, A. and P. A. Wilson. 1933. *The Professions*. London: Oxford University Press.

Christakis, George. 1988. "Lecture on the Greek Americans and the Workplace." Copernicus Center, Chicago, IL: Greek American Community Services.

Choi, Byoung Mohk. 1988. "Toward a Sociological Understanding of Koreans in Small Business in the United States: An Experimental Application of the Middleman Minority Hypothesis," Part of Ph.D. dissertation, Department of Sociology, University of Hawaii at Manoa.

College Rater. 1967. *A Composite Index of 700 Numerically Ranked Colleges and Universities.* Allentown: PA.

Coutsoumaris, George. 1988. "Greece" in Walter Adams (ed.), *The Brain Drain.* New York: MacMillan.

Cutsumbis, N., and Michael. 1970. *A Bibliographic Guide to Materials on Greeks in the United States 1890-1968.* New York, Center for Migration Studies.

Dendias, Michael. 1919. *Greek Colonies Around the World.* Athens.

Dye, Thomas. 1986, 1995. *Who's Running America*, Englewood Cliffs, NJ: Prentice Hall.

Edwards, Gilbert Franklin. 1959. The Negro Professional Class. Glencoe III: Free Press.

Feagin, Joe. 1989. *Racial and Ethnic Relations.* Englewood Cliffs, NJ: Prentice Hall.

Featherman, David L. "The Socioeconomic Achievement of White Religio-Ethnic Subgroups: Social and Psychological Explanations", *American Sociological Review* 36 (April 1971): 207-222.

Friedson, Eliot. 1970(a). *Profession of Medicine*. New York: Dodd, Mead.

_____. 1970(b). *Professional Dominance: The Social Structure of Medical Care*. New York: Atherton.

_____. 1973. *The Professions and Their Prospects*. Beverly Hills: Sage Publications.

Goode, William. "Community Within a Community: The Professions", *American Sociological Review* 22 (April 1960): 194-200.

Greeley, Andrew M. "The Ethnic and Religious Origins of Young American Scientists and Engineers. A Research Note." *International Migration Review* 6 (Fall 1972): 282-288.

Gross, Edward. 1958. *Work and Society*. New York: Thomas Y. Crowell Co.

Greenwood, Ernest. "Attributes of a Profession." Social WorkII/3 (July 1957): 45-55.

Hall, Richard. 1969. *Occupations and the Social Structure*. Englewood Cliffs, N.J.: Prentice-Hall.

Huber, Joan and William H. Form. 1974. *Income and Ideology*. New York: Free Press.

Hughes, Everett. 1963. "Professions," in Kenneth Lynn and editors of Daedalus (editors), *The Professions in America*. Boston: Beacon Press.

Institute of International Education. 1971. *Open Doors* 1971. Report on International Exchange. New York, Institute of International Education.

Karanikas, Alexander. 1985. "Greek American Prose Writers," in Modern Greek Studies Series, The University of Illinois at Chicago Circle and the Greek orthodox Diocese of Chicago.

Katzman, Martin T. 1969. "Opportunity, Subculture and the Economic Performance of Urban Ethnic Groups," *American Journal of Economics and Sociology*, vol. 28, No. 4, pp. 351-366.

Kluegel, James R. and Eliot R. Smith. 1986. *Beliefs About Inequality*. Chicago: Aldine.

Kourvetaris, George A. 1971(a). *First and Second Generation Greeks in Chicago*, Athens, Greece, National Center of Social Research.

_____. "Patterns of Generational Subculture and Intermarriage of the Greeks in the United States," *International Journal of Sociology of the Family* 1 (May 1971b): 34-48.

_____. "Brain Drain and International Migration of Scientist," *The Greek Review of Social Research* 15-16 (January-June 1973): 2-13.

_____. 1975. "Life Styles of Greek-American Families" to be published in an anthology entitled *American Minority Family Life-Styles: Racial, Ethnic, and Religious Variations*, edited by R. Habenstein and C. Mindel. New York: Rinehart and Winston.

_____. 1977. "Greek-American Professionals: 1820s-1970s." *Balkan Studies*, vol. 18, No. 2, pp. 285-317.

_____. "The Greeks of Asia Minor and Egypt as Middleman Economic Minorities During the Late 19th and 20th Centuries." *Ethnic Groups*, Vol. 7, (1987): 1-27.

Kuvlesky, W.P. and Victoria Patella. "Degree of Ethnicity and Aspirations for Upward Social Mobility Among Mexican American Youth", *Journal of Vocational Behavior* 1 (July 1971).

Kuvlesky, W.P. and K.A. Thomas. "Social Ambitions of Negro Boys and Girls from a Metropolitan Ghetto," *Journal of Vocational Behavior* 1 (April 1971): 177-187.

Light, Ivan H. 1972. *Ethnic Enterprise in America: Business and Welfare Among Chinese, Japanese, and Blacks*. Berkeley: University of California Press.

Lipset, Seymour Martin and Everett C. Ladd, Jr. "Jewish Academics in the United States: Their Achievements, Culture, and Politics," American Jewish Yearbook, 1971. American Jewish Committee and the Jewish Publications Society of America, N.Y.

Lovell-Troy, Lawrence A. 1982. "Ethnic Occupational Structures: Greeks in the Pizza Business," *Ethnicity*, 8, pp. 82-95.

Malafouris, Charalambos. 1948. "Greeks in America, 1528-1948," New York, Isaac Goldman.

Moskos, Charles. 1990. *Greek-Americans: Struggle and Success.* 2nd edition. New Brunswick: Transaction Publishers.

National Science Foundation. 1967. *Scientists and Engineers from Abroad 1962-1964,* Washington, D.C.: Government Printing Office.

_____. 1969. *Scientists and Engineers From Abroad-Fiscal Years 1966 and 1967,* Washington, D.C.: Government Printing Office.

_____. 1972. *Scientists, Engineers, and Physicians From Abroad: Trends Through Fiscal Year 1970,* Washington, D.C.: Government Printing Office.

Pavalko, Ronald M. 1971. *Sociological Perspectives on Occupations,* Itasca, Ill: F.E. Peacock Publishers, Inc.

Petersen, William. 1971. *Japanese Americans.* New York: Random House.

Portes, Alejandro and Robert L. Bach. 1986. "The Immigrant Enclave: Theory and Empirical Examples," in *Comparative Ethnic Relations,* ed. Susan Olzak and Joane Nazel. Orlando, FL: Academic Press.

Rassogianis, Alexander. 1982. "The Growth of Greek Business in Chicago: 1900-1930," M.A. thesis. The University of Wisconsin, Milwaukee.

Reiss, Albert. 1961. *Occupations and Social Status.* New York: Free Press of Glencoe.

Ritzer, George, G. Miller, Richard Bell, and V. McKeefary. 1974. "The Current Status of Occupational Sociology." Paper presented at the annual meetings of the Midwest Sociological Society, Omaha, Nebraska.

Roose, Kenneth D. and Charles Andersen. 1970. *A Rating of Graduate Programs.* New York: American Council on Education.

Roth, Julius, S. Ruzek, and Arlene Daniels. "Current State of the Sociology of Occupations," *The Sociological Quarterly* 14 (Summer 1973): 309-333.

Saloutos, Theodore. 1964. *The Greeks in the United States.* Cambridge: Harvard University.

Scourby, Alice. 1984. *The Greek Americans*. Boston: Twayne Publishers.

United States Bureau of the Census, Subject Reports. 1973. *National Origin and Language*. Washington, D.C.: Government Printing Office.

United States Dept. of Justice, Immigration and Naturalization Service 1962-1973. Annual Reports of the Immigration and Naturalization Service (for 1962-1973). Washington, D.C.: Government Printing Office.

_____. 1968-1974. Annual Indicator of the Immigration into the United States of Aliens in Professional and Related Occupations for Fiscal Years 1967-1973. Washington, D.C.: Government Printing Office.

Useem, Michael. 1980. "Corporations and the Corporate Elite" in *Annual Review of Sociology*, vol. 6.

Vavoudis, N. I. "The History of the Creation of Hellenic-American Intellectual Life," *National Herald* 11 (April 1925).

Vollmer, Howard M., and Donald Mills (eds.). 1966. *Professionalization*. Englewood Cliffs, N.Y.: Prentice-Hall, 1966.

Wilensky, Harold L. "The Professionalization of Everyone?," *American Journal of Sociology* 70 (September 1964): 137-158.

Yoon, In-Jin. 1988. "Korean Immigrants' Small Businesses in Chicago Black Neighborhoods," M.A. The University of Chicago, Department of Sociology, Chicago, IL.

CHAPTER 7
AN EMPIRICAL TEST OF GORDON'S ETHCLASS HYPOTHESIS AMONG THREE ETHNORELIGIOUS GROUPS[*]

Ethnicity and class constitute two major features in American society but no over-all sociological theory has been formulated to adequately explain the general linkage between them. In view of the current lack of critical analysis concerning the complex interrelationships between ethnicity and class, it is the purpose of this study to consider certain specific aspects of the relationship, with particular emphasis upon the idea of "ethclass," which has been advanced by Milton Gordon (1964). More specifically, the present research examines the influence of social class and ethnic factors upon one's primary group relations. The leading question is whether people actually confine their more intimate social relations to people within their own ethnic group, class and ethclass.[1]

THE ETHCLASS FRAMEWORK

Gordon's (1964:51) concept of ethclass referred to the subsocietal type created by the intersection of the vertical stratifications of ethnicity with the horizontal stratifications of social class. In simpler terms, ethclass refers to a person's own social class segment within his own ethnic group (e.g., middle class German Catholic). According to Gordon (1964:53) people of the same ethnicity, regardless of social class, share a sense of peoplehood or historical identification. People of the same social class, but different ethnic group membership, share behavioral similarities but not a sense of peoplehood. More specifically, the ethnic group member feels a general sense of identity with all those of his ethnic background, but he can feel comfortable in intimate or primary group social relations only with those who also share his own class background. Thus, class divisions tend to restrict primary group relations. In order to share both behavioral similarities and historical identification, individuals should be of the same ethnic group and social class, or what Gordon refers to as ethclass (which is also the locus of participational identity). Gordon's long range forecast for America calls for an informal social structure consisting of a series of ethnic subcommunities criss-crossed by social class, within which primary group relationships would tend to be confined. On the

[*] This chapter was originally published and co-authored with Betty A. Dobratz, University of Iowa, Ames, in the *Journal of Sociology and Social Research*, 1976, Vol. 61, No. 2 (October): 39-53.

other hand, secondary group relationships would often take place across ethnic group and social class lines as a result of the requirements of an urbanized industrial and post-industrial society.

PAST EMPIRICAL STUDIES

The literature on ethnic groups and social class is voluminous, but space permits citing only a few works relevant to the focus of this paper. It may be noted that no empirical tests which specifically refer to the concept of ethclass are known to the authors, although studies are often concerned with the class and/or ethnic dimensions of stratification or of primary group relations. Yet, while these studies consider the concepts, the linkage or interrelationships between class and ethnicity has not been thoroughly analyzed.

Relevant to the procedures employed in this paper are analyses of attitudes toward intramarriage, actual intermarriage patterns, and friendship patterns. For example, Kennedy's (1944, 1952) examinations of New Haven marriage records of the last seventy to eighty years revealed that different nationalities were merging but within three religious compartments rather than randomly. Protestant British-Americans, Germans, and Scandinavians intermarried while Roman Catholic Irish, Italians and Poles constituted a separate inter-marrying group; Jews remained endogamous. However, more and more Jews are marrying exogamously.

Another study of religious intermarriage based on the 1957 Current Population Survey of Religion and the NORC study of June, 1961, (follow up data collected in 1968) indicated that denominational homogeneity in marriage exists for at least three-quarters of the major religious denominations, including the various groups within Protestantism (Greeley, 1970:949). Greeley suggested that the broad categories of Protestant, Roman Catholic, and Jew were not comprehensive enough for the various denominations within the Protestant category which constituted important subcollectivities in the larger society. Yet another study (Abramson and Noll, 1966:12) suggested that the ethnic group may be considered the social basis for American Catholics in the same way as denomination has been for Protestants.

Hollingshead (1950) employed a 50% random sample of couples who were married in New Haven during 1948 and measured the influence of five factors (race, age, religion, nationality, and class) on the selection of marriage partners. Data were collected on the couples and their parents. No interracial marriages were recorded in New Haven; 91% of the marriages were between persons from the same religious group. Nationality within each religious group also was important but was more influential for the parental than for the present generation. The index of class position had six divisions based on an ecological analysis of the city. In 58.2% of the marriages, both persons came from the same class of residential area. Overall, Hollingshead (1952:686) concluded that the vertically differentiating factors of race, religion, and nationality combined with the horizontally differentiating ones of occupation, education, place of residence, etc., and produced a social structure that was highly compartmentalized.

Studies (Lenski, 1961; Anderson, 1968) on patterns of friendship have revealed that this aspect of primary group relationship often occurs within one's own religion. In particular, Laumann's (1969) Detroit study revealed that a large percentage of white Protestants' closest friends were members of their own denomination. He also found that, while a tripartite religious division of the American social structure was present, it alone provided a very inadequate representation of all his data. Although the structure of intimate associations was differentiated into the three broad groupings and within these groupings further divided along socioeconomic status lines, ethnic (nationality) differences were also playing a role in channeling the formation of friendships.

While Gordon postulated an ethclass hypothesis, he argued in his subsociety hypothesis that intellectuals were the only group in America that interacted quite frequently across ethnic lines. In an empirical study, Anderson (1971) found that ethnic characteristics were not important elements in the primary group relations of intellectuals although occupation certainly was important. While Anderson implied that the academicians were different from the rest of society on the ethnic dimension of primary group relations, the value of the study was limited since no direct comparison was made between academic professions and a general population sample.

SAMPLE

Members of three ethnoreligious groups were selected for analysis in a medium-sized community in the Midwest with a multiethnic population. This community will be referred to by the pseudonym "Forest City." The Greek Orthodox, the Italian Catholic, and the Swedish Lutheran ethnoreligious groups were selected mainly because they possessed diversified ethnoreligious characteristics within the American social structure. More precisely the Swedish Lutherans represent the dominant White Anglo-Saxon Protestant and northern and western European old immigrant sector of society. The Italian Catholics and Greek Orthodox are minority religious group members from southern and eastern Europe and represent the new immigrants. However, it should be noted that Italian Catholics, while a minority in the United States, are a much larger group than the Greek Orthodox.

In order to show that the ethclass tendency and subcultural differences persisted beyond the immigrant generation, only second and third generation were included in the sample. Because certain aspects of the study seemed to us particularly relevant to married persons (e.g., marriage patterns, preferred ethnic and class traits of potential marital partners for their children), only married couples were selected.

Because we felt belonging to a church was a nominal indicator of belief in a particular faith, church membership lists were used for the sample population. Three sources of information were used to help in selecting the churches and in identifying the nationality of their members: the personal observation of non-experts including the authors, the recommendations of men with religious training, and published or unpublished materials on the composition and distribution of various ethnic groups in the city.

The only Greek Orthodox church in Forest City was included in the sample. However, due to the small number of second and third generation Greek Americans that attended, it was also necessary to sample other Greek Orthodox communities within a 100-mile radius. In order to define a working universe for Italian Catholics, the membership lists of four of the eleven Catholic churches in the city were obtained. The parishes were selected to include the Italian national parish[2] and to represent various socio-economic strata. Since Catholic churches in Forest City generally have specific geographical boundaries, it was possible to arrive at some indication of the socioeconomic characteristics of each of these churches by comparing their boundaries with the various census tracts in the city for which income data were available. Results from the pretest had indicated that at least 50% response rate was feasible. Because we felt that one-hundred Catholic couples were sufficient for our sample, two-hundred names of couples were selected from the four church membership lists. A table of random numbers was used in the actual selection process.

In the case of the Swedish Lutherans, seven of the nineteen churches in Forest City were selected. (One Lutheran Church refused cooperation.) Originally many Lutheran churches were formed along nationality lines. Five of the seven churches were formerly Augustana Synod, which was initially composed of Swedish and Norwegian congregations. In order to give some representation to the Swedish not in the Augustana Synod, the sixth church also was from Lutheran Church in America, but from the United Lutheran Church branch. The seventh church, a member of the Missouri Synod, also had members of Swedish extraction. In a similar manner as done for the Italian

Catholics, two-hundred names were again selected using a table of random numbers. The final questionnaire concerning the major variables of nationality, religion, class, friendship and marriage patterns consisted of 36 questions and was four pages in length. An attempt was made to contact each of the couples selected from Forest City, explain the project to them, ask them to fill out the questionnaire confidentially, and return it in a stamped, self-addressed envelope. In each case a cover letter describing the project, the questionnaire itself, and the envelope were given to the couples. For those who did not complete the questionnaire, three follow ups were used to increase the response rate. The Greek Orthodox of Forest City were originally mailed questionnaires instead of being personally contacted.

Between the months of March to September, 1972, a total of 396 couples in Forest City were targeted to answer the questionnaires. Of these people 63.1% (250 of 396) adequately completed the questionnaire. However, 28 or 7.1% did not fulfill the criteria necessary for the study. An additional 27 couples were not given the questionnaire either because they had moved away or because in discussion with them it was concluded that they did not meet the criteria for the survey. The response rate of the Greek Orthodox outside the community was only 41%. The final sample consisted of 264 couples with 45 second and 8 third generation Greek Orthodox, 68 second and 35 third generation Italian Catholics, 61 second and 47 third generation Swedish Lutherans.

OPERATIONALIZATION OF CONCEPTS

Nationality, generation, and religion were determined by the responses of the male spouse. Two classes were formed based on the manual-nonmanual distinction in occupations, since many writings on stratification indicate that the greatest cleavage in the occupational system occurs between the white collar and blue collar dimensions (Roach, et al., 1969: 508). Heads of households with white collar positions were considered middle class and those in blue collar jobs were regarded as working class.

Marriage and friendship preferences were used as indicators for measuring primary group relations. Marriage preferences were determined by looking at the actual marriage patterns of the couples surveyed and by asking them their attitudes concerning prospective marriage partners for their children. Whether or not the husband married a person in the same social class as himself was determined by using the fathers' occupations as the indicators. That is, if the husband's father and the wife's father both had blue collar occupations, then the marriage was considered a working intraclass marriage. The same thing was true if both had white collar jobs. If one father had a blue collar job and the other a white collar one, the marriage was considered interclass.

A question, hereafter referred to as the "ethclass question," was devised to ascertain the feelings of the couples on this central issue. The couples were given three specific options of marriage partners for their children: a) one with similar ethnic (race, nationality, and religion) characteristics, b) one with similar social class characteristics, and c) one combining similar ethnic and social class traits, or what one might call a homogamous marriage. Also, it was possible to check a reply of "other (please specify)" if these alternatives were not regarded as appropriate. Concerning intimate friendship patterns, information was obtained on the nationality, religion (denomination, if appropriate) and occupations of the three best friends.

PRIMARY GROUP RELATIONS AND ETHCLASS: FINDINGS AND DISCUSSION

Marriage Patterns. On the separate dimensions, nationality, religious, and class endogamous marriage occurred for the majority of couples within the sample. Although the smallest nationality group, the Greeks had the highest intramarriage rate followed by the Italians and the Swedes. Members of each of the groups tended to marry wives of Anglo-Saxonic background, if they did not marry persons of their own nationality. Respondents were married to persons of the same religion more often than they were married to persons of the same class or nationality. The Lutherans had the highest religious endogamy rate followed by the Catholics and the Orthodox, respectively.

The patterns of class marriage for the sample revealed that 71% of the marriages occurred within the same class (19% between spouses whose parents both had white collar occupations and 52% with both parents having blue collar jobs). Within each ethnic group, intraclass marriage was strong and a chi square test revealed no significant difference among them. Class controls were used to see if intramarriage rates on the ethnic or class dimensions differed by social class. There were also no significant differences found between the middle and working class for nationality, religion, or class intramarriage.

While actual percentages provide some basic data on the marriage patterns, it is also helpful to have some idea of the expected (or at random) rate of selection. For example, if eight-tenths of the population was Protestant and three-tenths of the population was German, the probability by chance of marrying a Protestant was greater than the probability by chance of marrying a German. In order to provide a partial picture of the influence of religion, nationality, and class upon marriage patterns, one could begin with the assumptions that class, religion, and nationality were not associated with each other and that there was no tendency to marry within one's own group other than that of chance. The expected value would be what one would anticipate by chance. If the actual or observed rate was higher than that of the expected rate, then ethnic group and/or class membership may be considered important in the formation of intimate social relationships.

Table 7.1 presents the data on the expected and the observed percentages, frequencies (number in the sample), and the chi square value. The table clearly shows that the tendency of intramarriage was quite strong for all the dimensions. In every case the observed value was always higher than the expected. The larger the differences between observed and expected frequencies, the larger the value of chi square. (Chi square is zero only when all observed and expected frequencies are identical.) The chi square values for the Greek Orthodox for religion and nationality were quite high because of the combined effect of very low expected rates and high observed patterns. In every case except for blue collar intramarriage, the chi square result yielded significant differences at the .01 level.

It now seems appropriate to examine the interaction and interrelationships of ethnicity and class for the marriage patterns in order to further determine the relevance of the concept of ethclass. Some idea of the expected and observed percentages of the interrelationships seem necessary. More specifically, one may ask whether or not there were interactive effects with the three variables, or putting it differently, were people who are endogamous with respect to ethnicity, more endogamous than others with respect to class? If we take the marriage preferences of the individuals as given, the question becomes whether or not the number of marriages with partners similar on any two or all three of the criteria are any different from what would be expected from the independent influence of class, religion, and nationality preferences.

The actual data and the expected values for the marriage patterns are presented in Table 7.2. There were 85 cases in the ethclass category, which was five more than the expected based on the marginal results. While the difference was in the expected direction, it was not very substantial. The low expected numbers in certain of the "different" categories made chi square tests inaccurate here, but the data seemed to suggest that the additive model may be more appropriate with independent effects of class, religion, and nationality (and little interaction exists).

Importance of Intramarriage for Couple's Children. On all three dimensions the couples were asked how important it was for their child to marry someone of the same nationality, religion, and class. Here the relationship was not as clear cut as for the actual patterns of marriage for the couples. For nationality, only about 6% felt it was very important, another 28% believed it was somewhat important, and the majority (66%) did not feel that it was important. The ethnic groups themselves did not exhibit similar patterns of agreement on this question. Table 7.3 was constructed to show the results of the intramarriage questions by the three ethnic groups. The Greeks were more likely to believe that it was somewhat important or very important for their children to marry someone of the same nationality. In contrast, the majority of Italians and Swedes believed it was not important for them to marry someone of the same nationality.

Table 7.1 EXPECTED AND OBSERVED MARRIAGE PATTERNS OF COUPLES SAMPLED

	PERCENTAGE		FREQUENCY		CHI SQUARE*
	Expected**	Observed	Expected	Observed	
Nationality					
Greek	0.3	77	0.2	40	10 176.566
Italian	13	67	11.8	51	129.695
Swedish	30	55	32.1	59	22.472
Religion					
Orthodox	0.3	86	0.2	45	12 890.925
Catholic	20.3	96	20.5	97	285.476
Lutheran	24.6	98	26.6	106	237.006
Class					
White Collar	34	58	20.4	35	10.449
Blue Collar	66	78	82.5	97	3.300

* Chi square is computed by squaring the total of the observed frequency minus the expected frequency and dividing that by the expected frequency: $\frac{(fo-fe)^2}{fe}$.

Due to the small expected values in the Greek and Orthodox cells, chi square values should be regarded only tentatively.

** Expected values based on estimates of population for Forest City.

TABLE 7.2 EXPECTED AND OBSERVED PATTERNS OF MARRIAGE FOR NATIONALITY, RELIGION, AND CLASS COMBINATIONS OF COUPLES

	Same Class				Different Class			
	Same Religion		Different Religion		Same Religion		Different Religion	
Nationality	O*	E*	O	E	O	E	O	Exp
Same Nationality	85	80	0	4	33	33	1	2
Different Nationality	35	40	6	2	16	16	2	1

* O stands for observed
* E stands for expected

TABLE 7.3 IMPORTANCE OF NATIONALITY, RELIGION, AND CLASS INTERMARRIAGE BY ETHNIC GROUP

	Greek		Italian		Swedish	
Intramarriage	%	(N)	%	(N)	%	(N)
Same Nationality						
Not Important	31	(16)	75	(77)	74	(80)
Somewhat Important	50	(26)	24	(25)	22	(24)
Very Important	19	(10)	1	(1)	4	(4)
	$X^{2*} = 35.304$ 2df $p < .001$					
Same Religion						
Not Important	23	(12)	33	(34)	39	(42)
Somewhat Important	45	(24)	52	(53)	51	(55)
Very Important	32	(17)	15	(16)	10	(11)
	$X^2 = 13.471$ 4df $p < .05$					
Same Class						
Not Important	17	(9)	37	(38)	26	(28)
Somewhat Important	66	(34)	53	(55)	67	(72)
Very Important	17	(9)	10	(10)	7	(7)
	$X^2 = 10.918$ 4df $p < .05$					

Regarding religious intramarriage, members of all three ethnic groups most often indicated that such a marriage was somewhat important. However, as Table 7.3 shows, the Greeks were much more likely to believe that similar religion was very important in marriage. Again, the relationship was statistically significant.

The majority of each ethnic group thought that marriage within the same class was somewhat important. The Italians were the most likely of the three to believe it was not important. The difference among the ethnic groups was statistically significant at the .05 level.

A majority of the persons surveyed (66%) believed it was not important for their children to marry someone of the same nationality, and even 50% felt it was somewhat important for them to marry someone of the same religion. A majority of the respondents (62%) believed it was somewhat important for their children to have an intraclass marriage. However, a significant difference was found among the attitudes of the ethnic groups, with the Greeks most likely to favor marriage within the same nationality, religion, and class. It should be noted that while the actual marriage patterns of the couples showed the importance of similar religion, nationality, and class, when asked about their children, the respondents felt they were less important. This may be interpreted to indicate a possible attenuation of the ethclass idea.

"*Ethclass Question.*" This question provided information on the preferences of the parents regarding marriage partners of their children. About 64% of the sample indicated they preferred the ethclass combination for the prospective mate of their children, 17% indicated an ethnic preference, and only 8% favored class similarities. The other 11% either said they preferred other characteristics (a place was available for "other" with the request to specify the characteristics) or did not respond at all. Responses by ethnic group were remarkably similar on this issue. No more than a difference of four percentage points was noted between ethnic groups for responses to the question. (Chi square test for differences could not be used due to lack of an expected value of five in one of the cells.) No significant differences were found between classes on this item. The majority response, which indicated marital preferences of parents for their children, supported the ethclass notion.

Friendship Patterns. Data concerning this aspect of primary group relations also tended to substantiate the relevance of the "ethclass" concept. More than 50% of the couples responded that two or three of their best friends were of similar nationality, religion, and class. The expected number of Greeks having all three of their best friends being Greek was less than one in a thousand. However, 34% of the Greeks actually had these friendship patterns. Much the same pattern may be observed for the Italians and Swedes, although the expected values for all three friends from the same nationality were somewhat higher and the observed percentages were lower.

A similar picture for friends of the same religion and class was also revealed. The observed percentages for all three and two of the three best friends were considerably higher for each religious group. For class the observed also were higher for three and two of three in the blue collar sector and much higher than the expected for all three friends in the white collar division. The white collar respondents were much more likely to have their three best friends have white collar jobs than were the blue collar workers likely to have three associates from blue collar jobs (66% to 24%).

In addition to the high number of friends of similar nationality, religion, and class, the pattern of interrelationship among the three indicated a strong ethclass tendency. Table 7.4 is similar to table 7.2 for marriage patterns and presents both expected and observed values for friendship patterns based on having two or three friends of similar nationality, religion, and class. Taking the friendship patterns as given allows one to consider whether or not the number of friendships with persons of the same nationality, religion, and class are different from what would be expected from the independent influence of class, religion, and nationality. There were 87 individuals in the similar ethclass category although only 65 were expected based on marginal results. A chi square test indicated that the relationship was significant at the .001 level. Thus, while the analysis suggested an additive model for marriage patterns, the data for friendship patterns showed interaction effects as well as the independent influences of class and ethnic preferences.

In summary, the hypothesis that the members of the selected ethno-religious groups will associate on a primary group level with those of the same class and ethnic group was supported. However, results for actual marriage patterns tended to provide more convincing evidence than did the results from the questions regarding importance of their children's intramarrying on the ethnic, religious, and class dimensions. The general ethclass question showed that a large majority of respondents preferred a spouse who combined both similar ethnic and class characteristics. Actual friendship patterns revealed that the majority of couples had two or three of their best friends of the same nationality, religion, and class. Friendship patterns but not marriage patterns suggested that interaction between ethnicity and class existed with the ethclass couples occurring much more often than anticipated by additive effects alone.

TABLE 7.4 EXPECTED AND OBSERVED FRIENDSHIP PATTERNS
(TWO OR THREE FRIENDS) FOR NATIONALITY, RELIGION,
AND CLASS OF RESPONDENT

Nationality	Same Class				Different Class			
	Same Religion		Different Religion		Same Religion		Different Religion	
	O*	E*	O	E	O	E	O	E
Same Nationality	87	65	13	35	25	19	3	9
Different Nationality	24	46	47	25	7	13	12	6

* O stands for observed $X^2 = 65.94$ 3df $p < .001$
* E stands for expected

SUMMARY AND CONCLUSION

This study focused upon the relationship between ethnicity and class in primary group relations or what is known as the ethclass hypothesis. The proposition that Italian Catholics, Greek Orthodox, and Swedish Lutherans would associate on a primary group level with those of the same social class within their own ethnic group, that is to the ethclass, was supported by the data regarding both actual marriage and friendship patterns. The observed tendencies to marry or to form intimate friendships within one's own ethnicity and class were much greater than one would expect from random selection and chance probability. An examination of the ethclass tendency found interaction occurring for friendship patterns but not for marriage patterns of the couples.

Concerning the preferences of the couples for their children's prospective marriage partners, two types of questions were used. For the "ethclass question," the large majority of couples preferred a marriage partner for their children who combined similar ethnic and social class (ethclass) characteristics as themselves. However, in somewhat related questions asking how important it was for the couples' children to marry within the same nationality, the same religion, or the same class, the majority did not consider intramarriage on any of the three dimensions "very important." Overall, marriage within the same nationality was not important while religious and class intramarriages were somewhat important. The possible attenuation of the ethclass tendency from the actual ethclass patterns of the parents to the desired patterns for their children may suggest the need for further research on subsequent generations of ethnic group members.

In conclusion, this study attempted to empirically relate the concept of ethclass to selected ethnic groups. In contrast to what might be expected to occur by random selection, there seemed to be a very pervasive tendency to form intimate relations within one's own ethnicity and class. This was true regardless of one's social class. It may be suggested here that there is a need for more empirical research of the ethclass hypothesis rather than more general discussion of the importance of the separate variables of national origins, religion, and class. Using the same data Dobratz (1988) further explored the ethclass hypothesis and found similar results, namely regardless of socioeconomic mobility, people of Greek Orthodox, Italian Catholic, and Swedish Lutheran backgrounds tend to form intimate relations within their own ethclass. More consideration should be given to the possibilities of interaction occurring among these concepts. Such studies should have larger sample sizes, include more ethnic groups, cover a broader geographical area, and not restrict themselves to church members only. Other indicators of primary group relations could also be constructed. The major thrust of such studies should be comparative in nature so that knowledge can be obtained which will allow one to ascertain the relative position of various groups vis-a-vis other groups regarding the ethclass hypothesis.

ENDNOTES

[1]Following Gordon's definition, an ethnic group is set off or defined by race, religion, or national origins or some combination of these categories. By "ethclass", Gordon (1964) meant that primary-group relationships tend to be generated within one's social-class segment of one's ethnic group. He speaks of the intersection between ethnicity and behavioral-class similarities.

[2]In communities with a number of Roman Catholic churches, membership in a particular church is limited to a particular nationality regardless of where they live. Thus, an Italian Catholic may attend the Italian national parish church regardless of where he resides in the city.

REFERENCES

Abramson, Harold and Edward Noll. 1966. "Religion, ethnicity, and social change. *Review of Religious Research* 8 (Fall): 11-26.

Anderson, Charles H. 1968. "Religious communality among white Protestants, Catholics, and Mormons." *Social Forces* 46 (June): 501-508.

_____. 1971. "The Intellectual subsociety hypothesis." Pp. 227-245 in Charles H. Anderson and John D. Murray (eds.). *The Professors*. Cambridge: Schenkman.

Dobratz, Betty A. 1988. "Socioeconomic Mobility and Ethclass in Primary Group Relations." *Ethnic Groups* 7, 3 (227-257).

Gordon, Milton. 1964. *Assimilation in American Life: The Role of Race, Religion and National Origins*. New York: Oxford University Press.

Greeley, Andrew M. 1970. "Religious intermarriage in a denominational society." *American Journal of Sociology* 75: 949-952.

Heller, Celia S. 1969. *Structured Social Inequality: A Reader in Comparative Social Stratification*. New York: Macmillan.

Hollingshead, August B. 1950. "Cultural factors in the selection of marriage mates." *American Sociological Review* 15 (October): 619-627.

_____. 1952. "Trends in social stratification: A case study." *American Sociological Review* 17 (December): 679-686.

Kennedy, Ruby Jo Reeves. 1944. "Single or triple melting pot? Intermarriage trends in New Haven, 1870-1940." *American Journal of Sociology* 49:331-339.

_____. 1952. "Single or triple melting pot? Intermarriage in New Haven, 1870-1950." *American Journal of Sociology* 58:56-59.

Laumann, Edward O. 1969. "The social structure of religious and ethnoreligious groups in a metropolitan community." *American Sociological Review* 34 (April): 182-197.

Lenski, Gerhard. 1961. *The Religious Factor*. Garden City: Doubleday.

Roach, Jack L., Llewellyn Gross, and Orville Gursslin. 1969. *Social Stratification in the United States*. Englewood Cliffs: Prentice-Hall.

CHAPTER 8
THE GREEKS OF ASIA MINOR AND EGYPT AS MIDDLEMAN ECONOMIC MINORITIES DURING THE LATE 19TH AND 20TH CENTURIES[*]

Using the conceptual framework of middleman minorities advanced by Turner and Bonacich, an effort is made to look at the Greeks of Asia Minor and Egypt as middleman economic minorities during the late 19th and 20th centuries. Greeks met all the pre-conditions set out by Turner and Bonacich for the middleman economic minority hypothesis including a sophisticated infrastructure of intra ethnic organizations, an ethnic closure on the part of the Greeks and hostility of the host societies, and concentration in middle rank, entrepreneurial economic activities. The exodus of Greeks from both middle Eastern societies was due not only to the rise of nationalism in the region but to the economic and socio-ethnic factors including the entrepreneurial and the non-assimilative orientation of the Greeks in the predominantly Muslim societies.

"Middleman minorities" are ethnic groups which occupy a middle rank in the stratification system of the host societies. Turner and Bonacich (1980:146) define middleman minorities as migrants to a recipient society, who maintain distinct cultural traits (language, values, religious beliefs), live in separate subcommunities, cultivate high degrees of internal solidarity through kinship ties, endogamous marriages and school and religious organizations, and as a rule avoid politics unless their interests are affected. Furthermore, middleman minorities have somewhat tense relations with the majority population. They are targets of violent attacks, discriminatory laws, and negative stereotypes. However, the most distinguishing trait of middleman minorities is that "a substantial and disproportionate number of its members are engaged in small commercial enterprises" (Zenner, 1982: 457).

Greeks of the diaspora as well as those of Greece proper have played such "middleman roles" in the economic, political and cultural spheres throughout their modern history. Greeks are engaged primarily in small scale family businesses such as restaurants. They are a buffer between the large capitalist

---

[*] This is a revised version of a paper presented at the 9th International Symposium on "Modern Hellenism in the Context of Eastern Europe and the Eastern Mediterranean." The 1985 Modern Greek Studies Association Symposium held at Ohio State University, Columbus, Ohio November 7-10, 1985. This chapter was originally published in the Journal *Ethnic Groups*, Vol. 7 (1987): 1-27.

enterprises and the non-business people in host societies. One may find thousands of Greeks operating restaurants in the United States and other parts of the world, but only a few in the organized corporate world. Greece occupies the "middleman" economic position even in contemporary international money markets. Because shipping and tourism depend on international trade, the Greek economy is a dependent economy *par excellence*. Additionally, Greek emigrant remittances (the "invisible" revenues) complicate Greece's chronic problem of balance of payments (Botsas, 1985; Tsoukalis; 1981). Historically, the Greek economy has always depended on international markets and has influenced Greek migration to foreign lands. Botsas (1985) argues that the smallness of the domestic market, the scarcity of natural resources, and the deficiency in foodstuffs has made it difficult for Greece to be autarkic.

There is ample evidence that many ethnic and immigrant groups excel outside their homelands as traders, vendors, merchants, money lenders and shopkeepers in the host societies. The Greeks of the diaspora had well established commercial and trade centers in Odessa, Constantinople, Smyrna, the Slavic provinces of the Ottoman Empire, and in central and western Europe long before the Greek war of Independence of 1821. Between 1908-1918 there were about two million Greeks in Asia Minor. During this period Greeks were persecuted and massacred by Turks especially in Smyrna and Constantinople, and Turkish nationalism reached its peak. The Greeks had established a lucrative commerce in Smyrna even before the Western European penetration of Anatolia. In fact Greeks were in Asia Minor even before the coming of the Turks. From Smyrna they branched out to Odessa, Russia, Mazche (France), Marcheilles, Holland, and Alexandria, Egypt. The Greeks were the wheat and silk traders who competed with the Dutch, French, and British merchants in international markets. In addition, the Greek community in Smyrna included Greek bankers, shopkeepers, and innkeepers.

At the beginning of the 20th century, Greek emigration became transatlantic. During the first quarter of the 20th century, most Greek emigrants went to the United States and Canada, and later Australia. By and large the first-generation Greek emigrants were economically motivated (Kourvetaris, 1971). In part Greece solved its problem of unemployment and underemployment through emigration. Many Greeks who emigrated in the 1900s, and later those who left Greece in the 1950s, engaged in "middleman" economic activities such as restaurants, groceries, real estate, and service oriented occupations in general. In his study of Greek-American professionals, Kourvetaris (1977, 1989) found that the story of the successful Greek in the United States is that of the Greek economic entrepreneur (e.g. restaurateur) and not of the Greek-American professional.

Historically Jews, Armenians, Greeks, Indians, Chinese, Copts, Lebanese, Koreans, and others have excelled as small business entrepreneurs in alien societies and cultures. Porter (1982), for example, found both historical evidence for the "Middleman hypothesis" among the Jews in the Middle Ages and in more modern times in the United States and the Middle East. Marger (1985) believes that Jews, functioning as money lenders in medieval times, were a generally despised group. Zenner (1982) also found Arab speaking immigrants (such as the Syrian Jews, Syrian Christians, Lebanese Muslims and/or Christians) as middleman economic minorities in North America. Likewise, Yambert (1981) and Freedman (1955) found the "Middleman minority" thesis to be true among the overseas Chinese in Southeast Asia. Indians in East Africa and Arabs in West Africa have also engaged in middleman minority roles. The Chinese in the Philippines and East Indians in several eastern and central African nations have been successful businessmen; but at the same time, they have also been the target of much prejudice and discrimination (Hunt and Walker, 1974 quoted in Marger, 1985).

Many social scientists have examined why certain ethnic groups are engaged in entrepreneurial activities while others pursue occupations in agriculture, industry, government, and politics. There are those who seek to explain the relationship between ethnicity and small scale business activities on the basis of the internal dynamics of the ethnic subculture (i.e., ethnic cohesion, familism. and the like) (Turner and Bonacich 1980; Thompson 1977, 1979 mentioned in Zenner 1982: 458). Others look at the external or ecological environment, including the role which commerce and ethnic solidarity play in the survival of members of ethnic groups in different cultural, and the socio-economic and political contexts in the host societies (Van denBerghe, 1975 mentioned in Zenner, 1982: 458). Regardless of which of the two explanations is more credible, the phenomenon of "middleman economic minority" cannot be understood without explaining the link between ethnicity and political economy and/or politics in general.

One finds very little serious scholarship concerning Greeks in Asia Minor and Egypt as "middleman minorities." With the exception of a few studies by Alexandris, (1983), Kitroeff, (1983), Kitromilides (1979), Kalkas, (1979) or accounts of Arabs by Tsirkas and perhaps a few others, this important phenomenon of modern Greek entrepreneurship in Asia Minor and Egypt has been ignored. For the most part studies of the Greeks in these areas are historical accounts describing the ideological and political phenomena of Greek and Turkish irredentism and the nationalist movements of various ethnic groups against the Turks in the Balkans. The rise of nationalism in Turkey and Egypt increased economic antagonism toward Greeks, which led to their subsequent exodus from the Middle East, particularly Turkey and Egypt.

In light of the economic theory of "middleman minorities" advanced by Turner and Bonacich and by others, the experience of Greeks in Asia Minor and Egypt is as much a study of ethnicity as it is a study of political economy. The authors spell out the pre-conditions for the emergence of middleman minorities which include: a) the formation of intra-ethnic organizations among migrating ethnics, b) hostility toward the migrants by the host society, and c) the concentration in middle rank, entrepreneurial economic roles of migrants and the reinforcing interactions among (a), (b) and (c) which increase the probability of continued hostility, intra ethnic organization, and economic concentration. The Greeks in both Middle Eastern societies played such middleman economic roles.

Conceptually the pre-conditions are diagrammatically depicted in fig. (8.1) below.

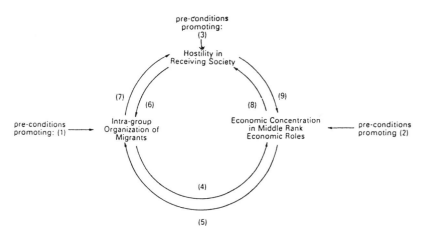

Figure 8.1 Key relations among classes of variables

THE GREEKS OF ASIA MINOR

Alexandris (1983:31-32) argues that the increasing importance of the Ottoman Greeks was by and large due to the economic, social, and demographic upsurge of the Greek element in the empire during the second half of the 19th century. Following the Anglo-Ottoman Commercial Treaty in 1838, an influx of foreign capital and entrepreneurs appeared in the Ottoman empire, including a cohesive entrepreneurial class of Greek and Armenian traders, brokers, moneylenders, and bankers in Constantinople. The Christian presence was more pronounced in finance and banking. The famous Galata bankers or sarrafs, who were predominantly Greek and Armenian, along with a number of European businessmen, furnished the Porte with 8,725,000 Ottoman liras in 1879 (quoted in Alexandris, 1983:31). The financial advisors of many sultans also belonged to the Christian minorities, especially the Greek and Armenian ethnic groups. Christian entrepreneurs became the local agents of British and French capitalists. Along with the middleman economic roles, the Greeks and Armenians staffed the liberal professions by becoming physicians, pharmacists, engineers, lawyers, bank managers, and teachers. In addition, they formed a white collar salaried middle class employed primarily by large European enterprises such as banks, railways, public utilities and industries. Even a greater part of the skilled urban working class in Constantinople was made up of Greeks. The powerful economic position of the Greeks is illustrated by the actual capital investment in the Ottoman empire in 1914.

Nationality	Percentage of Capital Investment
Greek	50
Armenian	20
Turkish	15
Foreign Nationals	10
Jewish	5

Source: (quoted in Alexandris, 1983:32).

This economic imbalance, according to Alexandris, helped divide Muslims and non-Muslims into hostile groups. To a large extent this stimulated the economic nationalism of the young Turks and ultimately undermined and destroyed the multi-ethnic and multi-religious foundations of the Ottoman empire.

The advent of nationalism among the ethnic groups of the Ottoman empire was as much a political phenomenon as it was economic. The creation of a

Greek nation state was based in part on the ideology of *Megale Idea*, or "Great Idea," which was predicated on the notion that there was a distinction between the concept of the "state" and the broader concept of the "nation." Most Greeks up until 1900 lived outside the boundaries of the Greek nation state. The Greek nationalist irredentism provoked Turkish reaction, and later found expression in the nationalism of the "young Turk's" Revolution of 1908 and the Kemalist nationalist movement against the Greeks in the 1920s. Greece's military landing in Asia Minor strengthened the Turkish nationalist movement and resilience against the Greeks. The failure of the Asia Minor campaign was a catastrophe and humiliation for Greece. With the Asia Minor debacle, the ideology of "Great Idea" died forever in Asia Minor in 1922.

The Kemalist nationalist movement, which was in part responsible for Greece's defeat, yielded the modern Turkish republic. The Young Turkish nationalist revolution of 1908 was simply the prelude to the Kemalist nationalist movement of the 1920s, which had far greater consequences for the Greeks of Asia Minor. Turkish nationalism resulted in the massive expulsion of Greeks from Anatolia. There were several pertinent questions raised by the expulsion. Was this massive expulsion of Greeks from Asia Minor, and later from Egypt, a result of ethnic/nationalist feelings or were the underlying reasons in part economic? First, to what extent were the Greeks of Asia Minor and Egypt engaged in economic "middleman" activities prior to and/or during the Turkish and Egyptian nationalist movements/revolutions? Second, to what extent were the Greeks of Asia Minor and Egypt integrated or assimilated in these societies? To put it somewhat differently, were the Greeks identified more with their European dominant groups or with the Turkish and Egyptian native groups?

According to Alexandris (1983) the Greeks continued to constitute the largest single non-Muslim ethnic group in Constantinople throughout the interwar period. Professor Frangakis also stated that Greeks were the most numerous among the ethnics in Asia Minor. According to her, during the 18th century and into the beginning of the 19th century, Greek merchants were the most important intermediaries between the Europeans and the Ottomans. During the 1930s there were 125,046 Greek Orthodox, of whom 108,725 were Grecophone. However, by 1935, of the 103,839 people who identified themselves as Greek Orthodox, only 88,680 declared Greek as their mother tongue. In addition to these numbers there were 8,124 Greeks in the islands of Imbros and Tenedos and 13,398 Constantinopolitan Hellenic subjects. The continued presence of Greeks in Asia Minor was due primarily to the sophisticated community or infrastructure which provided a self-identity for the Greeks. Citing Zervopoulos, Alexandris (1983:192) maintains that during 1933-34, the Greek community at large maintained 6 lycees and 38 schools with 7,667 students, 252 Greek, and 182 Turkish teachers. These, together with 54 churches, were administered by 48 parishes.

In general, the Constantinopolitan Greeks were a cohesive and distinct ethnoreligious group. During the institutional metamorphosis of the Turkish majority in the 1920s and 1930s, the Greek minority maintained part of its traditions. While Greek involvement in commerce continued, the cultural and social participation of the Greeks in modern Turkish society was minimal. The sharp distinction between Muslim Turks and non-Muslim minorities was partly the outcome of the Ottoman/Kemalist ideology and the Millet system.[1] Alexandris (1983:192) argues that the exclusion of non-Muslims, particularly the Greeks, from Turkish society and culture was in part explained by Greek ignorance of the Turkish language and the institutionalization of the Millet system. The latter accentuated the differences between the Greeks and the Turks, and created the "second-class citizens" status of the non-Muslim minorities.

During the Turkish rule (*turcocratia*) (1453-1827), the Greek ecclesiastical and administrative elites were granted certain privileges by the Ottoman authority, privileges which can be traced back to Christianized Byzantium. In other words, even during the Ottoman rule the notables played "middleman roles" between their co-religionists and their masters. The Greek notables were the mediators between the Greek people (rayas) and the Ottoman imperial structure. The central Ottoman administrative structure managed to control the vast empire indirectly through the ecclesiastical and religious elites of the various non-Muslim, ethnic-religious groups that constituted the Ottoman imperial system. In addition to their spiritual duties, the Greek Orthodox religious leaders were given quasi-secular duties. The concepts of ethnarch and ethnarchy had its origins here. These concepts were associated with the Millet system. An ethnarch was considered to be the leader of the subnationality or ethnic group; ethnarchy was a title extended to the religious leaders of the Greek Orthodox Millet system by Sultan, the Ottoman imperial ruler.

Turner and Bonacich (1980:149) recognize three major pre-conditions for the formation of an intra ethnic organization. These are: a) a relatively small but not an insignificant segment of the population; b) a distinctive subculture which sets them apart from the host society; and c) the continuation of ties to their homeland. The Greeks of Asia Minor met all three pre-conditions. According to Turner and Bonacich (1983:149), the concentration of minorities in a limited range of middle rank entrepreneurial economic roles is enhanced by cultural, contextual, and situational factors. The Greeks during the Ottoman rule had developed economic skills and knowledge of business transactions not only within their own ethnic communities but throughout the Ottoman empire.

They were the intermediaries between the Europeans and the Ottomans. Culturally, the Greeks developed religious and educational institutions within their ethnic communities, and, at the same time, created commerce and business institutions within and beyond them.

Contextually and structurally, the conditions in the Turkish society promoted middleman economic activities. The Ottoman/Turkish system was patrimonial/clientelistic with a rigid stratification that maintained the pronounced gap between elites and masses. The Greeks as descendants of Byzantines were considered cultured and were used as intermediaries in the Ottoman Empire not only in the economic sphere but in the diplomatic and administrative spheres as well.

Ottoman society was characterized by a high rank differentiation, low rates of mobility, and a high degree of solidarity within, but not across ranks. All these conditions were essential for the development of middleman economic activities by minorities. Greeks confronted a differentiated Ottoman/Turkish system of ranks in which low rates of mobility presented special opportunities for them. In addition, the middle rank entrepreneurial activities of the Greeks provided goods and services to the indigenous population at a low price. Turner and Bonacich (1980:150) argue that the middleman economic minority market exists only in a system in which rank differentiation, low mobility, and intra rank solidarity inhibits the indigenous population from entering the market. This is not the case among the migrant ethnic community which operates within its own ethnic cultural dynamics.

In addition, situational factors contribute to middle rank entrepreneurial success. Typically, middleman minorities, including Greeks, came from rural areas where they had to live frugally. This frugality enabled them to run their business thriftily, a necessary condition for small enterprises or shop-keeping. In general, Greeks of Asia Minor found all those cultural, structural, contextual, and situational factors which predisposed them to enter middle rank entrepreneurial roles. This pattern was repeated in Egypt and in other parts of the Middle East and indeed among all the Greeks of the diaspora.

Lewis (1969:454-455) argues that in the 16th century, the Turks had relied heavily on the Jews in matters of commerce and diplomacy. The gradual decline of the Ottoman Jews (along with the Ottomans) gave way to the rise of Christian middle minorities, namely the Greeks, Armenians, and Syrians. The political and economic positions of the Jews further declined during the 10th century, especially after the destruction of the corps of Janissaries with which many prominent Jews had been closely associated. As the Ottoman empire declined, the Greek and Armenian communities became stronger and more cohesive. They also profited from their commercial activities and cultural contacts with the Christian world in the West (Gibb and Brown quoted in Bernard Lewis, 1961:455). The influence of the Ottoman Greeks decreased after the creation of the Greek nation state in 1830. The chief beneficiaries were the Armenians who were already established as money-changers and bankers. The Armenians moved into many positions previously held by both Greeks and Jews and played an important role in the commercial and industrial development of the Ottoman empire in the 19th century.

By the mid-19th century the Christian merchants began to penetrate European commerce and investments. Many of them cherished national aspirations of their own, which Turks considered incompatible with Ottoman loyalty. The rise of a new Christian middle class that was prosperous, self-assertive, and potentially disloyal to the Ottoman empire led to a Muslim reaction.[2]   Later, the power of the Orthodox Patriarchate dominated by Greeks diminished due to the creation of Bulgarian and Serbian millet systems. By the beginning of the 20th century, the Greeks were not the only Christian group but one of the many competing Christian minorities within the Ottoman empire. The existence of an independent Greek nation state, with avowed irredentist aims, stirred up nationalist feelings among the Greeks, especially among those in European Turkey. It inspired other Christian ethnic minorities within the Ottoman praetorian system, such as the Serbians, to revolt.

In part, both the young Turkish revolt of 1908 and the Kemalist nationalist movement were economic in nature. In 1908, the "Young Turks" attempted to bring about economic reforms and political, and economic development in the disintegrating Ottoman empire. They tried to instill pride in Turkish products by organizing producers' and consumers' cooperatives, national banks, and the like. They also tried to foster Turkish commerce and industry. The Kemalist movement resulted in the exchange of populations between Greece and Turkey. The lands formerly held by Greeks were distributed among the Muslim immigrants and the Turkish veterans of war.[3] The radicalism of Kemalist reform, especially in agriculture and land reforms, moved Turkey toward westernization and secularization (Lewis, 1969:459-469).

The ultimate goal of modern Turkey was to completely eliminate the Greeks from Turkish national and commercial life. This policy of the Turkish economic nationalism was reflected in the discriminatory laws enacted by the Turkish state against non-Muslim minorities, especially the Greeks. The Greek merchants and professionals were taxed higher than their Muslim counterparts. According to a comparative list by professions, prepared by the Greek embassy in January 1943, the difference between the amounts of tax claimed from the Greeks and Muslim Turks was tremendous (quoted in Alexandris 1983: 226).

The taxation demands "meant nothing less than the complete extermination of the Greek community and represented a preconcerted plan to drive the Greeks out of business and take over their trade" (quoted in Alexandris 1983:227). Despite the fact that the Constantinopolitan Greeks constituted a small proportion of the total Turkish population (approximately 0.55 percent), the Greek merchants and professional classes bore 20 percent of the total taxation (Alexandris, 1983:22). The discriminatory laws against the Greeks were also evident in the sharp demographic decline of the Greek element in Turkey. According to the official population statistics, the following Greek speaking and/or Greek orthodox people were found in Asia Minor:

Date of Census	Greek-speaking	Greek Orthodox
1935	108,725	125,046
1945	88,680	103,839
1955	80,000	86,655
1960	65,000	106,611
1965	48,096	76,122

Source: Alexandris 1983: 291.

Alexandris (1983:50-51) argues that it is highly probable that the Greeks of Constantinople alone, between the 1870s and 1890s, ranged from 180,000 and 230,000 people, but that they feared to identify themselves as Greeks. By the early 1980s the Greeks of Asia Minor numbered 5,000-7,000. The mistreatment and discrimination that Greeks suffered,   along with that experienced by other non-Muslim and especially Christian Minorities in Turkey, contradicted the Treaty of Lausanne of 1923, which guaranteed the protection and freedoms of non-Muslim minorities. The decline and complete elimination of the Greek presence in Asia Minor has not been replicated, compared to the thriving Turkish minority in Greece who live primarily in Western Thrace which numbers over 150,000.

The forcible expulsion of Greeks from Asia Minor in the 1920s and 1950s was as much due to Turkish chauvinism as it was to class conflict between the prosperous ethnic minorities of Greeks, Armenians, and Jews on one hand, and the Turkish masses on the other.   These ethnic groups played "middleman minority" roles in Turkey, and they came into contact with the lower Muslim classes, which included the emerging indigenous middle classes.   The latter provided leadership to the Muslim masses and were in competition with their ethnic counterparts, the "middleman minorities." The emerging Muslim middle class was resentful of non-Muslim ethnic middleman minorities. Likewise, we can find an almost identical case among the Greek and Turkish Cypriots. One of the underlying reasons for the Turkish invasion of Cyprus in 1974 was the disparity between the prosperous Greek-Cypriot community and the impoverished Turkish-Cypriot community. The Turkish invasion facilitated the transfer of Greek property to the Turkish minority. What the Turkish-Cypriots could not obtain under more normal circumstances, or at the negotiation table in Geneva, were gained by the Turkish military's use of force.

Similar events have occurred in other times and places. In the 1950s, Turkish mobs attacked the Greek business establishments in Constantinople. The same happened to the Armenians who were massacred by the Kemalist nationalists in the 1900s. The Indians were expelled from Uganda in the mid-1970s by the dictator Amin. The Chinese in Vietnam had problems after the fall of Vietnam in the 1970s. In Malaysia and South Korea, Chinese entrepreneurs as "middleman minorities" encounter similar problems with the majority populations. In the 1950s the most extreme conflicts and massacres took place between the Hindu Indians and the Pakistani Moslems during the partition of India.

Greeks in Turkey experienced severe political and economic persecution and became easy scapegoats for Turkish ethnic chauvinism. The Greeks of Asia Minor were uprooted from their homes and communities where they had lived for generations, not only because of nationalism, but for economic reasons as well. The mass exodus of Asia Minor Greeks during the 1920s included many entrepreneurs and businessmen, including the late tycoon Aristotle Onassis. These Asia Minor refugees contributed to Greece's intellectual and economic development. A gradual dehellenization took place in Asia Minor, that including the closing of Greek schools, the expropriation/nationalization of Greek property, the changing of Greek names of historical sites and places, and demographic shifts. It was a policy of systematic Turkification or ethnic cleansing. A similar process followed in Northern Cyprus, especially after the Turkish invasion of the island in 1974.

By the end of World War II there were three major classes in Turkey: a new wealthy class, a peasant/wage earning class, and a bureaucratic/ military class. Separated from the dominant majority by both religion and language, the Greek, Armenian, and Jewish merchants as "middleman minorities" in Asia minor were not able to emulate the social and political roles usually played by the new middle classes in Anglo-Saxonic countries. These middleman minorities were not culturally assimilated and integrated in Turkish and Muslim society; they were marginal. This non-assimilation was due to their ethnic institutional autonomy in language, religion, traditions, and business, and to the hostility of the dominant Muslim population. The economic power of these middle class minorities was neutralized or diffused by the Ottoman communal and religious (millet) system, and this in turn prevented them from exercising much influence in Turkish society and state (Lewis, 1969: 473). The ethnic minorities either acted as a cultural buffer or became receptors of western impulses, but found themselves unable to transmit their ideas to the Turkish, Muslim heart of the Ottoman state and society.

The emergence of a genuinely Turkish middle class in the 1940s and the 1950s played an essential part in forming today's Turkish state and society. The appearance of a commercial class was changing the traditional ethos of Turkish society. However, the rise of this class was still not represented in the structure of the government by the 1940s. Of the 453 deputies elected to the Assembly in 1943, 127 were public servants, 67 were members of the armed forces, 89 were lawyers, and 59 were teachers. Only 49 were merchants, 45 were farmers, 15 were bankers, and 3 were industrialists (quoted in Lewis, 1961: 474).

In Turkey today there are two types of Greeks—those who are Greek citizens and those who are Greeks with Turkish citizenship. Most Greeks, however, have left Turkey. A systematic elimination of anything which enhances the Greek national identity has taken place. Greek history cannot be taught in the Greek schools in Constantinople. This is a violation of the 1923 Treaty of Lausanne which protects the Greek Orthodox Christians in Turkey. Greeks, like Armenians, were resented in Asia Minor especially after the emergence of the indigenous Turkish middle class. The "Young Turks" Revolution of 1908 and the Kemalist nationalist movement of 1920s brought forth the rise of the Turkish middle class which was resentful and antagonistic of Greek ethnic "middleman minorities."

THE GREEKS OF EGYPT

We can observe similar processes characterizing the experiences of "middleman economic minorities" among the Greeks of Egypt, whom many scholars describe as virtually the most prosperous and cosmopolitan of all Greeks of the diaspora. It is generally believed that the Greeks of Egypt make up the most important expatriate Greek community after that of the United States (Kitroeff, 1983). Most Greek communities in Egypt were established between 1843 and 1920. During this period the Greeks of Egypt reached the peak of their prosperity. As in Asia Minor the pre-conditions for the emergence of middleman minorities were also present in Egypt. Greeks established ethnic communities, ethnic organizations, and developed the infrastructure for entrepreneurial economic activities. Their economic activities were concentrated in a few occupations and industries, especially cotton, tobacco, shipping, leather manufacturing, and the like. However, unlike Asia Minor Greeks, the Greeks of Egypt were not expelled from Egypt where the hostility and discrimination against them were not as pronounced.

Professor Soulogiannis (1984) identifies four major historical periods concerning Greeks in Egypt. The first extends from the dynasty of Mohammed Ali, in 1830, to the British occupation of Egypt in 1881. During this period the Greeks settled in various cities and villages. The second period extends from 1882 to 1913, and is characterized by intense Greek economic entrepreneurial activities. It was during this period that Greeks established schools, churches, hospitals, and other institutions. While Egypt was under British control, the Greeks prospered. This progress stopped with the coming of World War I. The third period covers the years between 1914 and 1940. During this period the Greek community flourished. However, the ending of the British occupation of Egypt created the first anxieties among the Greeks concerning their future in Egypt. Finally, in the contemporary period, especially since the 1950s, Greeks have begun to leave Egypt. The revolution of 1952 in Egypt undermined, even further, the economic position of the Greeks there.

According to Soulogiannis (1984), during the middle of the 19th century European bankers and merchants, including Greeks, began to settle in Egypt. In 1843, the first large Greek community was established in Alexandria, followed by the second largest one in Cairo in 1904. During the second half of the 19th century other Greek communities were also established, such as Damiettis (1860), Minias (1860), Mansouras (1893), Tantas (1870), Sibin el Com (1870), Kafr el Zayiat (1872), and others. Due to its cosmopolitan and economic allure, Alexandria became the city in which most Europeans and Greeks settled. By 1927, 32.5% of Alexandria's population, or 140,736 people were foreign-born while 67.5%, or 432,327, were native-born Egyptians. (Kitroeff, 1983:14). In 1927, there were 22,000 Greeks in Egypt, while the 1907 census shows 32,451 persons of Greek Orthodox faith in Alexandria alone, which exceeded the number of Greek nationals (Kitroeff, 1983:14). Soulogiannis (1984) reports that about 200,000 Greeks organized themselves in 27 Greek communities in Egypt by 1930. In 1897, when the first census was taken, there were about 40,000 Greeks in Egypt. By 1927, there were about 76,000. At the end of World War II, it was estimated that the Greeks numbered between 100,000 to 150,000. Quoting from the work of Stratis Tsirkas (1958), Kitroeff (1981, 1983) points out the "disappearance of a group of wealthy Greek merchants in the 1870s and 1880s during the British control of Egypt and the emergence of a more anglophile Greek merchant group which became the community's *les nouveau rich.*"

From the early stages of Greek settlement in Egypt, Greeks followed capitalist and professional middleman entrepreneurial activities. The professional entrepreneurs included lawyers, journalists, teachers, scientists, and self-proclaimed men of letters who disseminated the official Greek ideology of irredentism and classic hellenism (Kitroeff, 1983). Alongside the professional and intellectual entrepreneurs were a number of Greek notables and middleman minorities or *les nouveaux riches* Greeks, especially in Alexandria. A list drawn on the eve of World War II contained 47 Greek names in Alexandria alone--7 lawyers, 6 directors of Greek newspapers, 3 judges of the mixed courts, and 2 professors. In addition, there were a number of writers, poets, artists, and critics who remained outside the community notables' ideological domain (Kitroeff, 1983:20). Around the turn of the century, other Greek communities in Egypt could boast of 79 doctors, 76 lawyers, 99 import-export merchants, 10 private bankers, 61 manufacturers, 52 restaurant owners, and 208 grocers. However, Soulogiannis (1984) reports that around 1930 there were 12,470 Greek workers and entrepreneurs in Alexandria and 6,960 in Cairo. In general, wealth and its accompanying bourgeois lifestyle were more characteristic of Greeks of Egypt than were intellectual and cultural activities beyond the schools and the church (Panayotopoulos in his study of Cavafy quoted in Kitroeff, 1983:20). One can observe similar trends among the Greeks in the United States (Kourvetaris, 1977, 1989).

The most important occupations of the Greeks in Egypt were in the cultivation and marketing of cotton. The Greek agriculturalists of cotton were considered among the first to cultivate and improve the quality and variety of cotton in Egypt. A second equally important occupation of the Egyptian Greeks was the tobacco industry. The leather industry also was almost exclusively in the hands of the Greeks. During the Muhammed Ali dynasty, a growing Greek merchant class, mostly exporters of cereals, tobacco, and cotton, encouraged many relatives of Greek middleman petty capitalists and merchants to migrate to Egypt. These included Greek shopkeepers and artisans. A steady flow of Greek immigrants left for Egypt to escape economic difficulties in Greece. Cotton was the main Egyptian industry during the 19th century, and exports were made by Greek firms until World War II. These cotton kings made large profits and diversified into banking, transport, and the stock market.

Subsequent events in Egyptian history, including the financial crisis of 1907, the outbreak of the nationalist movement in 1919, tariff autonomy in 1930, and the abolition of foreign privileges in 1937, undermined the economic position of the Greeks in Egypt. Europeans formerly had a set of privileges known as the Capitulations, which included immunity from taxation, from arrest, and from the local judicial system. Following the hardships of World War I, an Egyptian nationalist movement emerged which demanded the abolition of the Capitulations and independence from British control. A British-European treaty in 1936 abolished the Capitulations in 1937; the mixed courts functioned until 1949. The riots of 1919 and 1921 aimed against the British affected Greek lives and property as well.

In her study of 19th century Egyptian capitalism, Kalkas (1979) found that around the turn of the 19th century separate networks of Greek, Oriental Jewish and Coptic minorities controlled a large portion of the Egyptian economy. Kitroeff (1983) also found a substantial Greek capitalist class of shopkeepers, export-import merchants, private bankers, manufacturers, restauranteurs, grocers, and professionals (mostly doctors and lawyers) in Egypt. Greeks were known as the "cotton aristocracy" of Egypt at the turn of the 19th century: 22% of total cotton exports were made by Greek-owned firms in 1911-1912. According to Kalkas (1979) there were three separate networks or ethnoreligious subcommunities of capitalists: the oriental Jew, the Greeks, and the Copts. Members of each of the three ethnic and religious communities worked independently of each other. They married endogamously and developed intra-ethnic alliances and kinships which led to business relationships. Tables 8.1 and 8.2 describe the Greek kinship and family lines by birth and marriage.

TABLE 8.1 FAMILY RELATIONSHIPS AMONG THE GREEK ELITE, 1907.
Antonio Benachi

Michael *Sinadino*—Antone Vlasto Emm. Ant. Benachi—Sister of John *Choremi*

Alexander Benachi — Marie Sinadino
          Constantine J. Choremi — daughter of Antonio
          Steven Delta — daughter
          Alexander — Helen Tamvaco
          daughter — Michael *Salvago*

The Sinadino's were related to the Zervudachi's.
          Constantine George Zervudachi — daughter of Rodocanachi
          George Nicola

Source: Wright and Cartwright, *Twentieth Century*, 440, 289, 438, 328; *Egyptian Gazette*, January 5, 1912, p. 3.

(Taken from Barbara Kalkas's dissertation 1979:186.)

TABLE 8.2 FOUNDING DIRECTORS OF LARGE GREEK FIRMS
OPERATING IN EGYPT, INDICATING DATE OF FOUNDING.

Banque d'Alexandrie (1872)   *Banque Generale d'Egypt (1878)*

(L Stg. 1,000,000)   Constantine Sinadino*
J. Choremi* Themistocles Sinadino*
J. Antoniadis
C. Salvago* *Banque de Mitylene (1865-1911)*
Negreponte   George Zervudachi*
Zervudachi*
M. E. Benachi*   *Comptoir Foncier (around 1882)*
Constantine Sinadino*   George Zervudachi*
Basil Georgala
Ambrois Schylizzi

The Land Bank of Egypt (1905)
P. P. Rodocanachi et cie.*
Zafiropoulo et Zarifi et. cie. (Marseille)

C. M. Salvago et cie.*
Constantine George Zervudachi et Fils*
and other capitalists (Aghion, of the Jewish Sarraf-Bashas)

Source: Politis, *L'Hellenisme*, II, 262-65.
*Indicates that family is listed in Table 8.1.
(Taken from Barbara Kalkas' dissertation, 1979: 187)

Joint ventures between Greek and Jewish investors were also frequent during the first years of the 20th century. By 1907, of the 52 major firms operating in Egypt, 27 were coalitions of Greek and Jewish interests. Of the 59 "Normal"[4] firms, 12 were coalitions. The Greek family of Constantine G. Zervudachi was conspicuous in the Egyptian corporate elite. George C. Zervudachi inherited control of four banks, including the family bank. Zervudachi, like many other Greeks, was a land speculator. In 1907 a land crash came, and news of the failure came to public attention in 1911. As a result, Ambroise Zervudachi and Theodore Rodocanachi committed suicide; George and Nicola Zervudachi were imprisoned. By 1912-13, the Bank of Egypt and the Bank de Mytilene had failed, the Bank of Athens and the Bank

of d'Orient had reorganized, and a large number of Greek capitalists had fled
Egypt (Quoted in Kalkas, 1979:195).

Many of these early Greek capitalists lived lavishly, traveled frequently to
Europe (primarily to England and France), spent a great deal of money on
luxuries and entertainment, and, in general, emulated the European capitalist
class. Many Greek capitalists had Egyptian maids and servants. A number of
the wealthy Egyptian-Greeks gave donations to the Greek state. People such as
Tositsas, Salvagos, Benaki, Xenakis, Kasavetis, Aristofron, Demas, Gregoriou,
Kotsikas, Zervoudakis, Stournaras, Vassanis, Voltos, and Areroff were among
the most prominent benefactors. However, the Greek merchants and bankers
in Egypt were a tiny minority among the Greeks. Most of the business class
Greeks owned groceries, cafes, bars, pharmacies, and were tobacconists,
pharmacists, and cotton traders.

During the first half of the twentieth century, the social stratification of
Egypt resembled a pyramid. The broad base were the "fellah" or peasants and
urban workers, the middle sector were the petty bourgeoisie, and the upper
classes were landowners, merchants, and after 1930, a stratum of industrialists.
The social structure of Europeans including the Greeks looked more like a
diamond, with a small base of urban workers, a large petty bourgeoisie in the
middle, and an apex of wealthy businessmen. There was no direct class conflict
within European communities; the peasants and workers in Egypt were
exclusively Egyptian. The Greeks of Egypt as middlemen economic minorities
were the intermediaries between the British and French capitalists and the
indigenous Egyptian masses. It was the Greeks and other ethnic minorities who
had the shops and traded directly with the peasants and workers in the Egyptian
society.

Politically, the Greek Egyptian community was dependent on a secular
authority in Athens instead of a religious one in Constantinople. In Egypt, there
was a bifurcation between the church and community. The church was always
more autocephalous, and its income came from benefactors, people like
Tositsas, Antoniades, Familiades, Benakis and others.   There were many
African Orthodox bishops and priests who traveled to be educated in Greece
from such countries as Uganda and Tanzania.   Dependence on Athens made
home politics directly relevant to the Greek community in Egypt, and so Greeks
became an alien group on the Egyptian political scene.   When Britain took
control of Egypt in 1882, the Greek community interests fell under British
control.

Class politics in Egypt manifested themselves during the 1920s when a
small number of Greek blue and white collar workers and intellectuals, along
with a mixed Egyptian and European group, founded the communist party of

Egypt in 1920. It called for an anti-imperialist unity among all workers and intellectuals in Egypt irrespective of nationality. With the advent of World War II, the Greek Communist party members broke away to form an organization to promote the objectives of the resistance movement (EAM) in Greece. Kitroeff (1981) argues that, with a few exceptions, the Greeks of Egypt were more sympathetic toward the communist struggle than toward the Greek government in exile in Cairo. During the 1940s, the Greeks of Egypt prospered and contributed a great deal to the efforts of the Allies against the Axis.

While the Greek Egyptians were not active in the political events and processes taking place in Egypt during the 1920s, they were very much involved in the Venizelist-Royalist schism. The majority of Greek-Egyptians led by the notables supported Venizelos, viewing him as a bourgeois modernizer. Several of these prominent Greek Egyptians, who were mostly from Alexandria, traveled to Athens to help Venizelos, and two of them assumed cabinet posts. Ethnic interests took precedence over class interests in the Venizelist-Royalist schism. The progressive Greek bourgeoisie of Egypt supported Venizelos in contrast with the more conservative land owning classes of Greece who supported the king.

DISCUSSION AND ANALYSIS

Historically, a substantial number of Greeks in Asia Minor and Egypt engaged in "middleman" entrepreneurial activities. Those Greeks who engaged in economic and business activities were by and large a middle stratum of entrepreneurs. One can argue that ethnic groups are engaged in substantial numbers in middleman economic activities because many other occupational areas are closed to them. Greeks, for example, were not allowed to go into law or the military in the Ottoman empire. It was as much a matter of survival as it was the limited range of opportunities available to them.

Their forcible expulsion from Asia Minor, and later exodus from Egypt, was as much the result of the rise of Arab nationalism and political conflict as it was of class and economic rivalries between the Greek "middleman economic" minorities and the natives in these societies. The "middleman" status of the Greeks was further aggravated by ethnic, religious, linguistic, political, and cultural elements, which set them apart from both host societies. Greeks in both societies were not integrated even beyond the 2nd and 3rd generations. The emergence of nationalism in Turkey and Egypt was the culmination of a process that began with the resentment of western penetration into economic and political spheres in the Middle Eastern societies. By and large, those Greeks who engaged in business enterprises were part of the "middleman economic" petty bourgeois class. They were more Western than Middle Eastern in their business outlook and eventually unwelcomed.

The underlying causes of intense conflict between the Greeks and the "natives" of Asia Minor (modern Turkey) and Egypt were not only ethnic or religious but economic in nature. In both cases, during ethnic nationalist revivals, Turkish and Egyptian mobs were mobilized against foreigners, targeting the Greek business establishments and those of other ethnic minorities. The urban re-settlement of the Greek refugees from Asia Minor in the 1920s and Egypt during the early 1950s to Greece proper is an indicator of the non-agricultural nature of occupations among the Greeks of both of these societies. In a 1964 study of 909 refugees in Nea Ionia, Greece, Sandis (1972) found that the overwhelming majority of the respondents' fathers, mothers, and both paternal and maternal grandfathers, grew up in cities abroad. The occupations of these forebears were non-farming, and thus engaged in "middleman" entrepreneurial occupations.

The concept of the "middleman" minority has had political implications for the Greek ethnic identity in modern Greek history. The business and commercial classes were instrumental in popularizing the tenets of the French Revolution and the Enlightenment in the Greek communities of the Ottoman empire. Tsaousis (1983), in a comprehensive article on ethnic identity throughout Greek history, speaks of a horizontal or synchronic identity and of a vertical or diachronic identity. The diachronic vertical identity gives a sense of continuity in time and unity in space. The Greeks in the Middle East, especially in Asia Minor and Egypt, identified themselves primarily as Greek nationals and only tangentially as citizens of their host societies. They maintained their Greek ethnic identity beyond the first generation, rarely experiencing the need to relinquish their Greekness in order to prove themselves to others. They considered their Greek identity more desirable and preferred to set themselves apart from the Middle Eastern societies. They considered themselves "better off" and preferred their own Greek culture and European ways in general.

This non-assimilation into the Middle Eastern societies had both positive and negative consequences for the subsequent generations of Greeks in Egypt and Asia Minor. The most positive result was that the Greeks maintained their ethnic exclusiveness and Greek identity for many generations. The negative consequences were more obvious insofar as the Greeks set themselves up as easy targets or scapegoats during periods of political conflict between Greece and Turkey. During the 1920s, the 1950s, and the mid 1970s, Greco-Turkish relations deteriorated to the point that most Greeks left Turkey, some by choice, others by force. Similarly in Egypt in 1952, with the emergence of Arab nationalism and Gamal Abdel Nasser's rise to power, Greeks left that country fearing for their lives and properties. As Kitroeff (1981) points out, the Greeks of Egypt contributed to the development of Egypt, but at the same time, they enriched themselves at the expense of the Egyptians, especially from 1882 to 1913 when Egypt was under British rule.

Banton (1983) argues that "individuals utilize physical and cultural differences in order to create groups by the process of inclusion and exclusion." According to him, competition plays an important role in shaping racial and ethnic boundaries, and ethnic competition is often economic in nature. When Jews began to compete with Anglo-Saxon whites for upper-middle-class status, prejudice against them increased. Banton believes that "when members of one group compete with members of another group on an individual level, the boundaries between them will dissolve." However, this does not happen if ethnic and racial groups compete on a group level, in which case the group boundaries will be strengthened. Baker (1983) concludes that equal power relations lead to accommodations other than ethnic conflict.

Ethnic conflict is more likely to occur in asymmetrical power relations. One of the most important dimensions of ethnic power is economic. Overwhelming evidence from Belgium, Canada, France, the Celtic Fringe, Nigeria and elsewhere shows that only when subordinate groups improve their access to power and rewards and compete with the majority for jobs, housing, and political favors do they mobilize along racial and ethnic lines. One can argue this is also true among blacks and whites in the United States. Soulogiannis (1984) believes that the departure of the Greeks from Egypt in 1952 cannot be compared to the eviction of Greeks from Asia Minor in the 1920s. The Greeks of Egypt were not forced to leave Egypt as they were from Turkey. However, the 1952 Egyptian Revolution and the nationalization which followed made business and life for the Greeks precarious and problematic. The Greeks had to leave Egypt and so dispersed to different parts of the world including Greece, South Africa, Canada, Australia, and the United States.

CONCLUSION

Hellenism in Asia Minor and Egypt is, by and large, history. It seems that by the year 2000, or sooner, no organized Greek communities of any importance will be present in either Turkish or Egyptian society. As the older generations die out, there are no replacements. No Greek immigrants arrive to replenish these middle eastern Greek communities. Soon we will speak only of Americans, Australians, and Canadians of Greek extraction in Anglo-Saxon countries, because the Greeks of Asia Minor, Egypt and other middle Eastern societies will simply no longer be around. More and more, Greek identity abroad will be an Anglo-Saxonic phenomenon.

To what extent the exodus of Greeks from Asia Minor and Egypt was due to the Greek "middleman entrepreneurial" activities or to the use of ethnic nationalism and other causes has to be further investigated. It is up to future researchers to shed more light on this important phenomenon of the "middleman economic" minority status common among Greeks of Asia Minor, Egypt, and other communities of the Greek diaspora. Studies of this nature are useful as they have implications for ethnic conflict, ethnic politics, and political economy in general.

ENDNOTES

[1] The Islamic Ottoman ruling class granted self-government to the non-Muslim religious minorities of the empire which became known as the Millet system. The Millet Ottoman system recognized religion rather than nationality or linguistic affiliations. All the Greek orthodox peoples of the Balkans, Asia Minor, and Arab provinces of the Ottoman empire belonged to the Greek Orthodox Millet. The Orthodox Millet system remained in force from 1453 until 1923. The leader of each millet system (other non-Islamic Millets were those of the Jews, the Armenians, the Frankish, and the Lutherans) was the highest ecclesiastical office holder of the respective religious community. He was both the spiritual and ethnic leader (ethnarch), or Milletbasi, and he was directly accountable to the Sultan or the Ottoman central authority. Even the Milletbasi was a middleman, or a go-between leader, between the Greek ethnic religious community and the Imperial Ottoman authority (Passim in Alexandris, 1983).

[2] A similar reaction was present in the mid-1950s in the Arab and Muslim world due to the creation of the Jewish state.

[3] Something similar happened in Northern Cyprus in 1974 following the Turkish invasion of that island nation.

[4] Normal firms are those which do not include the highly capitalized Sarraf (bankers)-Basha Firms (See Kalkas, p. 281).

REFERENCES

Alexandris, Alexis. 1983. *The Greek Minority of Istanbul and Greek-Turkish Relations 1918-1974*. Athens: Center for Asia Minor Studies.

Baker, Donald G. 1983. *Race, Ethnicity, and Power: A Comparative Study*. London: Routlege and Kegan Paul.

Banton, Michael. 1983. *Racial and Ethnic Competition*. London: Cambridge Univ.

Botsas, Eleftherios. Nov., 1985. "Greece and the East: The Trade Connection, 1851-1984," paper presented at the MGSA, Ohio State Univ.

Freedman, Maurice. 1955. "The Chinese in Southeast Asia." Pp. 388-411 in Andrew W. Lind (ed.) *Race Relations in World Perspective*. Honolulu: University of Hawaii Press.

Glazer, Nathan and Daniel P. Moynihan. 1963. *Beyond the Melting Pot*. Cambridge, MA.: The MIT Press.

Hunt, Chester and Lewis Walker. 1974. *Ethnic Dynamics*. Homewood, IL: Dorsey.

Kalkas, Barbara. 1979. *Aborted Economic and Social Development in Egypt: New Leaders in an Old System*. Ph.D. Dissertation. Evanston: Northwestern Univ.

Kitroeff, Alexandros. 1981. "The Greek Community in Egypt and WWII: The Case of National Liberation Movement." (in Greek) in *Mnemon*, Athens.

_____. 1983. "The Alexandria We Have Lost," *Journal of the Hellenic Diaspora*, Vol. X, 1, 2 (Spring-Summer): 11-21.

Kitromilides, _____?. 1979. "The Dialectic of Intolerance: Ideological Dimensions to Ethnic Conflict," *Journal of the Hellenic Diaspora*, VI, 4 (Winter): 5-30.

Kourvetaris, George A. 1971. "First and Second Generation Greeks in Chicago: An Inquiry Into Their Stratification and Mobility Patterns," *International Review of Sociology*, Vol. 1, No 1 (March): 37-47.

_____. 1971. "Prejudice and Discrimination in American Social Structure," in P. Allan Dionisopoulos, ed. *Racism in America: An Interdisciplinary Approach*. DeKalb: Northern Illinois University Press, Pp. 28-49.

_____. 1973. "Brain Drain and International Migration of Scientists," *The Greek Review of Social Research*, No. 15-16 January-June. Center of Social Research, Athens, Greece.

_____. 1976. Book review of Charles Price, ed. *Greeks in Australia* in *International Migration Review*, Vol. 10, No. 4 (Winter): 531-532.

_____. 1977. "Greek-American Professionals: 1820s-1970s" in *Balkan Studies*, 18.2: 285-323.

_____. 1984. "Greek Armed Forces and Society in the 19th Century with Special Emphasis on the Greek Revolution of 1821," in *War and Society in East Central Europe* Vol. IV. Bela K. Kiraly (editor) New York: SUNY, Graduate Center.

_____. 1989. "Greek American Professionals and Entrepreneurs." In *Journal of the Hellenic Diaspora*, Vol. XVI, Nos. 1-4 (Spring, Summer, Fall, Winter): 105-128.

Marger, Martin N. 1985. *Race and Ethnic Relations*. Belmont, CA: Wordsworth Publishing Co.

Modern Greek Studies Association Meeting. Nov., 1985. Ohio State University.

Lewis, Bernard. 1969. *The Emergence of Modern Turkey*. London: Oxford University Press (2nd Ed.) paperback, pp. 15-16.

O'Brien, David J. and Fugita, Stephen S. 1982. "Middleman Minority Concept: Its Explanatory Value in the Case of the Japanese in California Agriculture." *Pacific Sociological Review* 25, 2, Apr.: 185-204.

Petropoulos, John A. 1968. *Politics and Statecraft in the Kingdom of Greece 1833-1843*. Princeton, NJ.

Porter, Jack. 1982. "The Urban Middleman: A Comparative Analysis: *A Comparative Sociological Research* 4: 199-215.

Saloutos, Theodore. 1965. *They Remember America*. Berkeley and Los Angeles: The University of California Press.

_____. 1964. *The Greeks in the United States*. Cambridge: Harvard University Press.

Soulogiannis, E. 1984. "The Greek Communities of Egypt" (in Greek) a speech under the auspices of the Egyptian Greek Association Athens, Greece.

Sandis, Eva. 1972. "The Asia Minor Refugees of Nea Ionia." *The Greek Review of Social Research* Vol. 14 (Oct.-Dec.): 186-188.

Tsaousis, D. G. 1983. 1981. "Hellinismos Kai Hellnikotita" (Hellenism and Greekness) in Tsaousis, D.G., ed. *Hellenism and Greekness*. Athens: Kollaros and Co.

Tsoukalis, Loukas. 1981. *The European Community and its Mediterranean Enlargement*. London: George Allen and Univ.

Turner, Jonathan and Edna Bonacich 1980. "Toward a Composite Theory of Middleman Minorities." *Ethnicity* 7: 144.

Van den Berghe. 1978. *Race and Racism: A Comparative Perspective*. 2nd Edition. New York: Wiley.

Wallerstein, Immanuel. 1974. *The Modern World System: Capitalist, Agriculture and the Origins of the European World Economy in the 16th Century.* New York: Academic Press.

Yambert, Karl A. 1981. "Alien Traders and Ruling Elites: The Overseas Chinese in S.E. Asia and the Indians in East Africa." *Ethnic Groups* 3, 3.

Zenner, Walter P. 1982. "American Jewry in the Light of Middleman Minority Theories." *Contemporary Jewry* 5, 2 (Spring-Summer): 11-30.

_____. 1982. "Arabic-Speaking Immigrants in North America as Middleman Minorities." *Ethnic and Racial Studies*, Vol. 5, No. 4 (October): 457-477.

CHAPTER 9
CONFLICTS AND IDENTITY CRISES AMONG GREEK-AMERICANS AND GREEKS OF THE DIASPORA*

The candidacy of Michael Dukakis as a Democratic nominee for the presidency of the United States in 1992 highlighted, once more, the ethnic dimension in American politics in general and the Greek-American ethnic experience in particular. Despite the fact that the majority of Greek-Americans supported the candidacy of Mike Dukakis, a substantial number of Greeks voted for Bush. This paper is an exploratory analysis of certain issues related to conflict and ethnic identity crises among the Greek Americans and Greeks of the diaspora.[1] This analysis will suggest a number of cultural, religious, bilingual, familial, and political dimensions of intra-ethnic and generational conflict and crises among the Greeks in the United States and the Greeks of the diaspora. Similar identity crises and ethnic conflicts can be observed among other ethnic groups in American society. The civil rights movement of the 1960s, spearheaded primarily by African Americans, gave a new impetus to ethnic, racial, and religious awakening in American society. Some welcomed this ethnic resurgence as a positive development; others viewed it as a manifestation of ethnic revivalism, albeit with some romantic overtones including nostalgia for the primordial and the folk. In the words of Patterson (1977), the ethnic resurgence in the United States may have carried with it a reactionary impulse against the most universalistic and humanistic values which transcend ethnic particularistic loyalties and identities.

ETHNIC CONFLICT AND ETHNIC IDENTITY: CONCEPTUAL CLARIFICATION

My intention in this paper is not to review the massive literature. For our purposes here, ethnic conflict will be defined as the conscious struggle that takes place within and among ethnic groups as one generation or ethnic group tries to gain advantages (such as power, status, prestige, class, and influence) over another. Related to the concept of ethnic conflict is the concept of ethnic competition, which may or may not lead to ethnic conflict. The concept of

---

* A revised version of an article originally published in the *International Journal of Contemporary Sociology*, Vol. 27, Nos. 3-4 (July-October, 1990): 137-153. The concept of *diaspora* dispersion becomes less and less applicable as the first generation dies out and Greeks no longer emigrate to other countries.

ethnic identity and/or ethnicity is related to the concept of ethnic minority which connotes a sense of powerlessness and subordination. Ethnic or racial minorities perceive themselves as objects of prejudice and discrimination that leads to exclusion. "Minority" has become a generic term that could ultimately apply to any one group according to some attribute or characteristic. Thus, we can talk about behavioral minorities (homosexuals), religious minorities (Jews), racial minorities (African Americans), national minorities (Italians), and of cultural minorities (Southern Whites). The word minority is meaningless without the concept of majority. A majority can be a numerical majority or it can mean a dominant group. Minorities, then, can be understood in terms of power relations. Numerical size may or may not be a dimension of power. For example, in the former apartheid regime of South Africa the white minority was the dominant group over the black majority. Even after the dismantling of apartheid, the whites still control the economic resources and wealth of South Africa. In the United States, women as a group are numerically in the majority, yet in terms of political and economic power, men (the numerical minority) continue to dominate.

In a general sense, the concepts of minority and ethnicity are not mutually exclusive. Most ethnic groups are minorities, but some minorities are the dominant ethnic groups. We all start as ethnic, racial, or religious minorities, and gradually we lose our ethnic minority status and become incorporated into the majorities or dominant groups. For example, most white ethnic Europeans, over a period of three generations, have been transformed from ethnic minorities into white Anglo-Saxonic dominant groups. Dworkin and Dworkin (1976) stress the dimensions of identifiability, differential power, group awareness, pejorative treatment, and mutually exclusive groups as aspects of the ethnic minorities' experiences.[2]

Ethnic identity or ethnic identification is an aspect of group identification—the linking of oneself to others through, ethnic, religious, national, cultural, or racial ties. Greek-Americans as an ethnic group are an ethnoreligious minority. In no other society outside Greece proper do Greeks represent a majority ethnic group. Even in Cyprus, where the majority of Cypriots are ethnically Greek Orthodox, the Turkish Cypriot minority in the North has foisted its secessionist and militant views on the island as a whole since 1974, supported by the most powerful patron Turkish state forty miles off the coast of Cyprus.

There are two basic factors of ethnic identity: a) the overall ethnic identity and ethnic consciousness of a particular ethnic group, and b) the intensity of one's ethnic identity. (These issues are applicable between *and* within ethnic groups.) Ideally, in the American context, it is not "who you are" (according to ethnic or other ascribed characteristics) but "what you can do" that determines one's social worth. However, one can argue it can be both. The civil rights movement of the 1960s, Affirmative Action, the various anti-discrimination laws of 1964 (including education, public accommodation, and voting), and the minority rights for women, Blacks, Asians, and Hispanics, all indicate the salience of one's ethnic identity. Needless to say, Myrdal in *An American Dilemma* has recognized since the 1940s the discrepancy between the lofty ideals of American society contained in its constitution and the realities in everyday intergroup relations in the United States.

In the United States, the "Anglo Conformity view" and the Americanization process has worked against the differentiated national/ethnic identities. An increase in intermarriage across ethnic lines undermines ethnic identity even further. As national origin identification declines in the United States, religious identification persists. The religious endogamy, however, is not as strong as it used to be. Ethnic identity remains a powerful factor in political, economic, and social life in the United States. Ethnically oriented clubs, societies, and associations proliferate among various ethnic groups in the United States.

The emphasis on ethnic identity and its intensity among different groups has ignored the fact that ethnic identification has many sources. We can note variations of ethnic identity depending on generational, class, political, and religious frameworks. For example, a large number of second-generation Greeks, despite their parents' efforts, rejected the identity of their heritage. For many second-generation children the question was a painful one: "Am I Greek or American?" Many children felt ashamed of their foreign-sounding names, or of their parents' strange foreign ways. Name changing or anglicizing foreign names, for example, from an Italian name Petrella to Peters and from a Jewish name Rosenberg to Rose, and from the Greek name Anagnostopoulos to Agnew, is one symptom of second generation rejection (celebrities especially have this tendency). Non-Anglo saxonic ethnics who change their name are not only rejecting their ethnicity, but also succumbing to societal pressures they feel would be more relieved if their names sounded more like those of the dominant group. In addition, changing one's name was also a matter of convenience, especially in the business world. Foreign sounding names were more difficult to pronounce and even school children made fun of their playmates who had long and foreign sounding names.

Historian Marcus Hansen formulated what is known as the "law of the third generation return," meaning that what was rejected in the second, was embraced by the third generation in a 'return to ethnicity.' Herberg took up this thesis: While the second-generation was striving to become 100% American, feeling insecure in American society, members of the third generation, conversely, were more secure in their Americanism, but no longer found it satisfying to be American.

The ambivalence that arises among an ethnic group's membership concerning its ethnic identification after the first generation is actually an ethnic identity crisis. The query "Who am I?" has preoccupied many Jewish-Americans, Italian-Americans, Greek-Americans, or any other ethnic group for a long time. Greeks in particular have experienced identity crises not only as members of ethnic communities outside Greece, but also in Greece proper as well. Greece as a nation state does not belong to any group of nations such as, for example, the Slavs, the Arabs, the Scandinavians, and the like. In the analysis below an effort will be made to identify a number of issues among the Greeks of the diaspora which create conflicts and crises of Greek ethnic identity.

CONFLICT AND IDENTITY CRISES AMONG THE GREEKS OF THE DIASPORA

Greek Church and Greek Koinotita (parish). To better understand the administrative structure of the Greek Orthodox church in the Americas and, indeed, throughout most of the Greek diaspora, it behooves us to detour and try to place the Greek Orthodox church within an historical and political context. The Orthodox faith is the eastern branch of Christianity and a religious minority vis-a-vis the Roman Catholic and Protestant branches of western Christianity. Within Orthodoxy, the Greek Orthodox faith is one of the many Eastern Orthodox Christian denominations. The religious part of the Greek ethnic identity is primarily a spiritual and ecclesiastical identity, a *koinotita* (close to the idea of parish) which can be traced to Christianized Byzantium in the East. Christianized Byzantium became part of the Ottoman Empire following the fall of Constantinople in 1453.

Within the Ottoman millet system there was an elite Greek social structure linked both nationally and locally to an Ottoman administrative structure. This Greek elite structure had both a religious and a secular component. Although this Greek elite structure held a subordinate position within the overall Ottoman system of political and social power, it had quite a different relationship to the Greek Orthodox subcommunity. The Orthodox millet subsystem recognized both religious and secular Greek leaders. The ecclesiastical leaders were bishops, archbishops, patriarchs, and the secular leaders, many of whom were *Phanariots* (named after *phanari*, a particular location in Constantinople.) The *Phanariots* were upper-class elites, descendants of Byzantines, who were associated with the Greek Orthodox hierarchy (Kourvetaris, 1984).

The Ottoman authority granted the ecclesiastical administrative elites certain privileges. Greeks had a certain power among their co-ethnics and co-religionists. They were the middlemen between the Greek people and the Ottoman imperial structure. The central Ottoman administrative structure managed to control the vast empire indirectly through the religious elites of the various non-Muslim ethnic-religious and cultural minority groups that constituted the Ottoman imperial system. In addition to their spiritual duties, the Greek Orthodox religious leaders were given quasi-secular duties. (The concept of *ethnarch* and *ethnarchy* had its origins here and originally meant the leader of the Greek nation.) The idea of *ethnarchy* was used during the Ottoman rule. The Ottomans recognized only religion as a group identity, not nationality, among the non-Moslem subjects in the Ottoman Empire.

The Greek ethnic identity crises and the conflicts among Greeks in the diaspora have become directly related to developments in Greece proper especially since the 1950s. Cultural divergence from the political/national status quo is evident not only in Greece proper (in the issue of the separation of church and state, for example), but it is present in Greek communities abroad. In the United States, the attenuation of ethnic identity among the Greeks started in the 1920s. Both the American Hellenic Educational Progressive Association (AHEPA) and the Greek Orthodox church have followed a policy of Americanization. The gradual replacement of Greek with English as an official language, AHEPA's insistence that Greeks become American citizens, and the replacement of Greek priests with American-born Greeks are just a few examples. Only recently, particularly since the Cyprus tragedy of the mid-1970s, have Greek-Americans begun to rediscover or show some interest in revitalizing Hellenism in America. While the bishops as administrators of the Greek Orthodox church still remain Greek-born, most of the parish priests are American-born Greeks. Most of these American-born Greek priests regard their parishes as spiritual communities rather than cultural entities. They do not identify with the political or national aspirations of Greeks in the diaspora. Their ethnic Greek identity is more symbolic than substantive. Like most second-generation Greeks, and like a large number of first-generation Greek immigrants, they have not internalized the Greek values of Hellenism. Their knowledge of Greek culture is more of a "dionysian" rather than of an "apollonian" nature. The religious dimension of Greek identity for most Greeks is defined by going to Greek religious services a few times a year. For first-generation Greeks, their identity is a given, it is ascribed. But for the majority of second-generation Greeks, Greekness is more symbolic: a convenient label for a good time indulging in Greek food and Greek festivals (*panygyria*).

Wherever we look we find turmoil behind the festive façade of most Greek communities in the diaspora. In Australia, for example, during the 1950s and 1960s a conflict arose between the Greek Australian communities and the administration of the Greek Orthodox church. In 1959, Archbishop Iakovos sent Archbishop Iezekiel from the United States to organize the Greek Australian communities on the model of Greek Archdiocese of the Americas. The communities were divided into two camps: those who supported the concept of individual communities with independent churches, calling themselves *koinotikoi* or secular oriented, and those who supported a more centralized administrative structure, or the *papadikoi* (priest oriented). The most conservatively oriented parishes support the official Greek Orthodox church, while the more liberal oriented support more independent Greek communities, hoping to pursue an autonomous Greek Australian Archdiocese. However, the movement to establish a federation of independent Greek Orthodox communities as church authority failed.

In Canada more than in the United States, newly arrived Greeks have challenged the traditional authority of the church, especially those who are better educated and more liberal politically (Chimbos, 1980). Greek Canadians have been critical and resentful of the political leverage of the archbishop. They are especially critical of the Greek Orthodox leadership for not protesting the Greek dictatorship (1967-1974). Montreal and Toronto have experienced the most conflicts. Most newcomers compete with old timers for administrative power of the church.

In Turkey, for the few remaining Greeks who live there, one can identify two types of Greeks—those who are Greek citizens and those who are Greeks of Turkish citizenship. For those Greeks who remain, both church and community work together. However, Greek education is under the strict control of the Turkish Board of Education; there is a systematic elimination of anything which enhances the Greek ethnic identity; and the mention of the Greek national holiday of March 25 (Greek Independence Day from the Ottoman rule) and that of October 28 (Greco-Italian war in 1940) have been eliminated from the Greek books in Turkey. Likewise, Greek history is not allowed to be taught in Greek language schools. Only Turkish is permitted to be taught. In Egypt, there is a bifurcation between the church and community. The church there was always more independent and its income came from benefactors such as Tositsas, Antoniades, Familiades, Benakis and others. There are very few Greeks left in Egypt.

In Sweden also, Greek schools and the Greek Orthodox churches function independently of each other. There is no religion taught in Swedish schools. The Greek Orthodox church, therefore, has no control over the schools or their auxiliary organizations. Mixed marriages are widespread among educated Greeks, but few occur among Greek workers. In the past, the tendency was to suppress the Greek language, but more recently the teaching of Greek has been stressed. In fact, during the 1980s a teachers' college with Greek professors trained Greek school teachers for the Greek children in Sweden. The teachers' salaries and the schools were paid by the Swedish government. Most Greeks of Sweden do not subscribe to the assimilative policies of the Swedish government. However, conflict begins to emerge in the second generation, especially when Greek children start going to public schools. Those who do not speak any Greek tend to be better adjusted to Swedish society. Only a small number of Greeks in Sweden are Swedish citizens.

Bilingualism. American society is a one-language culture. By contrast, India and Switzerland, for example, are multilingual. It can be argued that industrial capitalistic systems stress uniformity and discourage diversity or multilingual education. Only recently is there some emphasis on multiculturalism. Cultural or ethnic diversity is allowed but often at one's own expense. Public schools are not structured for multiethnic and multilingual curricula (excepting recent token attempts). Moreover, the American educational system is not committed to long-range bilingual education.

One of the most important issues in ethnicity is teaching the language of the immigrant generation to the children of immigrants. Language is one of the best indices of ethnicity. The issue of bilingualism was very popular in the 1960s and 1970s, especially among Hispanics. The resurgence of ethnicity through those years encouraged the rise in bilingualism. Some favor bilingual education, seeing the learning of another language as culturally enriching. In terms of ethnic identity, learning the language of the first generation enhances the individual's ethnic image and his understanding of his heritage. In the case of Hispanics, Spanish is often the child's first language. This is not always the case in Greek communities throughout the world. Bilingualism is a more complicated issue in large cities or countries with large Greek immigrant populations (e.g., Chicago, New York, Montreal, Toronto, Sydney, and those cities in Germany and Sweden that Greeks reside in). The first generation (both early and late Greek immigrants) is more likely to stress bilingual education in Greek and English while the second generation is more likely to stress English over Greek. By the third generation, the Greek language is usually no longer spoken by American-born Greek children.

Those who subscribe to the assimilationist view believe bilingual education is futile. The assimilationists are more likely to be American born. They argue that there are powerful environmental forces which mitigate against teaching and speaking another language. As the argument would go, the children themselves do not want it; it is easier for the American born to speak English. The pluralist or cultural traditionalists understand the obstacles, but insist that children should learn the rudiments of Greek language and culture. Those who subscribe to this view are more likely to be first generation immigrants.

The second and subsequent generations are more interested in maintaining ethnicity along the path of Orthodoxy (religion) rather than language (nationality). As it was pointed out, since the 1920s there has been a gradual erosion of national identity and sentiment among the second and third generation Greeks in America. It was, however, somewhat revived during the influx of the new Greek immigrants in the 1950s and 1960s. These new Greek immigrants gave a "shot in the arm" to Greek ethnicity in America. These Greek immigrants represented the new post-World War II Greek arrivals. Their progenies parallel the second generation of the earlier Greek immigrants. Ethnicity was strong in both immigrant groups but it began to decline among the second and subsequent generations of Greek Americans.

During the mid 1970s, Kopan (1974) mentioned 18 Greek parochial schools serving roughly 5,000 students, and 410 different Greek afternoon language schools serving 29,000 students. There is strong evidence that the Greek language is declining in the United States. Years ago, Bardis (1976) listed a number of causes for the decline of the Greek language in the United States. He included such obstacles as: the limited education of immigrants, the 1930s Depression, immigration laws (1921, 1924), assimilation of subsequent generations, the limited impact of Greek school, the decline of nationality, political factions among the Greek American organizations such as AHEPA, the American policy of Americanization, American public schools, social mobility of the Greeks, mixed marriages, the complexity of Greek language, and the Hellenization of English (boss—boshis, banker—bangathoros, basement—beshimo). All of these factors continue to operate as obstacles for Greek ethnicity. Many of these factors are not unique to the Greeks only. Other ethnic groups were faced with similar problems.

Language, for example, has been recognized as the single-most important factor of ethnic identity. Yet as one moves from the first generation to second, third, and subsequent generations, there is a concomitant decline in each generation's command of Greek. The first generation, of course, has Greek as its first language, and with it the strongest ethnic identity or Greekness. The average third generation, by contrast, neither speaks nor understands Greek. The third generation is the least Greek insofar as language is concerned. The second generation occupies an intermediate position between first generation and their American peers. They understand Greek more than they speak the language. The Greek language problem occurs primarily in Anglo-Saxon countries including Western European countries. Language was not a problem in Middle Eastern societies. As a rule, Greeks in non-Anglo Saxonic countries have maintained their ethnic identity through language beyond the second generation. The Greeks of Egypt and Turkey, for example, considered themselves more educated and more cultured than the average native in those societies. Speaking Greek and adhering to the Greek Orthodox faith gave them their ethnic distinctiveness and set them apart from the rest of society. The continuation of Greek identity in non-European societies was also due to the nature and character of non-caucasian societies, cultures, and states. English speaking countries such as Australia, United States, and bilingual Canada are considered immigrant nations whose very ethos demands that subcultures come into the mainstream. Countries in the Middle East, such as Turkey and Egypt, in which large Greek speaking people lived for centuries, do not encourage assimilation. Their leaders support ethnic divisions. It was unthinkable for a Greek to become a president or prime minister in these societies no matter how rich and influential. This may also be the case for other ethnic groups in these countries.

By the second generation, Greeks in the United States have lost most of their Greekness as measured by language, Greek customs, reading Greek newspapers, listening to Greek radio, or speaking Greek. They maintain their Greek names, their Orthodox membership, and their membership in Greek-American organizations primarily for business and professional reasons. While 40 years ago the Greek language was used widely in churches, organizations, and newspapers, in the 1990s English has replaced Greek in many Greek churches, especially in those which reflect second and third generations in their membership. Dan Georgakas (Written Communication, Spring, 1996) believes that Greek ethnic identity and Hellenism in general will be maintained only through an americanized form of "Greek" who is comfortable enough with being American but also Greek. The reverse, according to him does not work, as it leaves you in limbo.

Speaking or learning Greek is more than a matter of sentimentality or ethnic pride. It is the lifeblood of ethnic identity and consciousness. The Greek language is the best single indicator of Greekness. Learning Greek takes perseverance and commitment. It is more than a medium of communication. It is a dimension of Greekness and Greek heritage. The Greek language embodies the Greek culture itself with all its subtleties, ways of life, thinking, behaving, and symbolism. In most instances, the issue of language is the most important single factor in cultural conflict between people of different ethnic backgrounds and/or generations. In Canada, for example, conflict exists between Anglophones and Francophones. For the Greeks, generational conflict (strongest between first and second generations) is caused primarily by language barriers and differences in the perception of meanings attached to words or different expressions and idioms of the Greek language.

In general, children of first-generation Greeks or children of mixed parenthood are not eager to learn Greek. The pressure from American society to conform makes Greeks of the second generation more vulnerable to losing their ethnic identity. They don't want to be different, and in many ways they tend to overidentify with their non-Greek peers so they can prove their loyalty to the country where they were born. This overconformity stems primarily from a fear of rejection by their American peers. This was especially true during the 1920s and 1930s, which was one of the most racist periods in American history. Since the 1960s, there has been some relaxation of attitudes toward ethnic differences.

In general, learning Greek helps one to identify with or at least to understand the Greeks and things Greek. By the third generation, some believe there is a cultural atavism or a desire to go back to ethnic roots. This might include a desire to learn Greek, but it seems that most Greeks are occasional Greeks and enjoy things dionysian e.g., food, dance, music. Greek-Americans don't invest the time, the energy, or the commitment it takes to become knowledgeable in things Greek.

Another way of looking at conflict and identity crisis among the Greeks in the diaspora is to examine a host of social and social-psychological problems Greek immigrants encounter, such as social adjustment, prejudice, aging, discrimination, mental illness, divorce, loneliness, separation, and the like. Many of these problems are similar to American society as a whole and cannot be discussed here. Many Greek immigrants never made the adjustment or transition to the host society. While they were physically separated from loved ones in the old country, emotionally and nostalgically they were in Greece.

DISCUSSION, CONCLUSIONS, AND A COMMENTARY

As one moves from first generation to second, third, and subsequent generations, we can observe the gradual realignment of Greek ethnic identity. We move from an inner-directed ethnic Greek identity, most strongly represented by the immigrant generation, to other-directed identities in the second, third, and subsequent generations of Greeks in the diaspora. Concomitant to this transformation are changes in the correlates of Greek ethnic identity: a decline of Greek traditions; less awareness of Greek nationality; different family/kinship relations; a shift in loyalties; and the decline of language. The first generation were simply Greeks living in America with no identity problems. They had a Protestant work ethic and an entrepreneurial orientation. The fact that they crossed the Atlantic made them gutsy, daring argonauts, searching always for the golden fleece. Many of them found it, but a large number of Greek immigrants never managed to come near it. By the second generation, there is a gradual attenuation of ethnic identity. Thus, it can be argued that the ethnic identity crisis is primarily a second-generation phenomenon. Second-generation identity can be characterized as other-directed, that is, channeled into organizations such as the Greek Orthodox church, AHEPA, or United Hellenic American Congress. Second- generation Greeks preoccupy themselves more with status symbols. They tend to be sensitive about their hyphenated Greek-American ethnicity.

Athanasiades (1980) quotes the *Christian Science Monitor* of May 11, 1978, as saying that "both AHEPA and the Church a number of times have promoted goals that serve the political expediencies of American governments regardless if they don't agree with desires of the *homogeneia*, or greek larger community." Professor Athanasiades (1980) also cites Michael Novak who argues that the political maturity of PIGS (Poles, Italians, Greeks, Slavs) will not come through the church because it serves the interests of the Anglo-American capitalist class. Professor Athanasiades put it rather bluntly: "We need a deeper understanding," he says, "of our ethnic identity, something which goes beyond the Greek souvlaki, gyros, the Greek opa and the Sunday church." And Professor Athanasiades continues, "It does not matter if we are American born Greeks, or Greek Greeks, or Turkish Greeks and so on. . . . Our Greekness or ethnic identity must be measured in terms of what degree or to what extent we internalize the values, traditions of our Greek heritage, and to what extent we live by them. . . ."

Professor Moskos (1990) put forward a more conservative view of Greek-Americans as middle-class bourgeois, culturally conservative, and proud of their Hellenic civilization and culture. Greek-America, Moskos argues, "represents a new brand of Hellenism and we better consider and respect it in its own right and not as a pale reflection of an old country. . . ." But the issue now is that this new brand of Hellenism is lopsided. It is long on the dionysian, hedonistic side, and short on the apollonian side of Hellenic values and Greek *paedeia* (culture). The "new" Hellenism is too conservative and business (service establishments) oriented.

Moskos sets forth two versions of the Greek experience in America in the context of Hellenic diaspora. One defines an "homogeneia" or part of a homeland extension of the Hellenic diaspora, and the other a view of Greek-Americans as entrants and participants in American history. Then he asks which of the two versions we accept. Moskos says each of the two contains part of the truth. The diaspora view, Moskos argues, "implies that the Greek immigrant phenomenon is better understood as an outcome of political economy of Greece rather than as a minor theme in the American historical experience." But Moskos does not answer the pending question: Are Greeks serious in maintaining their Greek identity beyond the first generation in more than the dionysian aspects or not? Are Greeks committed to supporting Greece, the land of their forefathers, in her struggles? Greeks might occasionally visit her, they may enjoy their love boats in the Greek islands, but they stay detached from her. Greeks use the Greek names of food, dances, and music, but no more. They become proud when Greece is on our side or when Greece scores achievements, but Greeks stay away from her when she goes through tribulations.

The kind of Hellenism that Moskos is talking about is one diluted beyond recognition. Hellenism in Greek-America is defined by *souvlaki*, *gyros*, and *syrtaki*, at best as well as by a rich mystical Greek Orthodoxy with lots of atmospherics but no substance. Over 500 beautiful church edifices display icons and other religious paraphernalia, but Greek churches are empty of young people; indeed, overall membership in the Greek Orthodox church is very small.

A recent study of a Greek community in Akron, Ohio (Constantinou and Harvey, 1981) found a two-dimensional structure underlying Greek-American ethnicity. One they call *externalities* (that which pulls the Greek-American toward the place of origin), and the other *internalities* (that which binds Greek-Americans together as a community). While they found a variation across generations, the Greek language was definitely on the decrease. They found the first generation to be the most cohesive, tending to identify with the ancestral home, insofar as preserving the Greek language. The second generation was found to be the least cohesive of the three due to its transitional nature. The third generation was found to be less cohesive than the first but showed signs of ethnic revival. The authors concluded that no single factor is adequate to define ethnic identity. They examined 17 ethnically related factors including Greek language, Greek cooking, church membership, family, Greek press, and endogamy as the most important dimensions of ethnic identity.

Greek ethnic identity will survive if Greeks have something unique to offer beyond the *souvlaki*, *gyros*, and *syrtaki* dance to the societies in which they live. Greek-Americans have to internalize more of the apollonian aspects of Greek *paedeia* even if it is through translations of Greek literature and myths, through revivals of Greek holidays, Greek family traditions, and Greek music. They must not take our Greekness for granted. They must spend more time in trying to learn for themselves the essentials of our Greek identity. They must ask the leading question: Do Greeks really care to maintain their Greek identity within a pluralistic multiethnic society, or do they want to blend and totally assimilate into the dominant Anglo-American culture? If they are serious about their ethnic identity, then they have to commit themselves to investing more time and resources in learning about the Greek heritage. They must start with themselves, and then show others how proud they are of their illustrious past. But to be proud of something is not enough, they must continue to learn and keep current as much as possible. The Greeks have to do it themselves. The secret of Greek ethnic identity lies not in the other-directed American culture, but in the Greek inner strength of a 5000 year old Hellenic civilization. If Greeks have a common destiny as Professor Moskos (1990) believes, they must be ready to show it in words as well as in deeds. Greeks are like orphans, in that they do not have an extended ethnic family of nations such as, for example, the Latinos, the Slavs, the Anglo-Saxons, the Arabs, the Germans, the Blacks, and the Scandinavians have. They are more like the Jews of the diaspora. They have no "reference group" other than themselves. Needless to say, Greeks inherited a precious legacy from a distinctive ancient culture that has already offered much to our Euro-American civilization. It is that legacy the Greeks of the diaspora must try to keep and blend and share with others as much as possible. It is only then that Greek ethnic identity will survive beyond the first or second generation.

ENDNOTES

[1] The information for this chapter was based on informal interviews with participants of about 100 teachers and educators who participated in a conference on "Greek language" and "Greek education" organized under the auspices of the ministry of Greek education and the Archdiocese of North and South America, Department of Education. The conference was held in Athens and the island of Crete for 3 weeks in the months of July and August, 1980. Participants included teachers and educators from Alexandria, Egypt, Constantinople, Turkey, Nigeria, Jerusalem, Israel, Montreal, Toronto, United States, and Sweden. Secondary data included my own published work and research on the Greeks in the United States and elsewhere, and a number of recent publications on Greek-Americans, Greek-Canadians, Greek-Australians, and Greeks in Turkey and Egypt. This analysis on the Greeks of the diaspora is by no means exhaustive. Any conclusions or inferences should be at best tentative and exploratory.

[2] By identifiability is meant minorities are easily identified and as such become targets of discrimination. Differential power refers to the unequal distribution of power among various ethnic minorities in the United States. Group awareness is related to ethnic group identification. Bias treatment refers to the discriminatory treatment of minorities by majorities. Mutually exclusive groups are also referred to ethnic minority experiences as distinct social entities without much interaction with members of out-groups.

REFERENCES

Athanasiades, John. 1980. "Roots of Crises of Homogeneia." *NEA YORKH*, (Jan.): 35-44.

Bardis, Panos D. 1976. *The Future of the Greek Language in the United States*. San Francisco: R and E Research Associates.

Blauner, Robert. 1972. *Racial Oppression in America*. New York: Harper and Row, Publishers.

Chimbos, Peter D. 1980. *The Canadian Odyssey: The Greek Experience in Canada*. Canada: McClelland and Steward Ltd.

Constantinou, Stavros T. and Milton E. Harvey. 1981. "Basic Dimensional Structure and Intergenerational Differences in Greek American Community." A Paper Presented at 77th Annual Meeting of the Association of American Geographers, Los Angeles, CA.

Dworkin, Anthony G., and Rosalind Dworkin, eds. 1976. *The Minority Report: An Introduction to Racial, Ethnic, and Gender Relations.* New York: Praeger.

Kennedy, Rudy J. 1944. "Single or Triple Melting Pot? Intermarriage Trends in New Haven, 1870-1940." *American Journal of Sociology* 49 (Kamiaryu): 331-39.

_____. 1952. "Single or Triple Melting Pot? Intermarriage in New Haven, 1870-1950." *American Journal of Sociology* 58 (July): 56-59.

Kitroeff, Alexandros. 1983. "The Greeks in Egypt: Ethnicity and Class." *Journal of the Hellenic Diaspora,* Vol. 10, No. 3 (Spring-Summer).

Kopan, Andrew T. 1974. "Education and Greek Immigrants in Chicago, 1982-1973: A Study in Ethnic Survival." Ph.D. Dissertation. University of Chicago.

Kourvetaris, George A. 1976. "An Empirical Test of Gordon's Ethclass Hypothesis Among Three Ethnoreligious Groups." *Sociology and Social Research* (co-author) Vol. 61, No. 1 (October): 30-53.

_____. 1977. "Attilas 1974: Human, Economic, and Political Consequences of the Turkish Invasion of Cyprus." *Journal of the Hellenic Diaspora,* Vol. 4, No. 3 (September): 24- 27.

_____. 1973. "Brain Drain and International Migration of Scientists." *The Greek Review of Social Research,* No. 15-16 (January-June), Center of Social Research, Athens, Greece.

_____. 1971. "First and Second Generation Greeks in Chicago: An Inquiry Into Their Stratification and Mobility Patterns." *International Review of Sociology,* Vol. 1, No 1 (March): 37-47.

_____. 1984. "Greek Armed Forces and Society in the 19th Century with Special Emphasis on the Greek Revolution of 1821," in *War and Society in East Central Europe* Vol. IV. Bela K. Kiraly, ed. New York: SUNY, Graduate Center.

Moskos, Charles C., Jr. 1990. *Greek Americans: Struggle and Success.* 2nd Edition. New Brunswick: Transaction Publishers.

Myrdal, Gunnar. 1944. *An American Dilemma.* New York: Harper and Row.

Novak, Michael. 1971. *The Rise of the Unmeltable Ethnics.* New York: MacMillan Co.

Patterson, Orlando. 1977. *Ethnic Chauvinism: The Reactionary Impulse*. New York: Stein and Day Publishers.

CHAPTER 10
BRAIN DRAIN AND INTERNATIONAL MIGRATION
OF SCIENTISTS: THE CASE OF GREECE*

INTRODUCTION

One of the most striking by-products of modern science and technology following World War II has been the ever increasing mobility of scientific manpower. Not only has there been an internal movement of scientists within the peripheries and regions of a nation, but more profoundly it has become an outward international movement of far reaching proportions. This movement has generated the so-called "brain drain" controversy, for example the emigration of scientists, intellectuals, and professionally skilled people from one country to another. Usually the brain drain takes place from the less to more advanced countries of the world.

More than ever before, professional people are widely regarded as prime national assets. For a nation to survive in a modern competitive world it must encourage its most resourceful citizens—scientists and professionals in general, to contribute to its political, economic, and social development. The rise and decline of civilizations and cultures is partly attributed to the ability of the society to fully utilize and take stock of its human resources and to marshall its highly skilled manpower as a source of leadership and national development (Subcommittee on Immigration and Naturalization, 1968: 138).[1]

The issues and ramifications associated with the flow of skilled and talented people from the less developed countries to the more advanced ones are multi-dimensional and complex in nature. The problem of "brain drain" has an individual and social dimension attached to it. It is as much a product of individual human behavior (i.e., motivation, aspirations, ambition, intelligence, innate ability and the like) as it is a product of social structure and culture of the society in general (i.e., social institutions, social groups, occupational structure, history, traditions and the like). More specifically, one finds an interaction between human motivations, policies, purposes, and actions between individuals, groups, and nations that one can observe a diverse pattern of permutations and relationships between the gainer and loser nations.

While knowledge and scientific inquiry are transnational in nature—it has no boundaries—yet this international mobility of talent affects differentially the

---

* Originally published in the *Greek Review of Social Research* No. 15-16 (January-June, 1973): 2-13. The present analysis is updated and revised.

ability of the nation to develop and modernize its social structure. The promotion of the nation's welfare is problematic especially when some of its most talented and resourceful people decide to migrate. In short, the international migration of scientists has raised a number of political, social, economic, and moral issues. The decision of a professional to migrate, in the context of "brain drain" of a nation, has political and national consequences (SCIN, 1968: 139).

The purpose of this paper is to examine some aspects of "brain drain" in Greece in the context of international migration of scientists. More succinctly, given the international nature of "brain drain" which flows from the less developed to more developed countries, to what extent has Greece been affected by this outflow of its talents? What are the causes and consequences of Greek brain drain upon the social structure and development of Greece? It is through an analysis of secondary data and published reports on international migration of scientists including Greece that an effort will be made to address myself to this issue and its impact on the national development of Greece.

CONCEPTUAL PERSPECTIVES

In an effort to delineate and appraise some of these issues pertinent to the notion of "brain drain," as they impinge upon specific countries, a number of scholars have advanced various theoretical and conceptual frameworks of international mobility of scientists. These perspectives gravitate between the rights of individual scientists and the needs of states; there are basically three: the internationalist\cosmopolitan, the nationalist/local, and the differential push-pull explanation of international migration of scientists. According to Adams (1968) the internationalist/cosmopolitan model suggested by Harry G. Johnson of the London School of Economics and Political Science is predicated on the assumption that the international circulation of human capital (being scientists, scholars, engineers, or professionals), the genus in general is a beneficial process not only to immediate parties concerned—individual scientists and both countries of origin and destination of scientists—but more significantly it is a benefit to humanity itself. The principle of free movement is explicitly involved here, particularly the free choice of the individual scientist to seek what is best for the self-actualization of his or her talents and aspirations. This view recognizes the right of the individual scientist to freely choose his or her career and to pursue that right even if the scientist has to leave his or her own country.

Conversely, the "nationalist" model, proposed by Don Patinkin of Hebrew University, considers human capital as indispensable to economic, social, and political development of a nation. If a nation falls below certain minimum levels of human capital through its "brain drain," this can retard and endanger the growth potential of all resources in the economy. This model sees the question of "brain drain" as a serious problem for the loser nation when some among those who migrate are the best of its scientists from which the actual professional and managerial leadership usually comes for the development of the nation.

Adams (1968) presents a critical view of both aforementioned models. Regarding the "internationalist" model, the author argues that while it sensitizes us to the externalities in the form of scientific or other advances from which the losing and the highly developed nation benefits, it offers no panacea or prescription in curbing that part of the "brain drain" that justifiably should be checked. As regards to the "nationalist," Adams believes that this model fails to specify the means for achieving optimum allocation of domestically available resources.

Both in the internationalist and nationalist models two points of view are posed by the migration of skilled and talented people. On the one side, "brain drain" is seen by economists as a question of "manpower" involving the principle of supply and demand of human resources. "From this economic point of view the long range growth and development of a nation rest on its ability to develop and revitalize its major sectors of social life that are capable of attracting, stimulating, and rewarding talented individuals" (SCIN, 1968:18). On the other hand, the "brain drain" is seen in terms of needs and aspirations of the individual "scientist to move freely and to seek the actualization of his/her talents and aspirations in the fullest possible way." According to the latter view the right of the individual to choose the career, and the right even to leave his/her country of origin, can be a stimulant to the development of institutions and incentives that permit him/her to compete successfully in the human market of ideas (SCIN, 1968:18).

Lastly, there is the so-called differential push-pull approach explanation of international migration of scientists and professionals offered by Entique Oteiza of Latin America and Charles V. Kidd of the United States (Oteiza, 1965:445-461; SCIN, Charles V. Kidd testimony, 1968:76-84; Adams, 1968:120-134). The push factors are those which operate as centrifugal forces to many scientists and professionals in their effort to choose a career in their native countries, i.e. antiquated educational systems, rigid bureaucratic structures, political instability, emphasis on ascriptive criteria and nepotism rather than criteria of meritocracy and achievement. While these centrifugal forces push the scientists and other professionals from their native countries, concomitantly there are centripetal forces which operate to pull them toward countries where career prospects and opportunities for self-actualization and advancement are brighter in both economic and intellectual terms.

The question of "brain drain" is primarily an empirical one. It is in part the consequence of talented persons to be internationally mobile and cosmopolitan in nature and in part a product of the modern science and technology. Whether or not the accountability for the "brain drain" lies in the individual scientist or in the nation's social structure, the reality is that multiple factors contribute to the emigration of scientists. To some, the loss of such a talent is viewed as an anathema which is a severe impediment and handicap to national, economic, cultural, and intellectual development of a nation. To others, the loss of such talent is a blessing for if a nation is not capable of fully utilizing its human resources and talents, then it is in the interests of all concerned (individual scientist, home and host societies) that an international migration of highly specialized people exists.

THE CASE OF GREECE

In his survey of "Early Migration" of scientists, Steven Dedijer (Adams, 1968:9-28), draws five preliminary lessons from history. First, migration of scientists is as old as science itself. For example, until about 300 B.C., the center of attraction of scientists and scholars was Athens due primarily to Plato's Academy (388 B.C.) and Aristotle's Lyceum (335 B.C.) Historically, both became the first and long-lived institutions of learning and research in Europe. Around 300 B.C., however, Alexandria became the center of attraction of scientists. It was an exodus of talent from Greece to Alexandria. This reversal was primarily due to a conscious government policy by the first king of the Ptolemaios dynasty. Second, people in power in the past have acted to stimulate or prevent migrations of scientists, with many nations possessing specific policies. Third, it has been observed by many scientists that those in power have had a high degree of appreciation of the social value of science. Fourth, the development of a consistent foreign policy on science and on the migration of scientists is necessary yet very little appreciated. Fifth, those countries with the most sophisticated science policy are also striving to develop a consistent set of attitudes and actions on the question of migration. The United States, for example, has one of the most developed and sophisticated science policies.

Since Greece traditionally has been described as a country of "diaspora," it is only natural that she is among the heavy losers of human skills and talents (Coutsoumaris, 1968). Indeed, Greece has been found to be among the countries with the highest record of "brain drain" (Grubel and Scott, 1966; Coutsoumaris, 1968; Committee on the International Migration of Talent,[2]

1970). Other countries that lose large numbers of their talented people have been India, Iran, Turkey, Pakistan, the Philippines, Taiwan, Korea, Colombia, and Argentina. Only a few of the advanced countries—the United States, United Kingdom, Canada, Germany, Australia, and France—have received substantial numbers of these immigrants (CIMT, 1970:21-22).

Historically, it has been suggested (Geanakoplos, 1962; *Nea Estia*, 1955) that the Greeks of the Diaspora following the fall of Constantinople (1453 A.D.) constituted one of the most celebrated chapters in the making of modern Hellenic culture and civilization. According to Kohn, the Greeks of the Diaspora were extended from "Odessa up to Livorno, from Alexandria up to Manchester and from Vienna up to Massalia." The Greeks of Byzantium (Logioi), for example, who migrated prior to and following the fall of Constantinople contributed greatly to the Renaissance in the West. Later, the Greeks of Venice and of Western Europe in general had a profound impact on the Western attitudes and philhellenism toward the Greek National Revolution and the Greek Declaration of Independence from the Ottoman rule (1821-1827). The Company of Friends (Filiki Etaireia) was the first Greeks of Diaspora which started in Odessa, Russia, to organize and solicit support for the Greek National Independence (Prousis, 1994). Indeed, the roots of Greek National Independence must be sought among the Greeks of the Diaspora.

The transatlantic Greek immigration during the first quarter of the twentieth century reached alarming proportions but was offset somewhat by one and a half million Greeks uprooted from Anatolia (modern Turkey) who settled in Greece following the debacle of Asia Minor in the 1920's. There was a substantial number of Greeks who repatriated from America who could not make the adjustment in the New World (Saloutos, 1956). The story of these new argonauts of the New World and their contributions in the development of both the modern Greek nation and their adopted countries has been substantial. Only recently have scholars endeavored to investigate it (Saloutos, 1956, 1964; Vlachos, 1968; Tavuchis, 1968; Kourvetaris, 1971, 1977, 1987; Stathopoulos, 1971; Moskos, 1990; Scourby, 1984). During the 1950's, a new wave of Greek emigrant workers (roughly 300,000) sought work in Northwestern European countries, particularly Western Germany (Dimitras and Vlachos, 1971). Furthermore, while up to the mid 1950's the majority of Greek emigrants were designated as working class and/or blue collar emigrants, during the late 1950's a substantial number of Greek students and professional people migrated either temporarily or permanently to the Anglo-American countries (particularly to the United States) and Western Europe either to pursue a higher education or practice their profession.

It is perhaps against this synoptic framework of Greek diaspora that the phenomenon of Greek "brain drain" must be understood and explained. Indeed, Greek "brain drain" can be treated as a symptom or an aspect of a larger and more perennial problem of Greek emigration. While Greek immigration is an exceedingly important national problem, its cause is primarily socio-economic. However, the present analysis is limited to the "brain drain" aspect of Greek emigration.

Despite the absence of empirical studies on Greek "brain drain," there are some statistical data, particularly those collected by the United States Department of Justice, Immigration and Naturalization Service, for those countries (including Greece) which annually lose large numbers of scientists to the United States. In this part of the paper, an effort will be made to present some figures on Greek scientists and other professionals who have migrated to the United States for the last several years. Additionally, some statistics from the National Statistical Service of Greece and other secondary sources will be utilized for the purpose of elucidating the magnitude of Greek "brain drain." From the outset, it must be made clear that the exact number of Greek scientists who have permanently or temporarily settled abroad is not known.

SOURCES OF GREEK BRAIN DRAIN

Three major categories of Greek "brain drain" may be distinguished. These are the actual, the potential, and the hidden,[3] which also can be applied to other nations with a similar problem of "brain drain." The actual category includes all those professionals, technical and kindred workers (including scientists, engineers, and doctors) who, upon their completion of their professional training or thereafter, decide to migrate to more advanced countries particularly those of the United States, Canada, Western Europe, and Australia, and only secondarily to less developed countries in Asia, Africa, and Latin America.

The question can be asked, what is the magnitude of this type of Greek brain drain? It has been estimated (Coutsoumaris, 1968:169), for example, that between 1957-1961, Greece lost to the United States alone over one fifth of all her first degrees in engineering. Coutsoumaris believes that the total loss is even greater than this if one adds those who left for the other advanced countries of Western Europe and Canada; and include even those who migrated to the less advanced countries of the Third World. More specifically, the magnitude of Greek "brain drain" both in terms of professional specialties and professionals in general for the decade of the 1960s are given in tables 10.1, 10.2, and 10.3.

The figures presented in Table 10.1 by major professional subcategories show both the permanent and temporary nature of migration of professional people. However, it must be noted that a sizeable number of those who declared an intention for temporary emigration eventually settled abroad. Looking at table 10.1, nearly 35 percent of the graduates in engineering, over 27 percent in sciences, and 25 percent in the medical profession have left Greece permanently between 1961-65. Of course, the percentages are even higher if the final outflow of temporary emigrants is added.

Figures presented in Table 10.2 also indicate that from 1962 to 1969, a total of 1,066 scientists, engineers, physicians, and surgeons were admitted to the United States from Greece. Table 10.3 gives an overall picture of Greek professional, technical, and kindred occupations and total Greek emigrants admitted to the United States in the fiscal years 1962-1971 vis-a-vis total professionals admitted. Thus figures presented in Table 10.3 also indicate that for the decade of the 1960s, a total of 4,517 Greek emigrants in different types of professional, technical, and kindred occupations have been admitted under different immigration laws to the United States alone. It must be noted, however, that there is an overlapping in all three aforementioned tables, and it is exceedingly difficult to calculate the exact number of Greek "brain drain." Thus, although the exact number of Greek scientists and other professionals who temporarily or permanently migrated to other countries is not known, it has been estimated that Greece was losing about 1,000 young people with university training per year (Coutsoumaris, 1968:169).

The next source of Greek "brain drain" includes all those Greek students who are granted immigrant or non-immigrant visas by foreign consulates to pursue their education abroad and who potentially may be classified as the major source of Greek "brain drain."[4]   It has been estimated, for example, by Coutsoumaris (1968:169) that Greece has an annual average of well over 8,000 Greek students abroad, of whom about 10 percent are in graduate and 80 percent in undergraduate schools. This number represents about 15 percent of the total student body enrolled in institutions of higher learning in Greece. Despite the fact that no empirical studies have been conducted to determine the percentages of Greek students who receive undergraduate and graduate degrees from foreign universities, and the number of them who repatriate upon the completion of their studies, it is safe to speculate that a substantial number of them do manage to graduate, but the majority remains abroad after graduation, particularly those studying in the United States and Canada.

In a report by the Institute of International Education it was found that there were 144,708 foreign students enrolled in United States institutions of higher learning in 1970-71. Of this number, 37 percent came from the Far

East, 20 percent from Latin America, 13 percent from Europe, 12 percent from the Near and Middle East, 9 percent from North America (Canada), 6 percent from Africa, and 1 percent from Oceania (Open Doors, Report on International Exchange, Institute of International Education, 1971:3). To the question of whether or not they intended to remain in the United States, 33 percent of all foreign students said they did not plan to remain in the United States, and 18 percent reported they were undecided. Also, a large proportion of the 38 percent of students who did not answer the question at all do, in fact, intend to remain in the United States (Open Doors, Report on International Exchange, Institute of International Education, 1971:9).

In another study, Das (1969) examined empirically a sample of 1,400 international students representing 31 developing countries of the Third World. Attitudes of the students toward remaining in the United States upon the completion of their studies and the possible effect on the "brain drain" or "brain gain" in their respective studies were investigated. The author found that most of the African and Latin American students planned to return to their home countries but not the Asian students. Of the latter, those who planned to return were students in fields where there were employment prospects in the home country.

Concerning Greek students overseas, only some statistics for those in American institutions of higher education will be given here. A report by the Institute of International Education and Exchange indicated that a total of 1,968 Greek students were enrolled in the United States colleges and universities in 1971. (This number includes students who began their studies in 1968 and prior, 1969, and 1970). A distribution by sex, academic status, type of financial support, and major field of study of Greek students in 1970-71 reveals the following characteristics (see Table 10.4): There are about 2,000 Greek students in the United States colleges and universities, divided about evenly between undergraduate and graduate students. More than three-fourths were male and one-fourth female Greek students. Most of the students were self-supported (754), one fifth were financially supported by United States colleges or universities (436 students), but 642 of them did not answer this question at all. Finally 612 students considered engineering their field of major interest, with humanities, physical and life sciences, and business administration the second, third, and fourth highest, respectively. As part of a survey by the National Centre of Social Research concerning the migration and repatriation of Greek scientists, data were collected on 1,600 Greek students enrolled in United States institutions of higher learning in the academic year 1971-72. Figures for Table 10.5 show the total European and Greek aliens and students who adjusted

TABLE 10.1 GREECE: EMIGRATION OF SCIENTISTS AND OTHER PROFESSIONALS IN RELATION TO TOTAL FIRST-DEGREE GRADUATE, 1961-1965

	Stock According to 1961 Census	Total of New Graduates 1961-65	Persons Emigration Permanently 1961-65	% of Emigrated to Graduates	Temporary Emigration 1961-65	% of Temporary Emigration to Graduates
I. Total of Professional and Scientists	77,600	22,566	3,232	14.3	1,981	8.8
1. Engineers, architects, and similar fields first-degree graduates of higher education	5,000	1,876	650	34.6	191	10.2
2. Scientists (physicists, chemists, geologists, biologists, agricultural sciences, etc.)	5,700	2,200	600	27.3	233	10.6
3. Physicians, dentists, and trained persons related to medical profession	15,500	3,151	793	25.2	409	13.0
4. Teaching personnel	40,000	11,994	954	8.0	1,072	8.9
5. Lawyers	11,400	3,345	235	7.0	76	2.3
II. Managerial and Higher Administrative	28,500	5,804	470	8.1	125	2.2
Total of Groups I and II	106,100	28,370	3,702	13.0	2,106	7.4

Source: National Statistical Service of Greece: Statistical Year books taken from Coutsoumaris, 1968: 170.

TABLE 10.2 TOTAL, EUROPEAN, AND GREEK SCIENTISTS, ENGINEERS, AND PHYSICIANS AND SURGEONS WHO WERE ADMITTED TO THE UNITED STATES FOR FISCAL YEARS 1962-1969

Fiscal Year*	Total Number			European			Greek		
	Scientists	Engineers	Physicians & Surgeons	Scientists	Engineers	Physicians & Surgeons	Scientists	Engineers	Physicians & Surgeons
1962	1,357	2,940	—	780	1,651	—	17	52	—
1963	1,919	4,014	—	985	2,017	—	39	64	—
1964	2,037	3,725	—	1,041	1,941	—	26	53	—
1965	1,899	3,446	2,012	1,085	1,893	588	20	37	32
1966	2,290	4,915	2,549	1,041	2,371	739	51	57	48
1967	3,702	8,821	3,325	1,301	3,722	854	59	111	59
1968	2,959	9,310	3,128	1,101	3,601	691	29	108	34
1969	2,483	7,098	2,756	642	1,813	579	30	104	36
Grand Total	18,646	44,269	13,770	7,976	19,009	3,451	271	586	209

Sources: National Science Foundation and Department of Justice, Immigration and Naturalization Service.

*Each fiscal year ends June 30.

TABLE 10.3 GREEK IMMIGRANTS IN PROFESSIONAL, TECHNICAL AND KINDRED OCCUPATIONS AND TOTAL IMMIGRANTS AND PROFESSIONALS ADMITTED TO THE UNITED STATES, FISCAL YEARS 1962-1971

Fiscal Year	Total Admitted N	Total Prof. Admitted N	%	Total European Admitted N	%	Total European Prof. Adm. N	%	Total Greek Admitted N	%	Total Greek Prof. Adm. N	%
1962	283,763	23,710	8.4	119,692	42.2	10,979	9.2	4,702	1.7	261	5.6
1963	306,260	27,930	9.1	125,932	41.1	12,636	10.0	4,825	1.6	364	7.5
1964	292,248	28,756	9.8	123,064	42.1	12,759	10.4	3,909	1.3	268	6.9
1965	296,697	28,790	9.7	114,329	38.5	12,941	11.3	3,002	1.0	212	7.1
1966	323,040	30,039	9.3	125,023	38.7	12,059	9.6	8,265	2.6	374	4.5
1967	361,972	41,652	11.5	139,514	38.5	14,431	10.3	14,905	4.1	589	4.0
1968	454,448	48,753	10.7	139,515	30.7	15,955	11.4	13,047	2.9	512	3.9
1969	358,579	40,427	11.3	120,086	33.5	10,023	8.3	17,724	4.9	586	3.3
1970	373,326	46,151	12.4	118,106	31.6	10,294	8.7	16,464	4.4	697	4.2
1971	370,478	48,850	13.2	96,506	26.0	7,983	8.3	15,939	4.3	654	4.1
Grand Total	3,420,811	365,058	10.7	1,221,766	35.7	120,060	9.8	102,782	3.0	4,517	4.4

Source: United States Department of Justice, Immigrant and Naturalization Service.
*Each fiscal year ends June 30.

231

to permanent resident status in the United States for fiscal years 1966-71 under section 245 of the Immigration and Nationality Act. A total of 7,619 Greeks, of which 1,485 were students, adjusted to permanent resident status in the fiscal years cited.

TABLE 10.4 TOTAL FOREIGN AND GREEK STUDENTS IN THE UNITED STATES BY SEX, ACADEMIC STATUS, FINANCIAL SUPPORT, AND MAJOR FIELD OF STUDY: 1970-1971

Characteristics	Total Foreign Students	Total Greek Students
Sex		
Male	107,609	1,592
Female	34,564	355
No Answer	2,535	21
Academic Status		
Undergraduates	71,213	997
Graduates		
Pursuing M.Sc. degree	48,327*	568
Pursuing Ph.D. degree	17,532	269
Special***	5,132	98
No Answer	2,506	36
Financial Support		
U.S. Government	4,504	28
Foreign Government	5,297	16
U.S. College or University	23,527	436
Self	53,000	754
Private	8,101	61
U.S. College or University and Private or U.S. or Foreign Government	2,715	27
Private and U.S. or Foreign Government	626	4
No Answer	46,938	642
Field of Major Interest		
Agriculture	3,735	26
Business Administration	18,320	154
Education	7,896	42
Engineering	33,832	612
Humanities	25,334	390
Medical Sciences	6,994	42

TABLE 10.4 TOTAL FOREIGN AND GREEK STUDENTS IN THE
UNITED STATES BY SEX, ACADEMIC STATUS, FINANCIAL SUPPORT,
AND MAJOR FIELD OF STUDY: 1970-1971, (cont.)

Characteristics	Total Foreign Students	Total Greek Students
Field of Major Interest		
Social Sciences	17,936	258
All Other	703	6
No Answer	8,225	83

Source: Open Doors 1971 Report on International Exchange Institute of International Education.
*This figure includes 20,971 students who are pursuing graduate professional degrees of unspecified nature or no degree.
**This figure includes 235 Greek students who are pursing graduate professional degrees of unspecified nature or no degree.
***A "special" student is an undergraduate who is not enrolled for a degree.
Note: 446 out of 1,968 Greek students (22.7%) hold immigrant visas (and are unlikely to return to Greece upon the completion of their studies) while 26,732 of 144,708 foreign students (18.5%) hold immigrant visas.

TABLE 10.5 TOTAL, EUROPEAN, AND GREEK ALIENS AND STUDENTS
(BY PLACE OF BIRTH) WHO WERE ADJUSTED TO PERMANENT
RESIDENT STATUS IN THE UNITED STATES UNDER
SECTION 245, IMMIGRATION AND NATIONALITY
ACT, FOR FISCAL YEARS 1966-71

Fiscal Year	Total Number Adjusted	Total Students Adjusted	Total Europ. Adjusted	Total Europ. Students Adjusted	Total Greeks Adjusted	Total Greek Students Adjusted
1966	29,556	4,814	8,974	807	815	227
1967	38,619	9,957	13,025	1,059	1,305	320
1968	33,595	7,937	˜15,573	1,027	1,241	252
1969	29,257	7,493	11,737	769	1,133	211
1970	41,528	10,489	16,816	1,066	1,587	250
1971	49,239	11,693	16,901	962	1,538	225
Grand Total	221,794	52,383	83,026	5,690	7,619	1,485

Source: United States Department of Justice, Immigration and Naturalization Service.

In a study by the National Social Research Center (EKKE), at least 3,619 scientists repatriated to Greece since 1960. There appears to be, for instance, more than an adequate supply (compared to actual demand) of physicians, lawyers, architects, civil engineers, business, and public administrative posts. By contrast, there are serious shortages of well-trained people with industrial and managerial skills, of scientists in the agricultural sciences, research scientists in economics, and other fields of social science and modern technology (Coutsoumaris, 1968:171). However, during the 1980s and 1990s, these shortages may have been filled by the repatriation of many Greeks from the United States and other countries. In fact, there are indications more Greeks abroad are deciding to repatriate than emigrate to other countries for the first time in modern Greek history of emigration.

The exact number of Greek students who have graduated and adjusted their student visas to that of permanent resident and subsequently remained in the United States in the decade of the 1960s is not known. Perhaps it is safe to estimate that the majority of Greek students have remained in the United States by one way or another (some married to American or Greek naturalized citizens, some sponsored by their employers, and still others paid to remain in the United States). Regardless of how they managed to remain, the truth of the matter is that the majority of them did not return to Greece. The full drama of the Greek student abroad—his/her financial difficulties, his/her struggle with the language, the indifference of Greek and Greek-American affiliated institutions, and other similar problems of adjustment—has not been told as yet.

It must also be noted that while general external migration from Greece has almost stopped, a number of Greek students going abroad for studies continue to leave Greece. In December 1991, there were a total of 28,542 Greek students abroad. (Bank of Greece, reported in the Concise Statistical Yearbook of Greece, 1992: 85). The majority of the Greek students—both undergraduate and graduate—study in the following countries: England, Italy, United States, France, Bulgaria, Rumania, Germany, Hungary, Belgium, and a number of other European countries. Similarly, more recent data based on U.S. census and U.S. Department of Education also show a continuation of Greek students coming to the U.S. (see for example Table 10.6 below)

Against this outflow of actual and potential sources of Greek "brain drain," what is the "brain inflow" of trained and skilled Greek repatriates? To begin with, Greece has benefitted from repatriates because of war and political events in the countries of residence of Greek repatriates. Most of the benefit, however, came from the Greek entrepreneurial group. To mention only the most salient: one and a half million Greeks uprooted from Anatolia in the 1920's settled in Greece. During the 1950's a large number of Greeks came from

Egypt (during and after Nasser took over in 1952) and other Middle Eastern countries. Finally, a substantial number of Greeks repatriated from Rumania, Russia, and other Eastern European countries following the collapse of the communist regimes in 1989.

TABLE 10.6 TOTAL FOREIGN AND GREEK STUDENTS ADMITTED TO THE U.S. IN 1980, 1990, AND 1993

FISCAL YEAR	TOTAL FOREIGN	NUMBER OF GREEK
1980	286,000[*] (311,880)[**]	3,750[**]
1990	387,000[*] (407,530)[**]	4,360[**]
1993	———— (438.620)[**]	4,350[**]

[*] Source: U.S. Census 1994.
[**] Internal Center for Education Statistics. Digest of Education Statistics, 1994 U.S. Department of Education Office of Education Research and Improvement.

CAUSES AND EFFECTS: DISCUSSION AND ANALYSIS

That Greece has been losing annually a substantial number of actual and potential scientists and other professionals cannot be denied. Yet the question of Greek "brain drain" as such becomes a rather "mute issue" unless one is able to examine its causes and assess its effects upon the development of a nation. In this section of the paper, an effort will be made first to examine the causes of international migration of scientists and the conditions prevailing in less advanced countries (including Greece) that lead to "brain drain" and secondly, to consider some of the assets and liabilities; a resulting "balance sheet" will give us a picture of the extent of the Greek "brain drain."

It has been pointed out earlier in this paper that there are those who look at migration of scientists as a national hemorrhage which robs the nation of its human resources and retards the social, political, and economic development of a nation. On the other hand, there are those who view it as a blessing as long as scientists cannot be effectively absorbed by the socio-economic and occupational structure of their respective societies. The former subscribe to the "nationalist model" of the "brain drain" while the latter perceive it in terms of the "internationalist model".

In their efforts to advance viable causal explanations of international migration of scientists, a number of writers have focused their inquiries upon a multi-factor and multi-dimensional approach. To put it in a somewhat simplified way, there are two broad categories and constellations of factors in the "brain drain" controversy. There are those who look into the economic, demographic, cultural, institutional, and political factors, or the so-called objective and/or external forces, which push the scientists out of their home countries. On the other hand, there are those who look at the individual scientists and professionals themselves—both attitudinal and behavioral aspects of one's profession—the motives, goals, aspirations, values, professional ethos, and action orientations of the individual scientists and professionals in general.

A number of writers have primarily dealt with the so-called stock explanations: greater mobility for trained persons, greater cultural horizons, the desire to travel, the attractions of a well-informed international market for professionals, higher incomes, and the like. Part of this explanation is the supply and demand economic model, for oversupply of highly educated persons in certain fields but not in others is a problem as important as "brain drain" itself. An oversupply of certain professional skills without an effective absorption and demand in the professional marketplace leads to unemployment, underemployment, and finally leads to migration of scientists. If this is the case, one cannot speak of "brain drain" in the negative sense for the home countries (including Greece) but rather of "brain outlet" for the otherwise non-utilized human manpower. One important common characteristic of the losing countries is that the expanded educational system has produced more graduates than their economies can effectively absorb.

Powerful non-economic reasons are also at work that are equally counter-productive to the effective use of scientists and which retard the social, economic, and political development of a nation. The Committee on International Migration of Talent (1970:46) lists the following non-economic factors conducive to brain drain in the emerging countries of the Third World: the rigidity of government employment systems, the power of entrenched professionals, the extreme inertia of institutions, the lack of research funds, professional isolation, nepotism, lack of career mobility, inadequate recognition of talent in younger people, lack of hope for the future, and prejudice and discrimination based upon race, national origin, religion, or caste. Most of these factors are self-explanatory and are not discussed here.

Coupled with the non-economic factors are also professional considerations that further aggravate the situation and contribute to the "brain drain." For example, the quality of intellectual, professional, educational, and cultural life in the home country contributes to a large extent to the "brain drain." In addition, there is a lack of specialization and research that is frustrating to the individual scientists, the need for broad professional contacts and opportunities for both serious scholarship and dissemination of ideas will not be satisfied.

The lack of facilities for advanced training, research, and teaching in the home countries, particularly for highly specialized scientists, also leads to "brain drain." Another important professional consideration leading to "brain drain" is a feeling on the part of the scientists that their work and contributions are not appreciated and socially rewarded in their respective societies. A system of social hierarchies and stratification exists which is not based on the universal criteria of meritocracy and achievement, but rather it is based on the ascriptive criteria of birth, age, sex, family, class, race, caste, tribe, religion, geography, and political affiliation and ideology. This differential treatment based on criteria other than merit, achievement, and ability is what social scientists refer to as social discrimination and prejudice, which are contributing factors to the migration of scientists.

The rigidity of the stratification system also manifests itself in the lack of career mobility and promotion of young academic and research scientists. Career immobility and promotional freeze of highly talented people operate as deterrents of incentives and discourage competition in scholarship and excellence. The absence of vertical career mobility and promotion in both academic and non-academic professional occupational roles in the home country is an important determinant of migration of scientists. When professional needs, such as opportunities to be creative, a chance to effectively raise one's professional expertise and talents, to work with respected associates and colleagues, a feeling of social worth and usefulness in the community, are met, there is a tendency for professional people to stay home.

In some respects, the causes of "brain drain" in the less advanced countries are similar to and in other respects different from those of more advanced countries. One obvious difference, for example, is that the former are poor in natural resources and capital required to invest and provide adequate means and acceptable standards for professional and scientific work. Small nations such as Greece, which are poor in natural resources and located unfavorably with respect to external sources of materials or large markets, find it difficult to compete industrially with the more advanced countries in the West (Triantis, 1967). Immigration in general and that of scientists in particular seems to be a natural outlet for Greece's problem of unemployment and underemployment of its people. In this respect, the United States and other more advanced countries make a positive contribution to the less advanced societies by utilizing the otherwise under-utilized professional talents.

In short, while economic considerations are a powerful factor affecting the migration of exceptional people in less advanced and more advanced countries alike, a constellation of non-economic factors seem everywhere to be more important particularly in the more advanced countries to Europe.

The impact of brain drain on the development of the nation is different from one nation to another and from one time to another. Generally, the migration of scientists as that of emigration as a whole has both assets and liabilities for the losing nation. Indeed, the shortage of brainpower is not the only obstacle in the national development. An equally serious problem is the oversupply and saturation of certain specialized fields of scientists and other professionals that cannot be effectively absorbed in the occupational and economic structure of the nation.

India, for example, has an oversupply of engineers who until recently migrated to England. Greece also produces more engineers and lawyers than she can absorb. During the 1980s and 1990s there was a "brain drain" even in the United States. Due to the elimination or cutting of certain programs such as space exploration or military industry, a large number of engineers and physicists were laid off. Thus, a substantial number of American scientists of German extraction accept employment in West Germany. Likewise, many Jewish-American scientists move to Israel to work. A number of American public school teachers have in the past accepted employment in Australia.

In this respect, migration of scientists and other highly skilled people prevents (in principle) a waste of human resources and provides for effective utilization which may benefit both the home and host countries alike. The former indirectly receives advantages in the form of income remittances and other less tangible gains as well as by allowing opportunity for other scientists who remain behind to be fully and effectively utilized. It is also the receiving country which benefits from the skills and talents of the incoming scientists.

To truly assess both the assets and liabilities of "brain drain" for a given nation (including Greece), one should have a sustaining profile of scientific manpower both in diachronic and synchronic terms. The question of "brain drain" is not so much the number of scientists or other professionals who migrate from one country to another, but rather the type and quality of scientists that migrate. For example, there are thousands of doctors and physicians in a given society who practice medicine and yet only a few of them are engaged in medical research and epidemiology of human diseases. Illustrious scientists such as Fermi or Einstein, for example, who migrated from Germany and Italy, cannot be regarded as a statistical category. One particular scientist may be worth a hundred other scientists. A great discovery or invention beneficial to humankind cannot be measured in terms of statistical categories or in the numbers of scientists who migrate.

RECOMMENDATIONS

In view of the status of "brain drain" and scientific development of Greece, a number of long and short range recommendations may be offered that might genuinely alleviate the stream of "brain drain" and transform it into a stream of "brain gain" or "brain circuit," or even better, of "brain exchange" for the rapid process of modernization and development of Greece. These recommendations must be predicated upon two assumptions. One, the realization that "brain power" is a vital and indispensable force for the national development of the Greek nation and two, the willingness and determination on the part of national leadership in both its public and private sectors to re-examine and re-evaluate its domestic policies. Greece must shift its priorities and ensure that its "human resources" are utilized in the fullest possible way. "Brain drain" must not be seen as an isolated phenomenon. The concerted efforts should aim at diagnosing and treating the root of the problem and not its symptoms, of which "brain drain" may be considered a manifestation. And the root of the problem, it seems to this writer, lies in the nature and character of the Greek social structure and the manner in which human resources are utilized and rewarded in Greece.

Both the Greeks of Greece proper and those in the Diaspora must develop a professional class analogous to the entrepreneurial class. Greeks are known more as a nation of entrepreneurs rather than as a nation of scientists and professionals. The professional and academic community in modern Greece was, and still is, above all a national academic community. Greece has not succeeded in developing a broader scientific and professional base, one which can be used as a "frame of reference" by future Greek and non-Greek scientists and professionals, whether these scientists live in the United States, Western Europe, or in the nations of the Third World.

While the repatriation of "Greek scientists" should be a desirable and long range objective by private and public agencies alike, it seems to this writer that it is not sufficient to appeal to the national sentiments of the Greek scientists to return home. Greece must above all proceed to plan and solve its scientific manpower problem by revitalizing and restructuring its educational system along the model of more advanced societies, particularly the United States and Western Europe especially now that Greece is a member of the European Union.

A repatriation campaign and appeal to recruit Greek scientists working abroad must be based on a rational and realistic assessment of the nation's capabilities and needs. If a nation is not capable of effectively utilizing its human resources, it should not invite more scientists than it can absorb. It is usually in those nations with an oversupply or underutilization of scientists that the problem of "brain drain" is a serious one. Greece should not be known only as a country of leisure and tourism to the outside world but also as a country that offers excellent opportunities and facilities for teaching, research, and writing. Both scholarship and teaching should be rewarded. The subsequent specific and general recommendations are offered both as short and long range guidelines. In no way are these designed as either/or strategies of national development. In other words, these recommendations are not the only alternatives in bringing about directed social change in Greece. Unless an effort is made to re-evaluate and re-conceptualize Greece's human manpower, and on that basis restructure its policies, "brain drain" will continue to exist in Greece.

CONCERNING GREECE PROPER[5]

1. Conduct a careful dispassionate annual review of the numbers and kinds of specialists and/or scientists needed to achieve national development.

2. Develop a sustained national plan of development in which a list of priorities and long range goals of national development would be determined.

3. Stress quality over quantity by concentrating efforts upon the support of productive scholars and the elimination of the incompetent and lethargic. This would include the following aspects: (a) Provide a new system of incentives and rewards based primarily on merit and achievement rather than on ascriptive attributes (i.e. age, gender, class, etc.); (b) Encourage innovation and accomplishment; (c) Alter the ranking system of the professorial chairs by creating additional ranks in a manner similar to the American model of academic ranking and expand the present policies from those founded upon "sponsored mobility" and nepotism to ones based on universal criteria of "contest mobility", achievement, excellence in teaching, research, and administrative abilities of the university professors. Some of these suggestions have been implemented in Greece.

4. Restructure and redefine the role of the modern university and research organizations. Universities should cease to be feudal establishments and must change their curricula, modernize their structures and policies of governance. In this regard Greece has

expanded the university system and established a number of universities throughout Greece.

5. Expand the research activities of the present science research centers both at the university level and research organizations. Also, encourage and promote research at the universities in addition to that carried out by the research centers.

6. When developing new research centers or institutions of higher learning, attempt a program of decentralization in order to establish a better geographical balance.

7. Advance both organizational and professional skills, for both are indispensable.

8. Maintain academic freedom and a posture of value free intellectual honesty, objectivity, and responsibility in both the teaching and research aspects of science.

9. Develop a working relationship between the academic world and the larger community.

10. Increase the interest and seek greater professional support from the broader scientific community. For example, various science (physical and social) departments in major universities, grant giving institutions in other countries, and international agencies sponsor scientific training and research and also help disseminate the scientific findings in Greece.

11. Increase the number of scientific and professional journals and expand readership by using English and other languages as media of communication.

12. Expand the scientific base in Greece through membership in national and international associations. Sponsor and encourage Greek scientists to attend these international meetings, present scientific papers, and participate in panel discussions and professional symposia.

13. Invite various renown Greek and non-Greek scientists from overseas to teach and conduct research studies in Greece. This would tend to avoid parochialism in science.

14. Transform the Greek "brain drain" into "brain gain" or "brain exchange" by encouraging Greek scientists and their colleagues overseas to initiate a series of scientific publications using Greece as the research site and disseminate the findings by Greek and non-Greek scientists concerning modern culture and social structure in Greece.

CONCERNING GREEKS IN THE DIASPORA

1. Establish a Greek-American university in Greece supported jointly by Greece and Greek organizations and professional associations overseas.

2. Establish professional linkages between Greek scientists and institutions of Greece proper with those found in other countries. For example, invite Greek scientists from abroad to come more frequently to Greece and meet their colleagues or vice versa.

3. Encourage joint research projects and teaching seminars between Greek scientists overseas and those in Greece proper.

4. Increase and expand exchange programs and summer course offerings and institutes for Greek and non-Greek scientists concerning various aspects of the social structure of Greece. Initiate an exchange program of scholars and students and organize conferences and seminars to be held in Greece.

5. Organize charter flights to Greece for professional societies and students similar to those arranged by Greek churches and Greek organizations (i.e., AHEPA, Pan-Arcadian Federation, Pan-Macedonian, Byzantine Fellowship).

6. Compile directories of Greek scientists and students overseas.

7. Compile bibliographies of scientific works and studies by Greek and non-Greek scientists concerning various aspects of the social structure of Greece.

8. Establish at the ambassadorial level and in major cities where Greek consulates are located information offices concerning scientific developments and on-going research by Greek scientists proper and Greek and non-Greek scientists in other parts of the world.

SUMMARY AND CONCLUSION

In this paper an effort was made to dispassionately examine the Greek "brain drain" within the context of international migration of scientists. "Brain drain" was analyzed as a symptom and as an aspect of the Greek social structure and the problem of Greek migration in general. Certain conceptual and empirical aspects of "brain drain" controversy as they impinge upon particular countries including Greece were explored. Indeed, the purpose of the paper was primarily exploratory and diagnostic and only secondarily ameliorative in nature. Regarding the latter an agenda of interconnected specific and general recommendations were offered as pedagogical and policy guidelines. These recommendations, however, should not be construed as the only alternatives in bringing about change in Greece.

It is the opinion of this author that whatever changes should be initiated should first spring from within the Greek society. A rational long range plan grounded in past, present, and future realities and potentialities of "Greek brain" power should be initiated vis-a-vis the needs and prospects for the national development of the Greek nation within the European, Middle-Eastern, Balkan, and Mediterranean community of nations. In planning her future development, Greece can benefit and capitalize from Greek scientists in the diaspora without necessarily committing herself to a policy of their repatriation. Indeed, it seems to this writer that Greek "brain drain" can be transformed to a "brain gain" and/or "brain exchange" if the national and educational leadership in Greece adopt a cosmopolitan posture regarding science. This means Greece must encourage both Greek scientists in Greece proper and those Greek and non-Greek scientists overseas who are interested to carry out individual or joint research and teaching in Greece.

ENDNOTES

[1] The Subcommittee on Immigration and Naturalization of the Committee on the Judiciary, United States Senate, conducted hearings on the International Migration of Talent and Skills in March, 1967. It will subsequently be referred to as SCIN.

[2]The Committee on the International Migration of Talent will subsequently be referred to as CIMT.

[3]Hidden "brain drain" includes all those scientists and other professionals who while working in their respective countries might be employed by more lucrative foreign companies and/or research institutes that have branches or have investment in various countries. For the purpose of this report and because I was not able to collect any data on this source of Greek brain drain, my subsequent analysis will be based on the actual and potential sources of Greek brain drain only.

[4]In most instances Greek students studying abroad have finished their secondary education or have graduated from an institution of Greek higher education. If the Greek student completed both his undergraduate and graduate studies abroad, it is not clear to me whether or not one can classify him even as a potential source of Greek brain drain.

[5]An article on "Social Science with Emphasis on the Present Status of Sociology in Greece" by the author gives a profile of the state of the social sciences both as academic and research fields of study.

REFERENCES

Adams, Walter (editor). 1968. *The Brain Drain*. New York: MacMillan.

Baldwin, George B. 1970. "Brain Drain or Overflow?" *Foreign Affairs* 48(2):358-372.

Committee on the International Migration of Talent. 1970. *Modernization and the Migration of Talent*. New York: Education and World Affairs.

Coutsoumaris, George. 1968. "Greece", in Walter Adams (ed.), *The Brain Drain*, pp. 166-182. New York: MacMillan.

Das, Man Singh. 1969. "Effect of Foreign Students' Attitudes Toward Returning to the Country of Origin on the National Loss of Professional Skills." An unpublished Ph.D. dissertation, Oklahoma State University.

Digest of Education Statistics. 1994. U.S. Department of Education Office of Education Research and Improvement.

Dimitras, Elie and Evan Vlachos. 1971. *Sociological Surveys on Greek Emigrants, III*. Athens, Greece: National Centre of Social Research.

Geanakoplos, J. 1962. *Greek Scholars in Venice*. Cambridge, MA: Harvard University.

Grubel, Herbert G. and A.D. Scott. 1966. "Immigration of Scientists and Engineers to the United States 1949-1961." *Journal of Political Economy* 74 (August): 368-378.

Institute of International Education. 1971. *Open Doors 1971 Report on International Exchange*. New York: Institute of International Education.

Kourvetaris, George A. 1971. *First and Second Generation Greeks in Chicago*. Athens, Greece: National Centre of Social Research.

_____. 1977. "Greek American Professionals: 1820s - 1970s." *Balkan Studies*, Vol. 18, No. 2: 285-323.

_____. 1989. "Greek American Professionals and Entrepreneurs," in *Journal of the Hellenic Diaspora*, Vol. XVI, Nos. 1-4 (Spring, Summer, Fall, Winter): 105-128.

_____. 1994. "Social Science with the Emphasis on the Present Status of Sociology in Greece," in *International Handbook of Contemporary Developments in Sociology* edited by Raj P. mohan and Arthur S. Wilke. Westport, CT: Greenwood Press, pp. 461-482.

Moskos, Charles. 1990. *Greek Americans: Struggle and Success*. New Brunswick: Transaction Publishers.

National Science Foundation. 1967. *Scientists and Engineers From Abroad 1962-64*. Washington, D.C.: Government Printing Office.

_____. 1969. *Scientists and Engineers From Abroad—Fiscal Years 1966 and 1967*. Washington, D.C.: Government Printing Office.

Nea Estia. 1955. "O Hellinismos tis Amerikis" (Greeks in America). Athens, Greece: Nea Estia.

Oteiza, Entique. 1965. "Emigration of Engineers from Argentina: A Case of Latin American 'Brain Drain,'" *International Labor Review* 92 (December): 445-461.

Prousis, Theophilus C. 1994. *Russian Society and the Greek Revolution*. DeKalb, IL: Northern Illinois University Press.

Saloutos, Theodore. 1956. *They Remember America*. Berkeley and Los Angelos: The University of California Press.

_____. 1964. *The Greeks in the United States*. Cambridge, MA: Harvard University.

Scourby, Alice. 1984. *The Greek Americans*. Boston: Twayne.

Stathopoulos, Peter. 1971. *The Greek Community of Montreal*. Athens: National Centre of Social Research.

Subcommittee on Immigration and Naturalization of the Committee on the Judiciary, US Senate, 1968. *International Migration of Talent and Skills*. Washington, D.C.: Government Printing Office.

Tavuchis, Nicholas. 1968. An Exploratory Study of Kinship and Mobility Among the Second Generation Greek—Americans. An unpublished Ph.D. dissertation, Columbia University.

Triantis, S.G. 1967. "Population, Emigration and Economic Development" in *United Nations World Population Conference*, 1965, Volume IV, pp. 244-248. New York: United Nations.

United States Department of Justice, Immigration and Naturalization Service. 1962-1971. *Annual Reports of the Immigration and Naturalization, Service.* Washington, D.C.: Government Printing Office.

_____. 1968-1970. *Annual Indicator of the Immigration into the United States of Aliens in Professional and Related Occupations for Fiscal Years 1967-1969*. Washington, D.C.: Government Printing Office.

Vlachos, Evangelos C. 1968. *The Assimilation of Greeks in the United States*. Athens, Greece: National Centre of Social Research.

CHAPTER 11
THE BAHAMIAN GREEK COMMUNITY:
PAST, PRESENT, AND FUTURE[*]

Sixty miles off the South coast of Florida and stretching as far as Cuba, Haiti, and the Dominican Republic lies the Commonwealth of the Islands of the Bahamas. A coral archipelago of 700 islands, only 29 are inhabited, along with 2,000 or more rocks and cays. The Bahamas has a population of about 269,000 people, most of whom live on ten islands (New Providence, Grand Bahamas, Eleuthera[1], Abaco, Exuma, Long Island, Inagna, Cat Island, Bimini, and Andros[2]). With the exception of the 10 percent that are of European background, the rest of the inhabitants are of African descent and some of mixed parenthood. While Andros is the largest of the islands and the least explored and populated, New Providence is one of the smallest and most populated. The city of Nassau, located on New Providence Island, is the capital of the Bahamas, and has a population of approximately 150,000 people, which is more than half of the total population of all the Bahamian Islands.

The Bahamas is an English-speaking country that gained its independence from England on July 10, 1973. However, the Bahamas continues to be a member of the British Commonwealth. It has a British-type parliamentary system along with a prime minister and a governor general who is recommended by the prime minister, and who must be approved by the Queen of England. The parliamentary democracy has operated without interruption for 275 years.

The economy of the Bahamas depends predominantly on tourism, international banking, and other financial services. In addition, retail and wholesale distributive trade, light manufacturing, agriculture, and fisheries comprise the other sectors of the Bahamian economy. The gross domestic product (GDP) of the Bahamas exceeds $3 billion, 60% of which comes from tourist related activities. The per capita income of the country was $11,000 in 1994. The Bahamian dollar is on par with the U.S. dollar. Except for property taxes, there are neither income nor corporate taxes in the Bahamas.

---

[*]This chapter was co-authored with my three children, Andrew, Sophia, and Nicholas Kourvetaris. The data were collected during our Christmas vacation in Nassau, Bahamas in 1994.

THE DISCOVERY OF THE GREEKS OF THE BAHAMAS

On December 27, 1994, I visited Nassau, the capital of the commonwealth of the Bahamas. Two days later my daughter Sophia and my two sons Andreas and Nicholas joined me to spend the next couple of weeks in the Bahamas. Before leaving the United States, we had very little knowledge of the islands of the Bahamas other than the usual information of a tourist haven for those who wanted to escape the zero temperatures of the Midwest and to enjoy the sun and sea of the Caribbean Islands. What made our vacation more intriguing was the discovery in Nassau of a highly prosperous and successful Greek Bahamian community.

Initially, we were introduced to some members of the Greek Bahamian community, including the Greek Orthodox priest, through our host and hostess, Mr. Stephanos and Maria Antonas, who operate a Guest House[3] on Market Street in Nassau. Using a variety of approaches including participant observation, informal interviews with members of the Greek community, and extensive field work, we were able to collect some useful data about the Greek community of Nassau in Providence, Bahamas. In the next few pages we would like to present our joint report about our experiences and perceptions of the Greeks of Nassau.[4]

Three major questions guided our research of the Greek community of the Bahamas. When and why did the Greeks come to the Bahamas? What is the present socio-economic status of the Greek Bahamians? And how does the future look for the Greek-Bahamian community? In other words, our questions dealt with the past, present, and future.

THE BEGINNINGS OF THE GREEK BAHAMIAN COMMUNITY

In 1887, the arrival of 24 Greek sponge divers from the island of Kalymnos, one of the Greek Dodecanese islands in the Aegean Sea, marked the beginnings of the Greek presence in the Bahamas. The most likely sponsor of these men was the Vouvalis Sponge Packers and Exporters Company. The Vouvalis head office was in London and was established in 1882. (Public Records Office, Archives section, 1974:14). Indeed, the Vouvalis Company had been one of the first major firms to establish a sponge business and warehouses in the Bahamas. This company was Greek, which in the late 19th and early 20th centuries, expanded its operation to major sponging centers in Cuba, Africa, the Bahamas, and Tarpon Springs, Florida (Public Records Office, 1974:14). Three years later in 1890, the George Damianos Sponge Company was also established as packers and exporters of sponges in Nassau, Bahamas

(Public Records Office, Archives Section, 1974:16). It must be noted that the arrival of the 24 pioneer Greek Sponge divers was perceived by the native Bahamian sponge merchants as a threat to the local control of sponge fisheries. In a letter to the *Nassau Guardian* newspaper in December 1887, Joseph Brown, a leading sponge merchant at that time, wrote:

> Twenty-four aliens have arrived, experts in the gathering, clipping and packaging of sponge, and if I am rightly informed, determined to handle it themselves in all stages from the gathering to the packing, thus excluding native labor. If the experiment should be successful, it is quite probable that we should soon have hundreds of men in our midst, whose ways are not our ways, who would form a distinct section of the population, and who would only continue to remain here until such time as the sponge beds become exhausted or the business classes to be profitable" (*Nassau Guardian*, Dec. 28, 1887).

This letter had some discriminatory and alarming remarks against these early Greek men, and further suggested that a law be enacted to protect native sponge fisheries against the 'encroachment of aliens.'

Brown's letter triggered a similar wave of letters of protest sent to local papers to dramatize the threat which the entry of the two dozen Greeks in the sponging industry posed to native spongers. An additional demand for protective legislation against this alleged Greek "invasion" into the sponge business was made in a petition, signed by 14 of 29 members of the House of Assembly and 141 other citizens, and presented to the Governor of the colony in March 1888. (*Nassau Guardian*, 3 March, 1888). The argument in the petition was basically an urgent plea to protect local resources from foreign intrusion and from the dangers of attracting foreigners who would not easily be integrated into Bahamian society. Indeed, the thrust of the petition was outright anti-Greek arguing that the "Greeks by culture and race were not amenable to be integrated into the Bahamian society. The petition went on to state that the only objective of the Greeks was to gather that product of nature, the sponges, and thereby crush the backbone of our prosperity, and upon which the very existence of a large portion of this community exist" (*Nassau Guardian*, 3 March, 1888).

However, this anticipated "invasion" of Greeks into the sponge business never materialized. Some attempts by Greeks to bring sponge divers from the Greek Islands to compete with the natives proved to be an utter failure. The Greek sponge divers "could not compete with the natives and those who had embarked in the undertaking suffered to considerable loss in both time and money" (*Nassau Guardian*, 5 Oct. 1889). In general, Greek immigrants to the Bahamas concentrated on the buying, packing, and exporting of sponges. Initially, many Greeks came to the Bahamas as buying agents for the Vouvalis Company. Some of them established their own sponge business after accumulating some savings. As we mentioned, one of the earliest independent buyers of sponges was George Damianos and his son, who started their business in 1890. Other early Greek buyers of sponges were such individuals as Christofilis, Esfakis, Psilinakis, Mungos, Tiliacos, and Mailis (Transcript of interview with Mr. Psilinakis, 15 Oct. 1973, Dept. of Archives; also "The Greek Connection," *The Tribune*, 26 March 1981).

By 1924, the Greek community had established their control of the sponge/trade as buyers and exporters. Specifically in an editorial in the *Nassau Tribune*, August 1924, it was noted that the "Greeks practically control the sponge business of the island." It was estimated that they paid $20,000 annually in wages. However, despite the growing economic importance of the Greeks, they were not readily accepted socially by members of the white "Bahamian elite" (The "Greek Connection," *The Tribune*, 26 March 1981).

It must be emphasized that the Greeks prospered in the sponge business as sponge merchants and not as sponge divers. They were the buyers and traders. Native Bahamians actually went out on the boats and picked up the sponges on the sea floor of various Bahamian Islands, such as Acklins Island, Abaco, Mayaguana, Turks Island, and so on. The competition was most intense among the Greek sponge merchants and buyers themselves. Even brothers competed for the price of sponges. Over all, we believe it was the Greek merchants who benefited more from the sponge industry than the natives, who "always found themselves in debt." Dr. Gail Saunders, in the video on "The History of the Sponge Industry" also attended to this. The Greeks were essentially the middlemen and the entrepreneurs who bought the sponges and sold them throughout the world. This entrepreneurial ethos of the Greeks is similar in most Greek communities of the diaspora, and is one of the primary sources of economic prosperity of the Greeks.

About the same time in 1896, the first Greek man arrived in Tarpon Springs, Florida who later became the first pioneer of the sponge Greek community. His name was John Cocoris who came from Leonidion, Kynouria, the eastern province of Arcadia in south central Greece. John Cocoris became the driving force of the sponge diving industry and the builder of the Greek community of Tarpon Springs. (Frantzis, 1962:40). The history of sponge fishing in Florida began in 1849. Hook-spongers were natives of Key West, Cuba, and the Bahamas (Frantzis, 1962:38). In 1889, John K. Cheyney, a wealthy banker from Philadelphia, and a rich landowner in Tarpon Springs, entered the sponge business and built warehouses in 1890. Gradually, an influx of sponge merchants arrived from Greece, particularly from the Dodecanese Islands of Kalymnos, Halki, and Simi, and they established warehouses in Tarpon Springs (Frantzis, 1962:54-55). In Tarpon Springs the sponge industry was a multi-million dollar industry which flourished until 1950s when the industry declined due to the use of synthetic and plastic products. It must be stressed that the sponge industry became the focal point of Greek community-building in both Tarpon Springs, Florida and Nassau, Bahamas.

Although most early Greeks of the Bahamas engaged in the sponge trade, by the 1920s they began to venture into other businesses. For example, Theophilus Mungos established a bakery in 1924. By 1927, there were 4 branches of this bakery. Also the Mungos family opened the "Parisian Store" which sold womens' wear imported from Paris, including perfumes, and which catered to the lucrative tourist trade (*Nassau Tribune*, 17 Dec. 1927). Other Greeks owned fresh fruit stores and vegetables imported from the United States. One of these was the "California Fruit Store" owned by the Bantouvanis family. By 1930 two other fruit stores owned by Bahamian Greeks were established - the Olympia Fruit Store and the Acropolis Fruit Store ("Greek Connection," 26 March 1981; *Nassau Tribune*, 17 Dec. 1927; 10 Dec. 1930).

Another area of Greek enterprises was the restaurant business, which primarily depended on winter tourism. For example, D.N. Photiades, who had previously owned a central lunch stand, operated a fruit, vegetable, delicatessen, and light lunch business called The Grand Central in 1926. (*Nassau Tribune*, 21 Aug. 1926). Other restaurants owned by Greeks included Bahamas Restaurant (operated by steve Plakaris & Co.) and Prince George Restaurant (operated by Jim Glico) (*Nassau Guardian*, Sept. 1928; *Nassau Tribune*, 8 Jan. 1930). Although sponge trade was the first attraction that led Greek immigrants to the Bahamas, the sharp increase in the size of the Greek community after World War I was largely due to individuals joining friends and family members who had immigrated earlier (the "Greek Connection," *The Tribune*, 26 March 1981).

A PROFILE OF PRESENT GREEK COMMUNITY OF THE BAHAMAS

For years, the words "Greek" and "sponge merchant" were practically synonymous in Nassau, Bahamas. In 1939, a mysterious marine disease attacked the sponge beds and virtually wiped out one of the most lucrative businesses in the Bahamas (Bahamas Handbook, 1970-71:55). Though some species recovered from the blight, synthetics quickly took the profitability out of fishing for natural sponge. Today, the sponge industry is no longer an important source of income, though you can still find sponges in souvenir shops. In addition, a few merchants still maintain small sponge businesses but only as a sideline.

During the early 1930s, the Greek Orthodox Church was built largely through the efforts of master carpenter-builder James Mosko, who came from Kalymnos when Italy controlled the Greek Dodecanese Islands. At present, Mosko is considered one of the wealthiest Greek Bahamians. The Greek church in Nassau was the first Orthodox church in the entire West Indies. Since its founding, three priests, including Father Kolyvas, the present one, have served the church. Father Kolyvas, who by profession is also a printer, came to Nassau in 1953. He became the Parish priest, the Greek school teacher, and the printer who operated his printing shop from his home to supplement his income. In his words, "There was no other way to support myself and my family but to continue my printing business which I knew before I migrated to Nassau from Kalymnos, Greece." The community could not adequately support a full time priest and his family. However, the Greek community has provided him with a home that is adjacent to the church. A number of Greeks, concede that even if the priest retired he and his wife would continue to live in the present church home. Although retired from the priesthood at age 78, Father Kolyvas continues to serve as priest of the Bahamian Greek Orthodox Church. He enjoys the support of most of the Bahamian Greeks. For his services to the Greek community, the Greek Archdiocese of North and South America has given him an appreciation award. In addition, the Greek Government has awarded him an award for his contribution to the resistance movement against the German occupation of the Dodecanese and Greece during WWII (1941-45).

As mentioned before, the present Greek Bahamian community emerged out of the sponge industry of the *protoporoi* (pioneers), that is, all those who came primarily from the Greek Island of Kalymnos. Other Greeks in the Bahamas came from the Greek islands of Skopelos and Crete in the Aegean also. The nature and social structure of the present Greek Bahamian community reflects the beginnings of the *protoporoi*, but is not a pale replica of the early sponge industry which at one time was dominated by the Greek merchants. By 1940s and the coming of age of the second generation, the Greeks of the Bahamas, like their counterparts in Tarpon Springs, Florida, branched out in other types of businesses. From a sponge business community, the second generation of Greek Bahamians entered other areas of business and professions. As one would expect, the first generation Greek immigrants provided the economic base for their progenies, who, in turn, branched out in other business ventures and professions. Similar to the Greek communities in the United States, the early restaurateurs and other service establishments provided the economic base for the second generation (Moskos, 1990; Kourvetaris, 1987, 1994). Many second generation Greek Bahamians pursued careers in other occupations and professions such as medicine, law, architecture, construction, real estate, retail stores, restaurants, jewelry and perfume shops, hotels, accounting, carpentry, and teaching. In our view, we believe Greek Bahamians have achieved economically a middle and upper middle class status in the Bahamian society. In addition, at least a dozen or so millionaire Greeks from the U.S. and Greece live in exclusive areas of Nassau, along with other local and foreign elites. Most Greek shipowners have resort homes in the Bahamas and belong to exclusive clubs. For reasons that are unclear to us, we were told that these wealthy Greeks are not visible regularly in the Greek-Bahamian community. They usually appear once or twice a year in the Greek church. In this wealthy group of foreign Greeks there are at least half a dozen wealthy Greek Bahamians.

According to the Greek priest Father Kolyvas, the Bahamas in general and the Greek community in particular began to bloom in the 1950s. The closing of Cuba in 1959 contributed to a shift of tourism from Cuba to the Bahamas. In the last 30 years or so, the Bahamas and the Greeks have prospered due primarily to American tourism. There is a fear, however, that the re-opening of Cuba with the anticipated end of Castro's regime, might hurt the economy of the Bahamas.

At present, there are approximately 320 Greeks in Nassau, Bahamas of which, according to the Greek priest, 80-85% are members of the local Greek Orthodox Church. This includes first, second, and third generations, including mixed marriages. There are at least another 100 Greeks on other islands of the Bahamas. This includes first generation, their children (second generation), and grandchildren (3rd generation). Only a few families and individuals came to the Bahamas since the 1960s. Most second generation Greeks speak Greek but not the third generation. Similar to other ethnic groups, the Greeks of the Bahamas have married non-Greek spouses. Those who marry non-Greeks usually bring their spouses to the Greek church. By third generation, however, most marriages tend to be mixed and very few of the 3rd generation children speak Greek. Second generation parents no longer speak Greek to their children. Furthermore, the Greek language is not taught any longer by the Greek priest to the Greek Bahamian children. However, the liturgy at the church continues to be mostly in Greek. Only the sermon, readings from the epistles by Apostle Paul, and gospels are in both Greek and English.

The first generation Greeks came primarily as workers and eventually became entrepreneurs. They opened restaurants[5] (about 8-10), including one cafeteria, two carry-outs, and Dominos Pizzas. The second generation is mostly in the professional realm: 5-6 doctors, a dozen or so lawyers, about 1/2 dozen teachers, and (2 or 3) construction company owners. One of our sources told us that a Greek by the name Minas in Freeport, Bahamas, is famous for poultry. Mosko became wealthy in construction. We found several Greeks in the shoe store business, in women's clothing, jewelry, perfumes, and owners of such stores as "Gold," "Tick-Tack Shop," "Ocean Jewels," "International Jewelry," and "Express Limited." Many second and third generation Greek Bahamian children go to the United States, Canada, and England to pursue their higher education. After they finish their education many of them return to the Bahamas.

Granting independence to the Bahamas benefited all Bahamians including the Greeks. One of our interviewees put it this way: "Prior to independence, the British ruled the Bahamas with a local ruling elite. At present if you have an idea and want to work, you are free to make money." Indeed, the Greeks and other white ethnic groups in the Bahamas are doing well especially after the Bahamas gained their independence from the British. When Archbishop Iakovos, the primate of North and South America visited Nassau, the then Governor Sir Charles Dundas in the 1970s prior to the Bahamas independence, "told the archbishop that the best element in Nassau was the Greeks" (Bahamas Handbook, 1970-71:61).

FUTURE PROSPECTS OF THE GREEK BAHAMIAN COMMUNITY

In our interviews and participant observation, we have come to certain conclusions about the future of the Greek Bahamian community. Some of our observations are presented below in terms of tentative propositions for further investigation.

1.   The Greek Orthodox Church is the focal point of the Greek Bahamian community. However, the present structure and facilities of the church do not adequately serve the needs of a growing third and younger generation of Greek Bahamians and mixed parenthood children. The old timers, represented by the *protoporoi* (a few still alive) and by those Greeks who came during the 1950s, including Father Kolyvas, are attached to Greek traditions and to the Greek language. The young congregation and children of mixed marriages do not understand the liturgy, which is almost entirely in Greek (with the exception of the gospel, the apostle, and the sermon which are in both as was previously explained).

2.   We found no sense of strong ethnic Greek identity among the Greek Bahamians. The most salient characteristic of the Greek Bahamians seemed to be a pervasive entrepreneurial ethos bordered on individualism, competition, and enterprising. In the words of some Greeks who arrived in the 1960s to the Bahamas: "Greek Bahamians are for money . . . They don't talk to you if you are not well off . . . Even relatives and members from the same family are competing."

3.   Most Greek Bahamians, both old and new, came from the island of Kalymnos in the Dodecanese. Many of them are related. The new Greeks (who came here in the 1960s and later) are a minority and, as a rule, do not associate with old timers and their progenies, especially if the new Greeks were from different regions of Greece. We learned that many of the new Greeks who came during the 1960s to the Bahamas returned to Greece. Only a small number of the new Greeks remained, primarily because they already had relatives there. Some of the new arrivals came as sailors working on Greek ships in the Caribbean and decided to settle to make their living in Nassau, Bahamas.

In our question of what three things stand out about the Greeks of the Bahamas, one second generation respondent said: "Greeks are prosperous, law abiding, and Christian." Another second generation informant phrased it this way: "Greeks are now well accepted and integrated into the Bahamian society. The Greeks feel at home, and no serious problems exist between the Greeks and the rest of the Bahamians." We found no evidence of poor Greeks in the Bahamas.

In conclusion, we can say that Greek Bahamians have evolved from a limited number of original Greek sponge entrepreneurs to a full fledged Greek Bahamian community that has branched into various other small enterprises and occupations. As a rule, the early Greek immigrants started as workers or had small businesses. By second generation, some Greek Bahamians continued in the same line of business as their fathers, while others branched into such professions as law, medicine, architecture, and the like.

ENDNOTES

[1]Eleuthera is a fairly large island in the Bahamas. In 1649, English dissidents, in search of religious freedom, shipwrecked on the shores of this island, named it Eleuthera, from the Greek word "free" or "freedom."

[2]There is a similar Greek Isle in the Cyclades Islands of the Aegean Sea called Andros. The Greek Andros is famous for its ship owners. The Bahamian Andros was once famous for sponges. Some of the Greeks of the Bahamas believe the first Greeks who reached the island were from Andros. However, the most likely derivation of the name was from the British colonial Governor of Massachusetts and New England, who is said to have received a grant of land in the Bahamas from the Lord Proprietors. (Handbook, 1965-1966 fifth edition, p. 98). The name of the governor was Sir Edmund Andros.

[3]A guest house is a private house approved by the city to be used in part as accommodations for tourists. Guest houses provide shared bathrooms and showers, a communal refrigerator, and daily room services, including a change of sheets and towels. There is no radio or T.V. in the room. There is also a local telephone. Guest houses are usually cheaper than hotels or other accommodations.

[4]Interviews and participant observations were supplemented by a visit of the father and his son Andreas to the Department of the Archives where they met Dr. Gail Saunders, the Director, and a native Bahamian historian educated both in Canada and England. Dr. Saunders and her staff in the department were very helpful in providing us with available historical information in the Archives concerning the Greek community of the Bahamas. A brief video at the Pompey Museum on Bay Street in Nassau was also helpful in giving us an historical background and the social structure of the Bahamian society. Dr. Gail Saunders was the major speaker in that video.

[5]The names of five of the Greek-owned restaurants are Lums, Grand Central, Skans Cafeteria, Coco, and Imperial. Greek Bahamians also own and operate hotels such as the Olympia, El Greco, Parthenon (recently sold). There are 5 jewelry shops--which are mostly owned by second generation Greeks.

REFERENCES

Frantzis, George T. 1962. *Strangers at Ithaca.* St. Petersburg, Florida. Great Outdoors Publishing Company.

Bahamas Handbook. 1983. Nassau, Bahamas: A Dupuch Publication

_____. 1970-71.

_____. 1965.

_____. 1994.

The Bahamas Islander. Vol. 1, No. 2, 1994.

Curry, Robert. 1928. *Bahamian Lore.* Printed in France.

Johnson, Howard. 1986. "Safeguarding our Traders: The Beginnings of Immigration Restrictions in the Bahamas, 1925-1933" in *Immigrant and Minorities.* Vol. 5, No. 1, March 1986.

An interview with Dr. Gail Saunders, Director of Archives, Ministry of Education, Nassau, Bahamas, January, 1995.

Public Records Office, Archives Section, 1974.

Psilinakis, John. 1973. "Transcript of Interview with Mr. Psilinakis." Department of Archives, Nassau, Bahamas.

Eight interviews with Greek Bahamians (4 first generation and 4 second generation).

Kourvetaris, George. 1987. "The Greeks of Asia Minor and Egypt as Middleman Economic Minorities During the Late 19th and 20th Centuries" in *Ethnic Groups*, Vol. 7 (1-27).

_____. 1994. "The Greek American Experience and The Futuristics of Greek American Ethnicity" in *Hellenism and the U.S.: Constructions and Deconstructions.* Edited by Savas Patsalidis, Hellenic Association of American Studies. Thessalonikie, Greece: Aristotle University.

Moskos, Charles. 1990. *Greek Americans: Struggle and Success*, 2nd ed. New Brunswick: Transaction Publishers.

Nassau Guardian (newspaper). "Letter to the Editor," 28 December 1887.

_____. 3 March 1888.

_____. 5 October 1889.

_____. September, 1928

The Tribune. "The Greek Connection." 26 March 1981.

_____. August, 1924.

_____. 26 March 1881.

_____. 17 December 1927.

_____. 10 December 1930.

_____. 21 August 1926.

_____. 8 January 1930.

_____. 26 March 1981.

CHAPTER 12
THE FUTURISTICS OF GREEK AMERICAN ETHNICITY*

In order to make predictions about the future of Greek American ethnicity in the next century, it is important to take stock of our present achievements or failures so we can as Greek-Americans plan various strategies for our future survival as a Greek American community. In this last chapter I will concentrate on six major aspects of Greek American experience.

DEMOGRAPHICS

Estimates of Greek American population range from 3,000,000, according to the Greek Archdiocese, to 1,250,000 by various other estimates including those of Moskos (1978:2). The United States census does not go beyond the second generation. The 1970 United States census reported 177,275 Greek born Americans (first generation) and 257,296 native born Americans of Greek or mixed parentage (second generation), or a total of some 434,000 persons of Greek American stock in the United States. Needless to say, this number is low. One can never know the exact number of Greek Americans. However, we do know that since the mid 1970s, few Greek immigrants have been coming to the United States. This means that as the early immigrant generations are aging, repatriating, or dying out, Greek American ethnicity will be more defined by native Americans of Greek or mixed extraction, namely second, third, and subsequent generations of Greek Americans. The question is when do Greek Americans begin to lose their ethnic identity, if at all? This question will pre-occupy us throughout the paper.

Recently released census data shows the number of Greek Americans disappearing. According to the census report, between 1980 and 1990, in more than one out of three states in the United States, Greek Americans ceased to exist on the list of the top 25 American ancestry groups (*New York Review*, March, 1993:5). The 1990 United States Census reported about 1,100,000 Greek Orthodox Christians (United States Census, 1990). Of course, this does not necessarily mean that Greek Americans disappear altogether. It means that

---

* A version of this chapter was originally published in the *Journal of Modern Hellenism*, No. 7, 1990: 45-66. A somewhat revised version was also reprinted in *Hellenism and the United States* (edited) by Savvas Patsalides, American Studies in Greece Series. Thessaloniki: Aristotle University, 1994: 199-214.

other groups multiply faster. In 1992, the United States Department of Commerce had reported the number of immigrants admitted to the United States by country of birth between the years of 1961 and 1990. In general, we see a gradual decline of European immigrants. During the two decades between 1961-1980, there were about 184,000 immigrants from Greece admitted to the United States. However, during the years of 1981 and 1989 only 26 thousand, and in 1990 only 3,000 were admitted to the United States (United States Immigration and Naturalization Service Statistical Yearbook, annual 1992: 11).

INSTITUTIONAL/ORGANIZATIONAL

As we move from first generation to second, third, and subsequent generations, the institutional/organizational dimension of ethnicity is changing. For the first generation, and to a large extent the second generation, "nationality" and "religion" are the most important aspects of Greek ethnicity. Both the Greek school and Greek church are the most important ethnic institutions. However, as we move away from these two generations, Greek customs, Greek traditions, Greek endogamous marriages, and Greek benevolent societies, organized by village or regional societies (*somateia*), decline or change. The Greek language gives way to English, and nationality gives way to religious affiliation as an ethnic dimension. The Greek language schools are far less preferable in the subsequent generations. The church as an institution is also changing; from an immigrant church to a homegrown Greek American or mixed church. In every generation intermarriages are on the increase.

Leadership in these ethnic organizations and the church is also changing. As the old generation of priests is dying out, and few or no Greek priests are coming to the United States, the majority of our parish priests are of the American born second and third generations. Most bishops are still first generation, but as they age and pass on, they will eventually be replaced by American-born clerics. We find similar changes in the leadership of secular and lay organizations affiliated with the church, such as the American Hellenic Educational Progressive Association (AHEPA), the Hellenic American Congress, the Hellenic Institute, the Orthodox Forum, and other secular and supportive Greek Orthodox organizations. The ethnic press, at one time the most robust ethnic institution, and a predominantly Greek language press, gradually has adopted English for its Greek American readership. To name a few--*The Greek American*, the *Hellenic Chronicle*, the *Greek Star*, are all printed in English with little or no articles in Greek. There is some effort, however, to counter this trend by publishing some newspapers in Greek, most notably, the daily *National Herald* (which has been published for a long time), *The Proini*, and a number of weekly and bi-weekly Greek language newspapers. The *Atlantis*, a daily royalist paper was discontinued many years ago.

Despite these obvious changes this does not necessarily signal the end of Greek American ethnicity. Also, although the Greek language is an important component of our Greek national identity, its loss does not automatically lead to the loss of Greek American ethnicity. Our children and grandchildren speak English, yet they can still internalize some of the broader dimensions of Greek American ethnic subcultural forms and values. The problem here is that our emphasis is too much on the Dionysian and culinary aspects of our Greek American subculture and not enough on the Apollonian or more esoteric aspects of Greek culture. Greek literature, Greek American studies, Greek history, the Greek language, classics, Greek American scholarship in general are not usually stressed. We cannot maintain our ethnic identity and ethnic subculture beyond the second generation on the culinary and Dionysian aspects, the colorful parades, and church *panygyria*[1] of Greek culture alone. The "gyros," like other ethnic foods before, eventually will become Americanized. To build our ethnic identity on the "gyros" syndrome or other culinary and Dionysian aspects is indeed a shallow foundation which, it seems to me, will not carry us into the twenty-first century and beyond as a viable Greek American community. Our children and grandchildren must be exposed to the richness of Greek culture, including our rich Greek Orthodox tradition. Teaching and learning more about our Greek Orthodox heritage and culture strengthens our Greek and American identities. One reinforces the other.

STRATIFICATION AND MOBILITY

While our numerical significance becomes less consequential, our economic significance and economic mobility remains impressive. More and more names of Greek Americans appear among the wealthiest of Americans. For example, the number of Greek Americans who support the Greek Orthodox Church with a commitment of over $100,000 has reached to about 300. While this socioeconomic mobility of Greek Americans is admirable, it operates as a deterrent of ethnic identity and accelerates the assimilative process. A number of studies have documented the arrival of Greek Americans as a solid middle and upper middle class in the American society. Indeed, there is enough empirical evidence to suggest that Greek Americans have reached a middle class status in American society. However, the middle class status is not unique to Greek Americans only; other Euro-Americans such as Italian Americans, German Americans, Jewish Americans, Irish Americans, and Asian Americans, including Japanese Americans, Indian Americans (Asian), and other ethnic groups, have reached similar, and in some instances, higher mobility status than that of the Greeks.

It must be stressed that the very affluence and social mobility of Greek Americans is precisely one of the major factors of assimilation and, therefore, it contributes to a decline of Greek American ethnic identity. It seems ethnicity is sacrificed at the altar of economic success. Greek American ethnicity becomes symbolic rather than genuine and substantive. Greek Americans are no different than all those *nouveau rich*, the *neoploutoi*, whose newly acquired wealth is spent on such conspicuous consumption as Mercedes, minks, mansions, and elaborate weddings, and social gatherings. Meanwhile, Greek Americans spend little on things intellectual and cultural, or what I call "Apollonian." The latter would not only enhance our status but strengthen our cultural and intellectual presence, respect, and power in the United States. We desperately need more emphasis on Greek American studies, Greek American foundations, Greek American cultural centers (like the Maliotis Cultural Center, The Chicago Hellenic Museum and Cultural Center), Greek American scholarships, and Greek American exchange programs with Greece and other Greek communities of the diaspora. We have built beautiful and expensive Greek churches, but we need more libraries, more academic chairs, including Greek Orthodox theology, taught in American institutions. Our children and grandchildren have a limited understanding of our ethno-religious tradition. We must concentrate on the substantive not the external, superficial, or the ritual. It is rather ironic that while our numbers and Greek focus diminish, Turkish government expenditures and propaganda to change the Turkish image in the United States has accelerated. For example, Manatos has reported in *New York Review* (March 1993:5) that the Turkish government expenditures in Washington, D.C., on lobbying and public affairs (which are reported publicly), skyrocketed from $200,000 in 1983 to over $5,000,000 in 1992. Needless to say, much of this money is spent to counter the Greek American input and influence in the American public policy process. In addition, while Greek studies and Greek chairs in American institutions are almost non-existent, the Turkish studies and propaganda have penetrated the American universities in an alarming number. For example, Professor Spyros Vryonis, one of the leading scholars of Hellenic studies and former director of the Onassis foundation at New York University, warns that the Turkish government has both short and long term objectives. Turkey's long range aim is to become a regional power in the Middle East, especially following the demise of the former Soviet Union.

ATTITUDINAL AND SURVEY STUDIES

Another way to look at the nature of the Greek American community is to examine some studies by Greek American and American scholars concerning the Greek American experience. Since the 1960s and 1970s, there has been a growing interest in ethnic studies including Greek American studies. There is a growing number of Greek American scholars who, as Charlie Moskos put it, have "toiled in the vineyards of Greek American scholarship." A few such studies can be summarized here, especially those which have a bearing on the issues of Greek ethnicity, assimilation, mobility, and Greek Orthodox identity which we are concerned with here.

Greek American Ethnicity and Assimilation

Vlachos, in his study of the assimilation of 125 members of three generations of Greek Americans at Anderson, Indiana in 1968 found that: a) factionalism and internal conflict within the Greek American community leads to rapid assimilation; b) high structural assimilation of all three generations of Greeks occurs in the institutional area of economy; and c) the *first generation* was seen as adapting to a new American culture and as trying to perpetuate the Greek way of life, while the *second generation* was found to be the most confused, alienated, and marginal, trying to bridge the internal (Greek ethnic subculture) and the external (American) pressures and demands placed upon them. The *third generation*, while found to be more secure psychologically in its identification with American culture, tried to find certain elements of self-identification and social location within the ethnic setting. This Greek American ethnic identity of the third generation is a new composite of Greek American culture which encompasses certain traditional and often idealized Greek cultural patterns. Vlachos found no third generation Greek Americans who spoke Greek, which is an indication of assimilation and the decline of Greek national identity. Isolated and small town Greek American communities are more prone to assimilation.

Another study of "Greeks and voting" by Humphrey and Louis (1973) contradicts some of Vlachos's findings. The authors found that the Greeks had not reached full assimilation in American society even by the third generation. Despite the fact that by the third generation the Greek American identity decreases, one can argue that Greek Americans voted for both Agnew and Dukakis as fellow ethnics. Voting for Agnew and Dukakis, however, are not necessarily indicators of Greek identity.

In a study of "Greek American ethnicity," Scourby (1967) surveyed 160 individuals of Greek descent in the New York metropolitan area. She found that both American born and foreign born Greek Americans showed a strong attachment to their ethnic identity. According to the author, "social mobility did not result in abandonment of ethnicity and the Greek American community." In addition, as one would expect, Scourby found that the first generation was strongly identified with the ethno-religious dimension; for example, 75% of the first generation respondents expressed an ethno-religious identity as compared with 58% of the second generation, and 42% of the third generation. However, when the author asked questions that measured the larger ethno-cultural dimension of Greek ethnicity she found the reverse: 25% of the first, 42% of the second, and 58% of the third generation identified with the broader aspects of ethno-cultural values. Somewhat similar findings were reported by Tavuchis in his study of the Greek-American family in 1971. According to Tavuchis, social mobility of the second generation did not result in severing the relations with the second generation.

In another study of the Greek American community of Akron, Ohio, Constantinou and Harvey (1985:234-54) found a "two-dimensional structure" underlying Greek American ethnicity. One they called *externalities* (that which pulls the Greek Americans toward their place of origin), and the other they termed *internalities* (that which binds Greek Americans together as a community). While the authors found a variation across generations, knowledge of the Greek language always decreased. The authors found the first generation to be the most cohesive in its ethnic identity in preserving the Greek language. The second generation was found to be the least cohesive of the three due to its transitional nature. The third generation was found to be less cohesive than the first but showed signs of ethnic revival.[2] The authors concluded no single factor was adequate to define ethnic identity.

In a somewhat similar study, Constantinou (1989: 99-117) defined Greek-American ethnicity by looking at the dominant themes and generational differences among three generations of Greek Americans. Using data from six northeastern Ohio Greek communities, he found that language, socio-cultural activities, and politics were the three most important interrelated themes which define Greek-American ethnicity. Applying a multivariate analysis of variance, he concluded that the use of language is sharply declined by third generation, followed by a decrease in the interest in politics, and by a little variability in participating in sociocultural activities.

Greek American Ethnicity and Greek Identity

In a study of Greek ethnicity of two Orthodox parishes, one in Baltimore, Maryland and the other in Minneapolis, Minnesota, on the basis of an analysis of 553 returned questionnaires in the Spring of 1989, Demos found that all of the respondents thought of themselves as Greek ethnics. She also reported that most members of the two churches expressed a positive attitude towards both the Greek language and the Greek church. She also concluded that Greek ethnicity in both its religious and national dimensions gradually becomes attenuated as one moves from the first to the second, and third generations a finding consistent with a number of previous studies.

Greek Language, Subculture and Ethnicity

In her study of "ethnic language and subcultural continuity," Costantakos (1982:137-70) questioned 211 Greek Americans and found that the Greek language was a significant dimension of subcultural continuity. The Greek language, she found, holds symbolic meaning in ethnic identification, and represents the desire for ethnic maintenance and ethnic continuity. Paradoxically, she concluded that ethnic language maintenance is a progressive weakening in the process of subcultural continuity. In a somewhat similar study of "Greek American ethnicity and Greek American Orthodox identity" (for more extensive discussion on this issue see Chapter 3) the author surveyed, in 1989, a recently formed Chicago based Orthodox singles group of 248 members. Approximately 90 questionnaires were returned. The majority, or 55%, perceived themselves as Orthodox or Orthodox ethnic Americans, while 44% perceived themselves as simply American. When asked what was most important about their Orthodox identity, the majority of respondents ranked highest on the more *internal* aspects of Orthodoxy, such as theological or doctrinal beliefs, Orthodox faith, and spirituality. Less emphasis was placed on the more *external* manifestations of the .Greek Orthodox faith such as icons, Byzantine music, and Byzantine architecture. When asked how important the Orthodox faith was, 95% of the respondents replied important and very important. In response to a question asking them to choose between Orthodox or Greek ethnic identity, 33% preferred Orthodox, 22% Greek ethnicity, and 43% both. In choosing a marriage partner, "Orthodox faith" was more important than "Greek ethnicity" for 33% over 44%, respectively, but 40.7% would prefer both, and 20.7% neither. In questions concerning Greek ethnicity, the respondents considered the most important dimensions to be Greek family (44%), Greek culture (28%), Greek history (22%), and Greek traditions (17%).

To my question whether or not they favored panorthodox unity, the majority responded in the affirmative.[3]

Greek American Professionalism and Mobility

My own study of Greek American professionals, which covered the period of 1820-1970 and again 1970-1989, attests to the professional and business mobility of Greek Americans, especially following World War II. However, while Greek Americans have entered the professional and business world by the thousands, one finds few highly distinguished representatives in different professional and business occupations. We have many doctors but few outstanding medical scientists, many academic professionals, but few outstanding scholars in top elite universities or research foundations, many small business entrepreneurs but few top executives or presidents of major corporations. In politics, we have some members in both the house and the senate, but no cabinet members or Greek Americans occupying top positions in the government.[4] Over-all, the Greek American professionals are also concentrated in fewer occupations, such as in law, medicine, education, engineering and business--we find fewer of them in the arts, mass media, and the sciences, including the social sciences.

ISSUES OF CONTINUITY AND DISCONTINUITY OF GREEK AMERICAN ETHNICITY

In this last section, some of the issues that might contribute to the growth and revitalization and indeed the continuity of Greek American ethnicity in the 21st century will be discussed. This is what I call the "futuristics of Greek American ethnicity." On the basis of certain factors and my overall analysis, I will then try to suggest a number of possible strategies and scenarios for an emerging Greek American identity in the next century. Needless to say, without an assessment of our past and present, we cannot make valid predictions of our future course as a viable Greek American community. In view of our previous analyses, we can pose the following questions: What are some positive and negative aspects of Greek-American community? And what is the emerging model or models of the Greek American community in the future?

Factors of Continuity: How do We Maintain our Ethnic Identity?

We need a new crusade of Greek American renewal and revitalization that goes beyond the culinary aspects of Greek American culture. In practical terms, this means that we must have a deeper understanding of our ethnic heritage that surpasses the "gyros" and "opa" syndrome of Greek American ethnicity. We spend millions of dollars on colorful parades and other external elements of our Greek American culture, but we are short on the more esoteric and substantive elements of our Greek American cultural heritage. We build beautiful church edifices, but our young people have a shallow understanding of the spiritual, theological, and philosophical aspects of our Orthodox tradition. We have few libraries, Greek cultural centers, and Greek museums. We have very few or practically no Greek American studies centers at universities or courses that teach to younger generations the Greek American experience. It is only in the last few years or so that a genuine effort has been made to correct the situation. There are some universities that offer Greek studies (but most of these deal with Greece and give lip service to Greek American studies). In addition, there are few chairs of modern Greek culture in American institutions of higher learning and very little or nothing about the Greek American experience. In 1996, the Panarcadian Federation has initiated a campaign to raise funds for a chair in Greek Studies.

Our Greek American identity must be measured in terms of the extent to which we are willing to spend time, money, and energy to learn and internalize the values, traditions, and ideas of our Greek heritage and culture, and the extent to which we live by them. Most Americans, and indeed Greek Americans, have very little awareness and knowledge of Greek American artists, scientists, academicians, other professional Greek Americans, and our Orthodox faith, priests, and theologians. When Greek American professors ask the question in introductory courses in sociology, what comes to your mind when you hear the word "Greeks," the majority respond "gyros" and "restaurants." There is, of course, a truth to the stereotype that thousands of Greek Americans of first generation own or manage restaurants.

Our forefathers, during the long Turkish occupation of Greece, managed to survive the Turkish yoke because they had a deep desire and belief in their just cause, their historical legacy, their religious faith, and their national identity as a distinct cultural and ethno-religious group. Today, we are conversely being assimilated and swallowed up by the banners of the Anglo-Saxon dominant culture. In the name of "economic success," Greek Americans give up their ethnic identity and subculture easily. Once we lose it, it is difficult to regain it.

It seems to me that we must mobilize all our economic, spiritual, and intellectual forces and talents in our Greek American communities. We need both the "cultural conservatives" and the more "liberal elements" in our Greek American communities. We need to forge what Dan Georgakas has called an 'alliance between the two.' Dan Georgakas makes a number of useful suggestions including Greek American studies, Greek language dailies, and support for the feminist movement within the Greek church. We must use the broader framework of Greek culture and ethnicity, or a balance of the Dionysian and Apollonian dimensions. In this endeavor, we must establish links with Greece and other Greek communities in the diaspora. We must make available the contributions of modern Greece and Greek Americans to our succeeding Greek American generations and to the larger American culture and society. We must have a long range agenda which goes beyond the colorful parades and picture-taking in the local Greek newspapers. I believe we must reach out beyond our Greek American communities.

On the same issue of ethnic continuity, Konstantellou (1990) has suggested Greek ethnic education as a means of empowerment for minority cultures, including the teaching of ethnic values. Konstantellou argues that strengthening parochial education is compatible with cultural pluralism and complements the dominant educational system. Konstantellou believes strengthening ethnic educational institutions contributes to the continuity of Greek American community and presence in American pluralist society.

Factors of Discontinuity

What are some factors which are inimical to the growth and maintenance of Greek American ethnicity? There are many such factors which cannot be discussed in detail here. I would like to mention a few major ones which, in my judgment, operate as assimilative agents and contribute to the decline of Greek American ethnicity. These are *mixed marriages, social mobility* and *affluence, the decline of the Greek language, factionalism, and ethnic conflict* among Greek American communities. Intermarriage or mixed marriages have been called "the final test of assimilation" and the attenuation of ethnic identity. It has been documented that the fusion of ethnic subcultures and ethnic identities into an Anglo-Saxon dominant monoculture is in large part accomplished through the process or processes of assimilation. With few exceptions, there is a dearth of Greek American studies on the frequency of generational mixed marriages. In general, the picture as it emerges throughout the Greek American communities is one of rampant frequency of mixed marriages. If we look at the 1990 Handbook of the Greek Orthodox Archdiocese, for example, which keeps vital statistics of Greek Orthodox and mixed marriages, in the last 17 years we find mixed marriages run almost 50-50 up to 1980, and later they run 2 to 1 and higher over Greek-to-non-Greek marriages. In other words, we have two mixed marriages to one in which both spouses are of Greek extraction.

Greek Americans have embraced the Protestant ethic and the capitalist ideology. In the past, to move up on the social economic ladder in the United States you had to give up your ethnic roots and become Americanized, or you suffered social discrimination and exclusion from the economic, political, and educational resources of American society. This is not so in the 1990s and beyond. Greeks, along with other ethnic groups who emigrated around the turn of the century, experienced intense social discrimination, and they felt the need to conceal their identity. Saloutos (1964) argued about the emergence of respectability for Greek Americans in the 1940s. Related to this, Moskos, twenty years later, titled his book *Struggle and Success* (1980, 1990). The ideas of respect, status, and success have a socioeconomic ring to them, and indicate the struggle for Greek Americans to make it economically in the United States and be accepted as equal American citizens with other old type Americans. In the 1990s, Greek Americans, like other hyphenated Americans, do not have to give up their ethnic identity to be successful. It is a fallacy to assume that by imitating the Anglo-Saxons, Greek Americans will be embraced and accepted by other Americans.

We can be Greek and proud of it, and, at the same time, successful Americans or Greek Americans. Our Greekness is an asset to our over-all Greek American experience. Our Greekness strengthens and indeed re-enforces our American identity. The resurgence of ethnic identity and the civil rights movement of the 1960s gave a new respect for ethnicity. Americans began to rediscover their ethnic roots and, literally, everybody wanted to be an ethnic. As Greek Americans, we are caught between our ethnicity and our American core values of affluence, cultural conservatism, and the business ethic. Dukakis was the personification of a split personality. On one hand, he tried to be proud of his Greek American ethnicity to appeal to his ethnic constituencies (all the hyphenated ethnic Americans), but at the same time, he wanted to be seen as an American. Bush and the Protestant establishment succeeded in portraying him as neither. The fact that he was a successful Greek American who embodied the American dream and spoke for the less fortunate Americans did not matter. Neither his "Americanism" nor his "ethnicity" helped him to win the White House.

GREECE, AMERICAN GREEKS AND PHILHELLENISM

A recent commentary by Philip Spyropoulos on "Greece and Greek Americans" appeared in the December issue (1994) of the *Greek American* bi-weekly. The author's major argument was that there is "natural separation" and a "widening schism between many Greek Americans and their ancestral homeland." Mr. Spyropoulos went on to suggest that in the last analysis, "the single most important condition for the survival of Greeks in the diaspora is the ongoing existence and well-being of Greece." The author contended that while Greece has survived throughout the millennia, at present Greece is undergoing a series of regional challenges that may terminate her existence. Because of this, the author believes that Greek Americans should not take Greece's continuous existence for granted. I would like to add to the equation of "Greece and Greek Americans" and the "survival" of Greek American identity the notion of "Philhellenism."

It is my belief that the survival of Greek American communities and Greek communities in other Anglo Saxonic pluralistic societies in general, can be re-enforced and enhanced by a movement of philhellenism. In this analysis, philhellenism will be defined as the genuine cultivation of friendship and appreciation of things pertaining to Greek culture both in its "dionysian" and "apollonian" dimensions. The major reason for the need of philhellenism is the fact that Greeks do not reproduce themselves in great numbers as other ethnic groups. They easily become assimilated in Anglo-Saxonic societies.

We cannot maintain our ethnic identity by relying only on the dionysian aspects of our Greek American subculture. We must strive for a dionysian-apollonian nexus of Greek American identity. We must nourish and develop a Greek American identity and subculture which links the past with the present, bridging our Greek cultural roots. The Greeks as inheritors of such a magnificent culture only give lip service to that culture. Since the 1920s, Hellenism has been shrinking. By the end of this century we will speak of Americans, Australians, and Canadians of Greek extraction in Anglo-Saxonic countries only. Increasingly, the hyphenated-Greek identity will be an Anglo-Saxonic phenomenon (with some exceptions, of course, in Europe, Africa, Asia, and Latin America).

Our ethnic identity in the Anglo-Saxonic world will survive if Greeks have something different or unique to offer beyond the dionysian aspects or Greek material culture (the material artifacts including food culture in these societies). We have to internalize the apollonian aspects of Greek *Paedeia* even in translations—i.e. Greek literature, Greek philosophy, Greek myths, Greek holidays, Orthodox religion and theology, Greek family traditions, Greek music, etc. We must not take our Greekness for granted. We must spend more time in trying to learn for ourselves the essentials of our Greek apollonian culture.

I believe we can enhance our ethnic identity and culture both in Greece proper and among the Greek communities around the world by a new movement of philhellenism. Needless to say, it was this movement in Europe and elsewhere that helped the Greek nation to win its freedom from the oppressive yoke of the Ottoman Turkish rule in the middle of the 19th century. However, philhellenism then was inspired by the tenets of the Enlightenment, the French Revolution, the Romantic Movement, and the legacy of classical Greece. The closing decade of the 20th century and the commencing of the 21st century have moved away from the ideals of 19th century. We live in a world of "multinationalism and global economy" on one hand, and the resurgence of "ethnic nationalism" on the other. One force moves the nations toward a convergence model and the other toward a divergence. Greece is faced with a number of regional challenges that question the status quo both in its Aegean and northern frontiers. Even books like "Black Athena" by Martin Bernal[5] challenge Greece's classical legacy as a mother of western civilization.

The need for philhellenism can come from two basic sources: a) from within our Greek American communities, and b) from without the Greek American communities. We cannot survive as a viable Greek American community by relying only on our own internal communities and resources. We must organize both a panhellenic and philhellenic world movement. We have to learn to promote and cultivate both. In the next few lines, I would like to spell out what I believe is the nature and strategy of philhellenism both from within and from without. In other words, how do we cultivate, sustain, and promote friendship among co-ethnics and Americans (Australians, Canadians, and so on) of Greek extraction toward Greece and Greek culture beyond first generation of Greek immigrants from within? How do we cultivate, sustain, and promote friendship toward Greece and Greek culture among non-Greeks from without?

Philhellenism has to be promoted on both fronts with emphasis on the non-Greeks. In other words, how do we inform the national concerns of Greece to our American (Australian, Canadian) friends, neighbors, co-workers, colleagues, business partners, co-religionists, and the like? First, we will briefly discuss how we promote Philhellenism from within, and second we will expound on how we promote Philhellenism from without.

From the outset, we must be realistic and not take our Greek American identity for granted. Greek American ethnicity is not a given beyond the third generation. We cannot assume and insist American Greeks of third, fourth, and subsequent generations of Greek extraction be as equally concerned and knowledgeable about Greek national issues the same way as the first generation immigrants and Greeks in Greece proper. Our strategy beyond third generation should be the promotion of philhellenism among our children and grandchildren and not the insistence of making them pale replicas of Greeks. In this respect, the programs and the role of the Greek Orthodox Church in the Americas, the Greek American cultural and professional societies, such as AHEPA (American

Hellenic Educational Progressive Association), UHAC (United Hellenic-American Congress), KRIKOS (link of the United States and Greece), MGSA (Modern Greek Studies Association), ENOSIS (Union of Greek and Greek-American Organizations), SAE (Council of Greeks Abroad), ethnic mass media, the Greek parochial schools, and the hundreds of Greek regional and village societies, federations, organizations, and other groups, should promote philhellenism and Greek culture at both the dionysian and apollonian levels. For example, we must promote and expand organized and well planned cultural and educational field trips for children of Orthodox and non-Orthodox marriages to their ancestral homes of their forebears. I believe the dissemination of Greek culture should be carried out by teachers and scholars of Greek civilization (ancient, Byzantine, and modern). The present structure of Greek language schools, and private Greek schools is inadequate. It is my contention that beyond the third generation, the Greek culture should be taught in English and be taught to all children of mixed and Orthodox marriages (the former is the majority of marriages now) and be taught free of charge.

How do we generate the necessary funds for this task? I suggest 30% of the proceeds of the Greek Orthodox picnics (panygyria) should be earmarked for the purpose of promoting secular Greek culture and philhellenism among Americans of Greek extraction. One strategy here should be the promotion of philhellenism among Americans of mixed and Orthodox marriages beyond third and subsequent generations by offering the best what the "Greek Culture" has to offer. In this regard, we must go beyond the entrepreneurial and dionysian aspects of material Greek culture, such as Greek food or parades, and include the more cognitive apollonian dimensions of Greek culture and ethnicity as well.

In order to establish a frame of reference of Greek American scholarship and Greek American culture, Greek American parents must encourage their children and grandchildren to specialize in areas of learning beyond such lucrative professions as law, medicine, business, and other technical areas of specialization. We need more Greek American scholars and intellectuals. We should not promote only consulting or client-dependent professions (e.g., lawyers, doctors, realtors, accountants, engineers), or those professions who provide services to various clients for profit. More profoundly, we need colleague-dependent professions (e.g., academic and research professions or all those professions in the humanities, social, behavioral, natural sciences, and the arts who produce or create knowledge by carrying out basic research in universities and research institutes). As one very good Greek American friend and colleague of mine in history once put it: "If Greek Americans are not interested in modern Greek culture and history, someone else is going to specialize and re-write modern Greek history." I would also add, rewrite ancient Greek history. Indeed, this is already happening in the "age of revisionism and "ethnic nationalism": in the Balkan imbroglio, in "Black Athena", and more recently by the movie "Before the Rain," in which Alexander the Great is depicted as a Slav who was born in the former Yugoslav Republic of Macedonia (FYROM).

Of course, there are other ways of promoting philhellenism from within. The Greek government and the private sector in both Greece proper and those outside of Greece can develop coordinated strategies of promoting philhellenic sentiments among the children of mixed or Greek marriages. We must develop young ambassadors to Greece, not career bureaucrats or individuals whose main interest is self-promotion and picture-taking in local Greek American newspapers. We need dedicated and genuine students of Greek culture and civilization.

How do we promote philhellenism from without? The inception of the modern Greek nation state in the middle of 19th century was not only the result of the struggle of the Greek people from within (those called the autochthones Greeks) but also the contribution of thousands of non-Greeks and Philhellenes, friends and supporters of the Greek liberation movement against the Turkish yoke from outside of Greece, and from the Greek communities of the diaspora (or the heterochthones). Indeed, we must not forget that the beginning of the Greek Revolution and "lytrosis" (redemption) of Greece from the Ottoman Turkish oppression was as much a contribution from Greeks in Greece proper as it was from Greeks and Greece's friends outside of Greece (see for example an excellent book by Theophilus Prousis on the Russian Philhellenism and the Greek Revolution, 1994).

Greece, now more than any other time in its modern turbulent history, needs a long-range strategy of promoting philhellenism, not only among the non-Greeks, but also among its own Greek communities around the world. The Greek government cannot take for granted the diverse Greek Orthodox communities nor can it treat all the Greeks as economic immigrants of the diaspora. Immigration from Greece and most other European countries has stopped since the mid-1970s. More and more, when we talk about Greeks of the diaspora, we refer to Orthodox communities of Greek Orthodox or Greek families in which one spouse is Greek and the other is non-Greek. More and more Greek Americans, and for that matter Greek Canadians or Greek Australians, will be a homegrown phenomenon. It is for this reason that we need to develop strategies of philhellenism. There is no longer diaspora of Greek immigrants. In most Anglo-Saxon societies the majority of Greeks are born overseas.

For a century or more, Greek pioneers (the *protoporoi*), along with their progenies, have built beautiful Orthodox edifices and some community centers. Yet most Orthodox communities do not promote or allocate funds for the promotion of the apollonian or cognitive aspects of modern Greek culture (including the theology of Eastern Orthodox) other than the dionysian aspects of Greek culture. Trying to find any books or libraries on modern Greek secular culture in our Greek Orthodox *Kinotites*, is usually in vain. Books on Greek culture are usually not found in our Greek Orthodox communities. Greek afternoon and some daily schools are supported primarily by Greeks who came during the 1950's and 1960's, who have children of school age, and who wish their children to learn Greek. I believe Modern Greek secular culture is more supported by non-Greeks than Americans of Greek extraction. Classes in modern Greek studies taught at a few American universities are not usually supported by Greek American students but rather by Americans in general. In a course this author taught on the "Sociology of Greek Americans" and Modern Greek Culture," only one out of 15 students who registered for the class was Greek.

The blame for the neglect of Greek secular culture taught and disseminated among the Americans of Greek extraction and American friends in general does not rest only in Greek Orthodox communities overseas, but in the lack of planning and long range strategy of Greek governments. Greece gives the impression to the outside world that it is a country of political disunity and polarization. Greece needs to develop a national strategy of philhellenism which goes beyond partisan politics. Only recently one can see some signs in that direction. It seems that while Greeks as a rule prosper and advance outside of Greece, in Greece proper one gets the impression that nothing works. It seems also that in general Greeks and Greek Americans are over-critical of Greece but rarely critical of the United States. In short, I believe there is a need for the development of philhellenism both within and outside our Greek communities whether they're Greek American communities, Greek-Australian, Canadian, etc. It is only then that we may have hope for survival as an ethnic community in the 21st century.

SOME SUGGESTIONS AND TENTATIVE PROPOSITIONS

One thing we can say for sure is that as we move from first generation to second, third, and subsequent generations, one can observe a gradual attenuation and re-alignment of Greek American ethnic identity. We move from an inner-directed, or *esostrophic*, ethnic Greek identity most strongly represented by the immigrant or first generation, to an other-directed, or *exostrophic* identity more characteristic of the second, third, and subsequent generations of Greeks in the diaspora. More and more we have to re-define our ethnic identity as a process or ethnogenesis, namely as an ongoing, dynamic adaptation, and not something as a static product or unchanged over the generations. Concomitant to this transformation, one can observe parallel changes in the correlates of Greek American ethnic identity; a decline in knowledge of Greek language; fewer observances of Greek family and kinship traditions, holidays, and customs; and the virtual disappearance of Greek pride and *philotimo* after the second generation. A shift in loyalty from Greece, the country of origin of the first generation, to the United States, the country of American born Greeks, has been taking place. Greek America is more and more a second, third, and subsequent generation Greek American Community.

In the first two generations, Greekness and Greek Orthodoxy converge. By the third generation, however, a differentiation and divergence emerges. "Greekness" (nationality) gives way to "Americaness" and "religiosity" as aspects of Greek American ethnic identity. As one moves from the first generation to the second, to the third, and to subsequent generations, there is also a gradual shift of our ethnic identity and realignment. This is not unique to the Greeks. This pattern also characterizes other ethnic groups. When nationality declines as an index of ethnic identity, religion takes its place. In turn when religion declines, race takes its place, and if race declines, then social class becomes the major differentiating factor in American society.

What are the Future Prospects of the Greek American Community into the 21st Century?

It is a mixed bag. The pessimists are apocalyptic and define their gloomy predictions in terms of an assimilationist model. The optimists and ethnic pluralists, on the other hand, acknowledge the forces of assimilation, but they argue that we can do more to arrest the erosion of our ethnic identity. We must struggle not as individuals but as community and as an ethnic group to maintain our dual or hyphenated identity, one Greek and one American, or Greek American. This Greek American identity is going to be a metamorphized or transformed identity of an American vintage. We cannot maintain our ethnic identity by relying only on Dionysian aspects of our Greek American subculture. We must strive for a Dionysian-Apollonian Greek American nexus. We must nourish and develop a Greek American identity and subculture which links the past with the present, creating bridges of our Greek cultural roots. The Greeks as inheritors of such a magnificent culture only give lip service to that culture. The vehicles or institutions of Greek American ethnicity must be broadened and reach out beyond the Greek American ethnic community, which is basically a religious community. We must have our proportionate voice, or affirmative action so to speak, in American society. We must try to penetrate the power structure of the United States without losing our ethnic identity.

What is the Future Like?

I believe that, more and more, Greek ethnicity will be defined as a homegrown phenomenon, or as sociologists term it, "ethnogenesis." Those who understand and know the dynamics of this process must assist in shaping that type of Greek American who is proud of his Greek heritage, and knows enough to transmit it to the next generation, and the next to the next, and so forth. We must guard against self-depreciation of our Greekness. Our ethnic identity is a process rather than a product beyond the immigrant first generation. Immigration from Greece has, more or less, stopped. For the first time in many decades more Greeks are repatriating than leaving Greece. Since the 1920s Hellenism has been shrinking. By the end of this century we will speak of Americans, Australians, and Canadians of Greek extraction in Anglo-Saxon countries only.

Our ethnic identity in the Anglo-Saxon world will survive if Greeks have something unique to offer beyond the *souvlaki*, *gyros*, and *syrtaki* dance in these societies. We have to internalize the Apollonian aspects of Greek *Paedeia* even in translations--i.e. Greek literature, Greek myths, Greek holidays, Greek family traditions, Greek music, etc. We must not take our Greekness for granted. We must spend more time in trying to learn for ourselves the essentials of our Greek identity.

We must ask this critical question: Do we really care to maintain our Greek identity within a pluralistic society or do we want to be absorbed totally by the dominant Anglo-American culture? If we are serious about our ethnic identity, then we have to invest more time and resources in learning more about our Greek heritage. First we must start with ourselves and then show to others how proud we are of our illustrious past. But to be proud of something is not enough. We must avoid the disease of *ancestoritis*. We must be educated in Hellenic matters. We must take a conscious effort to share Hellenism with others. The Greeks have to do the Hellenizing. In this respect, I would like to suggest a "*Hellenistic model for the modern Greek diaspora*," not so very different from what Alexander the Great and his heirs espoused as they set out to Hellenize Asia and parts of Africa. Why not broaden our Greek American *polis* to encompass the greater American community? We must allow our Greek American Hellenistic culture to Hellenize, so to speak, the non-Greeks, and not be Americanized by them only. It must be mutual. After all, Greek culture is the language of the New Testament--the *Koine*--which is the basis of Christianity, just as classical Greece is the basis of Euro-American secular civilization. In the words of Shelley, "we are all Greeks," our culture has its roots in Greek *paedeia*. Parallel to the Hellenistic model, I believe the emerging model of Greek American ethnicity will be understood more and more within a religious dimension of Greek American or Eastern Orthodoxy.

Integration of Greek American Studies and Modern Greek Studies

For a long time modern Greek studies as exemplified by the Modern Greek Studies Association (MGSA), which started in 1968, was oblivious of the Greek American Studies which has involved a smaller number of Greek American scholars. What we need is the integration of both. As Konstantellou (1990) put it, "the rich Greek American experience has been long overdue." It is encouraging to see that Greek American Studies has been part of the Modern Greek Studies Association conference in 1995. It took almost 20 years to have the Greek American Studies recognized by the Modern Greek Studies Association. A more extensive conference, under the auspices of MGSA, was held in 1976 at the University of Chicago.

I believe that without the Greek cultural component in our ethnic identity, we will not survive in the Anglo American world as a dynamic and vibrant community in the twenty-first century and beyond. Greek culture and civilization are the basis of our Western and American culture. By being Western and American, we are also Greek. We must strive to maintain our Greek heritage and culture as much as we can. In order to accomplish that we must develop bridges between Greece and the Greek communities, between the *autochthones* and *heterochthones*. We must develop within our Greek American communities (and outside) cultural and educational institutions including institutes of modern Greek studies at American universities. We must go beyond the Greek school, the annual festivals (*panygyria*), and the colorful parades. We must look at the substance and the Apollonian aspects of our heritage more than the Dionysian and external, materialistic aspects of Greek American ethnicity or, at least, maintain a balance between the two. We must stress modern Greece and modern Greek culture and avoid a sterile total subservience to the glory that *was* Greece. Americans know about the classical part of our history but have little or no knowledge of the Byzantine and modern components of our Greek civilization. Few Americans know the struggles and tribulations of Greece as a new emerging nation in the middle of the nineteenth

century. If we do what we must do as Greek Americans, then I am optimistic
for the future of our Greek American community in the twenty-first century.

ENDNOTES

[1]Unfortunately the dionysian aspects of Greek culture are also stressed in Greece proper. Most Europeans and Americans think of Greece primarily as a country of tourism, Greek islands, and beaches to have a good time. With exception of literature (poetry) and shipping, modern Greek achievements are not known outside of Greece.

[2]In many papers and studies on Greek Americans, I find little evidence of a genuine Greek ethnic revival. At best most of this cultural atavism is more of dionysian nature rather than Apollonian.

[3]The panorthodox unity has been the long range policy of Greek Archdiocese in the United States. For example, for a number of years all the Eastern Orthodox denominations have established "SCOBA" (Standing Committee of Orthodox Bishops of America). This committee represents all the Eastern Orthodox denominations and meets frequently to discuss various issues including unity among all Eastern Orthodox churches. The visit of Patriarch Demetrios to the United States in 1989 was a shot in the arm for all the Orthodox denominations in the United States. However, the Turkish government exploited the visit of the patriarch to promote its own agenda and dispel the negative reputation and record of human rights violations Turkey has in the United States, Europe, and around the world.

[4]More recently Stephanopoulos, the Greek American press celebrity for Clinton, was designated to some kind of senior advisor position to the president.

[5]In an edited reader by Mary Lefkowitz and Guy MacLean Rogers entitled *Black Athena: Revisited* (1996), twenty leading scholars in a broad range of disciplines have challenged the claims made by Martin Bernal in his book *Black Athena: The Afroasiatic Roots of Classical Civilization* Vol. I (1987).

REFERENCES

Bardis, Panos. 1977. "The Future of the Hellenic Language in the USA: Causes and Solutions." Paper presented at the International Seminar, Athens, Greece, July 28.

Bureau of the Census. 1992. Barbara Everitt Bryant, Director United States Department of Commerce, p. 11.

Constantinou, Stavros. 1989. "Dominant Themes and Intergenerational Differences in Ethnicity: The Greek Americans." *Sociological Focus*, Vol. 22, No. 2 (May): 99-117.

Constantinou, Stavros and Milton E. Harvey. 1985. "Basic Dimensional Structure and Intergenerational Differences in Greek American Ethnicity," *Sociology and Social Research*. Vol. 68: 234-54.

Costantakos, Chryssie M. 1982. "Ethnic Language as a Variable in Subcultural Continuity," *The Greek American Community in Transition*. Ed. by Harry J. Psomiades and Alice Scourby.

Demos, Vasilikie. 1989. "Maintenance and Loss of Traditional Gender: Boundaries in two Greek Orthodox Communities." *Journal of the Hellenic Diaspora*. Vol. XVI, No. 1-4 (Spring-Summer-Fall-Winter): 77-93.

Georgakas, Dan. 1989. "Greek America in the Nineties." *Greek American* (a weekly newspaper) (Dec): 15-16.

Gordon, Milton. 1964. *Assimilation in American Life: The Role of Race, Religion and National Origin*. New York: Oxford Univ. Press, p. 71.

Greeley, Andrew. 1974. *Ethnicity in the United States*. New York: John Wiley, pp. 308-09.

Herberg, William. 1955. *Protestant-Catholic Jew*. New York: Doubleday and Co.

Humphrey, Craig R. and Helen Brock Louis. 1973. "Assimilation and Voting Behavior: A Study of Greek Americans." *International Migration Review*.

Kennedy, Ruby. 1944. "Single or Triple Melting Pot: Intermarriage Trends in New Haven, 1870-1940." *American Journal of Sociology*.

Kopan. 1981. "Greek Survival in Chicago: The Role of Ethnic Education 1890-1980." *Ethnic Chicago*, Grand Rapids, MI: R. Ferdmans Publ. Co., pp. 80-139.

Konstantellou, Eva. 1990. "Education as a Means of Empowerment for Minority Cultures: Strategies for the Greek American Community." Paper presented at the second annual conference Oct. 19-21, 1990, Brookline, Mass.

Kourvetaris, George. 1990. "Conflicts and Identity Among the Greek Americans of the Diaspora." *International Journal of Contemporary Sociology* 27/3-4, (July-Oct):137-54.

_____. 1989. "Greek American Professionals and Entrepreneurs," *Journal of the Hellenic Diaspora*. Vol. XVI, Nos. 1-4 (Spring-Summer-Fall-Winter):105-28

_____. 1989. "Will the Greek American Community Survive into the 21st Century?" KRIKOS: An American Quarterly, Vol. one, pp. 26-28.

_____. 1989. "Greek Orthodox and Greek American Ethnic Identity." An unpublished paper based on a survey of 248 members of a Chicago based Orthodox singles group.

_____. 1988. "The Greek American Family," in *Ethnic Families in America*. Ed. by Charles H. Mindel and Robert W. Habenstein. New York: Elsevier, pp. 776-108.

_____. 1977. "Greek American Professionals: 1820-1970s," *Balkan Studies*. Vol. 18, No. 2: 285-317.

_____. 1973. "Brain Drain and International Migration of Scientists." *Greek Review of Social Research*. (January-June), No. 15, Athens, Greece.

_____. 1971. *First and Second Generation Greeks in Chicago*. Athens, Greece: National Center of Social Research.

_____. 1971. "Patterns of Generational Subculture and Intermarriage of the Greeks in the United States." *International Journal of Sociology of the Family*. Vol. 1 (May): 34-48.

Lefkowitz, Mary R. and Guy MacLean Rogers, (eds.). 1996 *Black Athena: Revisited*. Chapel Hill and London: The University of North Carolina Press.

Lopreato, Joseph. 1970. *Italian Americans*. New York: Random House.

Manatos, Andrew. 1993. "The Disappearing Greek Americans," in *New York Review* (a monthly Greek American magazine) (March):5. (It has been renamed *Greek American Review*.)

Moskos, Charles Jr. 1978. "Greek Americans." Presented at the Illinois Sociological Association, Chicago, IL. October 27-28, p. 2.

_____. 1980. *Greeks in America: Struggle and Success*. Englewood Cliffs: Prentice Hall. (Also a revised version was published by Transaction Publishers in New Brunswick in 1989.)

Rosen, Bernard. 1959. "Race, Ethnicity and the Achievement Syndrome." *American Sociological Review*. xxiv: 47-60.

Saloutos, Theodore. 1964. *The Greeks in the United States*. Cambridge: Harvard Univ. Press, p. 6.

Scourby, Alice. 1984. *The Greek Americans*. Boston: Twayne Publishers, p. 26.

Tavuchis, Nicholas. 1972. *Family and Mobility Among Greek Americans*. Athens, Greece: National Center of Social Research.

Vlachos, C. Evangelos. 1968. *The Assimilation of Greeks in the United States*. Athens, Greece: National Center of Social Research.